E. B. White: The Children's Books

Twayne's United States Authors Series

Ruth K. MacDonald, Editor

Bay Path College

TUSAS 621

E. B. WHITE IN 1961.

Photograph by Stanton A. Waterman. Courtesy E. B. White Collection, Division of Rare and Manuscript Collections, Carl A. Kroch Library, Cornell University.

E. B. White: The Children's Books

Lucien L. Agosta

California State University, Sacramento

Twayne Publishers
An Imprint of Simon & Schuster Macmillan
New York

Prentice Hall International
London Mexico City New Delhi Singapore Sydney Toronto

#32240885

Illustration on p. 28: illustration copyright renewed ©1973 by Garth Williams.
Illustration on p. 92: illustration copyright renewed ©1980 by Garth Williams.
Illustration on p. 144: illustration ©1970 by Edward Frascino.
Reprinted by permission of HarperCollins Publishers.

Twayne's United States Authors Series No. 621

E. B. White: The Children's Books
Lucien L. Agosta

Copyright © 1995 by Twayne Publishers

Twayne Publishers
An Imprint of Simon & Schuster Macmillan
866 Third Avenue
New York, NY 10022

Library of Congress Cataloging-in-Publication Data
Agosta, Lucien L.
E. B. White : the children's books / Lucien L. Agosta.
    p.   cm. — (Twayne's United States authors series ; no. 621)
    Includes bibliographical references and index.
    ISBN 0-8057-4631-5
    1. White, E. B. (Elwyn Brooks), 1899– —Criticism and interpretation. 2
Children's stories, American—History and criticism. I. Title. II. series.
PS3545.H5187Z524   1995
818'.5209—dc20   95-8467
                                          CIP

For Phyllis Bixler

Contents

Preface

A book on E. B. White as a children's writer needs little justification. White is universally recognized for his "substantial and lasting contribution to literature for children," as his citation accompanying the 1970 Laura Ingalls Wilder Award notes.[1] Despite the wide acclaim his books for children continue to enjoy, no complete study of these three works has yet been written. Indeed, White as a writer has been the subject of only one full-length critical assessment, the 1974 Twayne volume by Edward C. Sampson, which is no longer in print. Sampson's book, however, accords White's children's works only a scant 12 pages. *E. B. White: The Children's Books* is written to rectify this neglect: herein I discuss in full and offer a survey of critical commentary on *Stuart Little* (1945), *Charlotte's Web* (1952), and *The Trumpet of the Swan* (1970).

Chapter 1 offers a reassessment of White's career as a children's writer and draws from sources not available to Sampson in 1974, especially Scott Elledge's definitive 1984 biography. Chapter 2 consists of a full-length discussion of *Stuart Little*, White's first important work for children. Like all of White's works for juveniles, *Stuart Little* has never been out of print and still commands an enthusiastic readership. Indeed, by January 1977 total sales of the book, not including translations, amounted to more than 2.5 million copies, and its success in the marketplace has not diminished. According to Peter Neumeyer's assessment in *Twentieth-Century Children's Writers* (1983), *Stuart Little* "has won its place among contemporary classics."[2]

Charlotte's Web, White's masterpiece, was met with a chorus of praise on its publication in 1952. That praise has, over the years, grown more insistent. Eudora Welty called the book "just about perfect, and perfectly effortless and magical in the doing."[3] John Rowe Townsend in *Written for Children* called it "astonishingly full and rich,"[4] while Peter Neumeyer judged it to be "lyrical, suspenseful on its primary level, and philosophical under all. Its individual excellences have been recognized almost universally, and its profundity has been understood by sensitive readers" (1983a, 817). Neumeyer's concluding assertion that *Charlotte's Web* has secured White's place "permanently among the great writers for children" is borne out by the book's having sold more than six million copies (1983a, 818). It has been translated into at least 20 languages and was the overwhelming winner in a 1960 poll conducted by *Publishers Weekly* to discover the best children's book written between 1930 and 1960. Between 1963 and 1973 the novel topped the annual *New York Times* best-seller list for children's books, and in 1976 it was number one on the *Publishers Weekly* poll of teachers, librarians, authors, and publishers asked to name the 10 best children's books written in America since 1776. Since 1960 *Charlotte's Web* has consistently outsold such children's classics as *Winnie-the-Pooh*, *The Wind in the Willows*, and *Alice in Wonderland* in the American book market.

Chapter 4 offers a full consideration of White's last work for children, *The Trumpet of the Swan*. Though not as widely acclaimed as *Stuart Little* or *Charlotte's Web*, *The Trumpet of the Swan* has its defenders, including John Updike, who thought it "the most spacious and serene" of White's three books for children, the book of White's "most imbued with the author's sense of the precious instinctual heritage represented by wild nature."[5] John Rowe Townsend called it "a loving book as well as a funny one" (243), while Peter Neumeyer, noting the tempered praise accorded it, nevertheless acknowledged that the novel would generally be recognized as "a splendid accomplishment" had it been written by a lesser writer (1983a, 818). *The Trumpet of the Swan* clearly merits the serious critical treatment it is accorded in this chapter.

The fifth chapter provides a summary examination of White's themes, settings, and characters in his children's works and discusses some of his theoretical positions on the writing of fiction for juveniles. Before he came to write his three novels for children, White penned two essays—"A Boy I Knew" (1940) and "Children's Books" (1938)—in which he took inventory of some of the concerns central to him that would find their way into his novels for juveniles and in which he discussed his critical positions in regard to children's books. These two essays provide an enlightening retrospective on White's achievement in this field.

In writing this book, I am greatly indebted to Scott Elledge's 1984 biography of E. B. White, from which I gathered many of the details of the biographical first chapter, as well as helpful points of departure for my own critical assessments of White's three children's books. White was fortunate in his collaboration with Dorothy Lobrano Guth as editor of his collected letters (1976); her volume is a necessary source for understanding White's creative process.

From California State University, Sacramento, I received a 1991 Summer Faculty Research Grant, as well as units of release time from teaching during the fall 1991 and spring 1992 terms. Without this support I would have been considerably longer in completing this project. For her continuous friendship I would like to thank Professor Phyllis Bixler of Southwest Missouri State University, Springfield. I am especially grateful to John Robert Castro for his love and encouragement, as I am to Kevin Moen, who lent me his apartment in Washington, D.C., during the summer of 1992 so that I could write without distraction. Professor Uli Knoepflmacher of Princeton University unwittingly inspired me to work on White as a result of his insightful observations on *Charlotte's Web* during his 1986 NEH summer seminar on children's fairy tales, which I was fortunate to participate in. Finally, I am grateful for the helpful criticism given me on this project by my Twayne editors, Ruth MacDonald, Barbara Sutton, and Mark Zadrozny.

Chronology

1949   *Here Is New York.*

1950   Receives honorary degree from Bowdoin College.

1952   *Charlotte's Web;* receives honorary degree from Hamilton College.

1954   *The Second Tree from the Corner;* receives honorary degree from Harvard and Colby College; wins Page One Award for Literature from Newspaper Guild of New York.

1957   Retires from New York to the farm in Maine.

1959   *The Elements of Style* (with William Strunk).

1960   Receives Gold Medal for Essays and Criticism from the National Institute of Arts and Letters.

1962   *The Points of My Compass.*

1963   Is awarded the Presidential Medal of Freedom.

1970   Receives the American Library Association's Laura Ingalls Wilder Award; *The Trumpet of the Swan; Letters of E. B. White.*

1971   Is awarded the National Medal for Literature.

1977   Katharine S. White dies on 20 July; *Essays of E. B. White.*

1981   *Poems and Sketches of E. B. White.*

1985   Dies on 1 October.

Chapter One

"First Person Singular": The Life and Career of E. B. White

"The Minutes of His Own Meeting"

In the twentieth-anniversary issue of the *New Yorker* (17 February 1945) E. B. White noted the wartime pressure on writers to serve government interests by becoming propagandists, advocates of causes, and mouthpieces for agencies with diverse agendas. He concluded, however, that "the deepest instinct of a creative person is not to promote the world's cause but to keep the minutes of his own meeting."[1] This statement provides the key to understanding White's life and career, which consisted essentially of a successful effort to record "the minutes of his own meeting" fully and faithfully in a series of highly personal essays and in his three works for children. "I am a member of a party of one," he later wrote as an assertion of artistic and personal independence, and, indeed, throughout his life he was to refuse to join most societies and clubs, feeling, as he wrote in 1948, "that I can function more effectively and honestly if I don't join a group and accept a group program, however sympathetic to it I may feel."[2] White's insistence on personal and artistic independence as embodied in these assertions provides a leitmotiv in his life story and an illuminating perspective on his long and productive career.

Consonant with this determined artistic independence was White's insistence, unwavering throughout his career, that the subject of any writer's art must be the self, must be a record of an individual's passionate engagement with the world. If not carried to extremes, he wrote as a young man just out of college, "self is the most interesting thing in the world, . . . and life would be far less gallant and exciting if men were not continually absorbed with watching what they're doing with their own hands and marvelling at the stew which is simmering in their own heads."[3] Though White may not have realized it at the time, this early statement—situated, as it seems to be, in youthful egocentrism—was to become the aesthetic center of gravity for his work and for the life he explored—and exploited—during his long career.

After some initial difficulties in discovering a way to support himself while exploring the individual plight, White found his medium in the *New Yorker*, where he became a staff writer in 1926. There, he later recalled, he made "the enormously important discovery that the world would pay a man for setting down a simple, legible account of his own misfortunes." There followed, he added, "a long vista of profitable confession."[4] "Writing is translation," he wrote at the end of 1951, "and the opus to be translated is yourself" (*Letters,* 346). "If a writer succeeds in communicating with a reader," he added in 1956, "I think it is simply because he has been trying (with some success) to get in touch with himself—to clarify the reception" (*Letters,* 417). These mid-career assessments of his work and purpose echo, with remarkable consistency, similar statements White offered at the beginning of his professional life. In a letter to his brother written in early 1929, White indicated "that sometimes in writing of myself—which is the only subject anyone knows intimately—I have occasionally had the exquisite thrill of putting my finger on a little capsule of truth, and heard it give the faint squeak of mortality under my pressure, an antic sound" (*Letters,* 85). A crucial understanding of White's career and many of his life decisions, then, emerges from a consideration of his often reiterated aesthetic—that "the first person singular is the only grammatical implement I am able to use without cutting myself," that his works, as he said particularly of *One Man's Meat* (1942), his favorite collection of essays, are strictly "of, for, and by an individual."[5]

These persistent statements of aesthetic intention and lifetime dedication are essentially twentieth-century reiterations of Henry David Thoreau's opening statement in *Walden:* "I should not talk so much about myself if there were anybody else whom I knew as well." They indicate White's intention to fulfill Thoreau's requirement that a writer must provide "a simple and sincere account of his own life, and not merely what he has heard of other men's lives."[6] White's lifelong dedication to keeping "the minutes of his own meeting" originated, perhaps, from his early reading of *Walden.* The book's effects on him were certainly profound. "*Walden* is the only book I own," White wrote at midpoint in his career. "Every man, I think, reads one book in his life, and this one is mine." White kept *Walden* always by him—"for relief in moments of defluxion and despair," as he put it—and Thoreau's nineteenth-century "morning call" everywhere resonates in White's life and works.[7]

Thoreau's influence on White manifested itself in other ways as well. White's life is a record of his attempt to live "deliberately" (to use Thoreau's term), to remain free and unencumbered in a materially rich twentieth-century America, to stay connected and in tune with the self despite the lure—and possession—of fashionable New York apartments, sloops and sailing vessels, roadsters and touring cars, a Maine farmhouse, and ever-increasing domestic and professional claims on his time. White was leery of too-insistent familial and work-related obligations, and, though he successfully satisfied both, he was careful throughout his life not to let either encroach too nearly on his independence and freedom as a writer and an individual. He clearly feared what Thoreau termed the "life of quiet desperation" lived by the majority, the entrammeled life White likened to a "spectre," its amorphous outlines determined by "the shape of a desk in an office, the dreaded tick of the nine-to-five day, the joyless afternoons of a Sunday suburb."[8]

White's life may thus be seen as the successful attempt to avoid that spirit-withering bondage that both he and Thoreau saw most human beings laboring under, as the attempt to quit the desk, as White put it in Thoreauvian accents, in order "to call on a bayberry bush, . . . to see a pond about a man; . . . to find spruce gum, look under a rock, test rain for wetness and fertility; . . . to look for Life Everlasting."[9] White pursued writing as a career because he was good at it and because it left him free: "To write a piece and sell it to a magazine is as near a simple life as shining up a pushcart full of apples and vending them to passersby. It has a pleasing directness not found in the world of commerce and business" (*Letters,* 85). Independence, the simple life, freedom from all constraints on the act of writing—these are the values everywhere celebrated in White's life and in his works.

Thoreau and White share two other important characteristics as well—their intense love for nature and their attempts to remain ever attuned to the child within, an aspect of crucial importance in any consideration of White as a writer for children. White's personal letters are fluent with references to nature and the natural world, and many of his works, most notably *Charlotte's Web,* are essentially catalogs of the abundance and rich diversity of creation. "All that I hope to say in books, all that I ever hope to say, is that I love the world," wrote a middle-aged White to an early admirer of *Charlotte's Web* (quoted in Elledge, 300). He associated what he called a "passionate love of the natural world" with "the scheme of inheritance" from a father who took him each summer for a month in the Maine woods (*Letters,* 389), and he repeatedly employed the egg as a shorthand metaphor for the germination and regeneration that so moved him in nature and without which the earth would "grow old and die."[10] "I am sending you," he wrote in 1973 to a class of sixth-grade admirers, "what I think is one of the most beautiful and miraculous things in the world—an egg" (*Letters*, 647).

Closely allied with this lifelong celebration of the natural world was the high value White put on the perennially childlike and the attempt always to remain connected to the child in himself. Like Wordsworth, like Thoreau, he saw in the child's perspective the key to remaining ever in contact with the world's wonder, with direct, unmediated observation and experience in the natural sphere, and with the sense of humor necessary to live in the world with style and grace. Once again, Thoreau's elegance of phrasing and cogency of perception must have impressed White: "Not by constraint or severity shall you have access to true wisdom but by abandonment, and childlike mirthfulness" (quoted in Elledge, 129). White accepted P. L. Travers's assertion "that anyone who writes for children successfully is probably writing for one child—namely, the child that is himself," and he surmised that unsuccessful books for children result from some kind of "internal barrier that separates the child from the man" (*Letters*, 368).

White's carefully maintained independence, his unflinching focus on the self as the appropriate subject for his writings, his intention to live simply and deliberately, his passionate love for the natural world, and his desire ever to remain in touch with childlike mirth and perception are the motifs that unify his life and literary production. White is perhaps the premier American spokesperson for these principles in the twentieth century as Thoreau was in the nineteenth. White's necessary and largely successful compromises between these values and twentieth-century technological complexity are nowhere more clearly evident than in his domestic arrangements at his home in North Brooklin, Maine. White lived and often worked in a large farmhouse, where daily he had to attend to "the thousand and one exciting little necessities which spring from a 12-room steam-heated house standing all alone in a big world" (*Letters*, 189). Still, he wrote *Charlotte's Web*, certainly his masterpiece, in a simple boathouse furnished with only "a chair, a bench, a table, a nail keg for a wastebasket, and a wood stove" (quoted in Elledge, 323–24). This boathouse, edging away from the mailbox, telephone, radio, and other modern distractions of the farmhouse and perched on the edge of a windy cove of an often unruly sea, was exactly the same size as Thoreau's cabin at Walden Pond—a spare, deliberate 10 by 15 feet.

"All Beginnings Are Wonderful"[11]

Elwyn Brooks White was born on 11 July 1899 in Mount Vernon, New York, a fashionable suburb 25 minutes by train from New York City. His mother, Jessie Hart White, was a daughter of the artist William Hart, a member of the Hudson River School and first president of the Brooklyn Academy of Design. His father, Samuel Tilly White, worked himself up, in Horatio Alger fashion, from errand boy to president and one of the principal shareholders and trustees of Horace Waters & Co., a prosperous New York piano manufacturing concern.

White's childhood was spent comfortably among loving and indulgent parents and five solicitous older siblings in a spacious house on a quiet, tree-lined street. This house and its occupants provided him with security and safe harbor from his boyhood adventures in neighboring backyards and stables, in Wilson's Woods, in open fields, and on nearby Siwanoy Pond, ideal for winter skating. He was, from the first, surrounded by animals and green, growing things, by the fertility and abundance of nature both wild and domesticated, allowing him "a sense of living somewhat freely in a natural world" and providing him with that enduring love for nature and its creatures which would play so strong a role in his works and in his life. During this secure and happy near-rural boyhood, with its long days and free-ranging adventures, White experienced what he called his "first and greatest love affair," the object of his love being "freedom," a "lady of infinite allure . . . who restores and supplies us all" (quoted in Elledge, 18).

White claimed for himself a large share of the normal fears of childhood: "I was uneasy about practically everything: the uncertainty of the future, the dark of the attic, the panoply and discipline of school, the transitoriness of life, the mystery of the church and of God, the frailty of the body, the sadness of afternoon, the shadow of sex, the distant challenge of love and marriage, the far-off problem of a livelihood" (*Letters*, 1). He was, however, blessed with sufficient economic and familial security needed to confront these fears successfully. According to Elledge, White did not exaggerate his early fears: "Much of the story of the life of E. B. White is the story of how he has come to terms with his fears; and that story begins early" (23). One of the most potent armaments against this "unusual number of worries" was a firm belief in the essential benevolence of regenerative nature. White was sustained by "a faith nourished by the natural world rather than by the supernatural or the spiritual" ("A Boy I Knew," 34). This faith was revitalized each year during the family's annual sojourns (beginning in August 1905) at a rented camp on Great Pond, one of the Belgrade Lakes in Maine. These trips—"four solid weeks of heaven," as White remembered them—were the highlights of his youthful years and were to form in him a lifelong love for Maine itself and for boats, which, according to Elledge, White saw as "exciting symbols of freedom" (28). White's later writing is threaded by vivid and affectionate remembrances of these summer idylls in Maine.

This host of childhood worries and fears could also be routed by an additional weapon—writing, which White commenced very early in order "to assuage my uneasiness and collect my thoughts" (*Letters,* 1). Even at the age of seven or eight, according to White, he knew, while looking at a blank sheet of writing paper, that "this is where I belong, this is it" (*Letters,* 281). Perhaps it is no accident that *Charlotte's Web,* White's most important work for children, ends with Wilbur secure in the natural world of the barnyard, all his fears vanquished forever through Charlotte's wondrous web-writing.

White's success as a writer began early with a prize from *Woman's Home Companion* for a 1909 poem about a mouse, one of the many predecessors of Stuart Little. This award was followed by a silver badge at 13 and a gold one at 14 from *St. Nicholas Magazine,* the leading periodical for juveniles at the beginning of this century. Early on, he began to keep a daily journal that he disciplined himself to write in for the next 20 years. The early success of his writing seems to have provided him his most important satisfactions as a student in elementary and high school. Formal education he regarded as a necessary tedium to be endured in order to arrive at summer vacations and his much-coveted freedom. In his senior year at Mount Vernon High he was assistant editor of the *Oracle,* the school literary journal, and published several stories there as well as an editorial and a parody of Longfellow's *Song of Hiawatha.*

After graduation from high school, White, following the example of his two older brothers, entered Cornell in September 1917, having won two scholarships totaling a thousand dollars (tuition at Cornell was then only one hundred dollars a year) and having failed the physical examination required for enlistment in the wartime army. Cornell was a good choice for White because of its natural setting and its emphasis on educational freedom. Situated among the gorges, woods, and hills of the beautiful Finger Lakes region of upstate New York, the school promoted intellectual openness and the freedom for students to make choices concerning their own educational priorities. Cornell had a seminal and shaping influence on White. There he earned a name for himself, both literally and figuratively. Dubbed "Andy" after Cornell's first president, Andrew D. White, a nickname he welcomed in lieu of his own more cumbersome and thoroughly disliked given name, he was to be called "Andy" for the remainder of his life by those close to him. He also earned a name for himself as a promising writer through his association with the student newspaper, the *Cornell Daily Sun*. A reporter on the *Sun* during his freshman year, White was elected during his sophomore year to the paper's board of editors. Faculty members and fellow students wrote letters of praise for his succinct, informative news stories and lively interpretive pieces as well as for his humorous poems and one-liners. During his junior year he was elected editor-in-chief of the paper. His success as journalist and editor of the *Sun* was the most important formative influence of his years at Cornell. His receiving the Arthur Brisbane Award for an outstanding editorial was but the first of many awards he was to receive for his mature writing.

An English major, White was a mediocre student at Cornell, preferring to put his energies into his work for the *Sun* rather than grind for his classes. He had, however, the good fortune of working with four professors at Cornell who were to have a profound influence on him. From his advanced writing course with William Strunk, White learned how to hone the English sentence into a clear, graceful, bold, concise conveyance of thought. In 1959 White was to promulgate Strunk's stylistic precepts in his expanded and rewritten edition of Strunk's brief, pithy, privately printed pamphlet *The Elements of Style*. At the Manuscript Club, founded and hosted by Professor Martin Sampson for the encouragement of young writers, White found a critical yet sympathetic audience for his works, and at Professor Bristow Adams's Monday night gatherings, White formed many of his attitudes and sharpened his thinking and his conversational wit during the wide-ranging discussions on diverse issues. From Professor George Lincoln Burr he imbibed the convictions that were to structure his life and career. Calling his encounter with Burr "the greatest single thing that ever happened in my life," White credited Burr with providing him "with blinding clarity" the realization of "how vital it is for Man to live in a free society." "The experience enabled me to grow up almost overnight," White continued; "it gave my thoughts and ambitions a focus." He claimed that this transforming insight "caused me indirectly to pursue the kind of work which eventually enabled me to earn my living," and, most important, "it gave me a principle of thought and of action . . . for which I shall gladly continue to fight for the remainder of my life" (quoted in Elledge, 58–59).

White's success at Cornell was unqualified. He had formed himself as a writer, had gained social and intellectual skills which fitted him for a place in the world, and had come under the influence of four men from whom he had received a set of values and a sense of commitment that would guide him personally and professionally throughout his life. His graduation from Cornell in June 1921, however, thrust him into a world arena not as tidy and clearly orchestrated as his college campus had been. Prepared to succeed in that world, White set out to find a situation after a summer as a counselor at Camp Otter, a boys' camp near Dorset, Ontario. In Ontario he fell in love with a Nature much wilder than that encountered during his summers on the Belgrade Lakes.

There followed a series of briefly held jobs in Manhattan, to which White commuted from his parents' home in Mount Vernon. The first of these was a stint of several weeks duration as a reporter for the United Press, a job he found uncongenial because he did not relish writing about assigned topics according to a deadline. After savoring a few weeks of freedom, he took a job in public relations, writing press releases and editing an in-house publication for a silk mill. After several other jobs of equally brief duration, he went to work for the American Legion News Service doing publicity work. To relieve the tedium of his days on the job and the too-quiet domesticity of his evenings with his elderly parents in Mount Vernon, White wrote poems that appeared in various New York daily literary columns, including Franklin Pierce Adams's "Conning Tower" in the *New York World* and Christopher Morley's famous "Bowling Green" in the *New York Post*.

Dissatisfied with the jobs then available in New York, not knowing exactly what he wanted to do instead, not ready to commit himself to his ongoing but inconclusive relationship with a Cornell student named Alice Burchfield, White decided in February 1922 to seek the open road in his Ford Model T, dubbed "Hotspur." On 9 March he and Howard Cushman, a friend from Cornell, set out to see America. Their intention was to stay at various chapter houses of their fraternity Phi Gamma Delta and to earn traveling money by doing odd jobs along the way and by syndicating a daily humor column detailing their adventures and parodying traditional travel accounts. Though this writing venture did not come to fruition, the exhilarating combination of youth and freedom saw them through hungry and uncomfortable times as they made their way West, sometimes on roads marked only with a painted arrow tacked to a power-line pole or two wheel-ruts disappearing in the tall grass of the plains. This transcontinental trek was to resonate in White's later writings, especially in the nostalgic essay "Farewell, My Lovely!" published in 1936 in the *New Yorker* and in the lovingly recounted journeys in *Stuart Little* and *The Trumpet of the Swan*. White's journey west was an American alternative to the expatriate sojourns in Europe of other American writers of the 1920s.

Once they reached Seattle, Cushman returned home and White signed on with the *Seattle Times* as a reporter. Unhappy in Seattle and finding his job as reporter as uncongenial as he had found similar work in New York, White nonetheless remained at his post until March 1923 when the *Seattle Times* publisher asked him to write a daily personal column consisting of brief comments, anecdotes, paragraphs, and poems along the lines of the literary columns in the great New York dailies. In this column White served the true apprenticeship for what was to be his life's work, hitting upon his uniquely personal and autobiographical subject matter and inventing and refining the forms he would most consistently use in the *New Yorker*'s "Notes and Comment" section that he was later to make such an outstanding success.

Three months later, however, White was complaining about the restrictions of a daily deadline. After producing almost 80 columns, he was laid off in June, to little discernible regret, and, after a month longer in Seattle, he booked a first-class passage on the S. S. *Buford* bound for Alaska and Siberia. At Skagway he changed from privileged passenger to saloon-boy and eventually worked his way back to Seattle, where he boarded the Canadian Pacific for the long trip home by rail. In the fall of 1923, a 24-year-old White presented himself at his parents' home, discouraged and with no clear prospects, but with a wealth of experiences to recount.

"Here at the *New Yorker*"

In late 1923 White went to work in the Frank Seaman advertising agency in the layout department, commuting from Mount Vernon each morning. He satisfied his creative urges by continuing to publish verses in "The Conning Tower" in company with Dorothy Parker, Don Marquis, John O'Hara, William Rose Benét, and other New York wits. During the two years that White was performing his uncongenial advertising duties at Frank Seaman's, his future boss, Harold Ross, was putting together a new weekly magazine with financier Raoul Fleischmann. This weekly, to be called the *New Yorker*, would publish short pieces of satire, humor, news, and light verse as well as brief reviews, profiles, character sketches, and sports commentary—all in a relaxed, albeit sophisticated, package intended for any New Yorker who wished to be in the know about doings in the city. White acquired the first issue (21 February 1925) at a newsstand in Grand Central Station and was immediately attracted by its brief articles and casual, witty tone. As White recalled, the generally unnoticed appearance of Ross's *New Yorker* on the scene "was a turning point in my life, although I did not know it at the time" (*Letters,* 72). He immediately began submitting short pieces, including poems, receiving small checks and no little satisfaction in return.

In 1925 White quit his job at Seaman's and moved to a furnished Greenwich Village apartment, which he shared with three friends from Cornell. He continued to submit to the *New Yorker* articles that soon came to embody for Ross, and for his editorial assistant, Katharine Sergeant (Mrs. Ernest) Angell, the exact tone and authorial voice the magazine was looking for. By 1926, on the recommendation of Mrs. Angell, Ross had made White several offers to join the *New Yorker* staff full time. When White stopped by the magazine's offices, he was met by Mrs. Angell. White recalled the introduction many years later: "I sat there peacefully gazing at the classic features of my future wife without, as usual, knowing what I was doing" (*Letters,* 72).

Ross persisted in offering the skittish White a job. Finally, after much hesitation and negotiation, Ross in late 1926 worked out with his reluctant quarry an agreement whereby White would work half-time for the *New Yorker* and half-time for the advertising firm of J. H. Newmark, where he was then employed. As his duties increased at the magazine and as he found them congenial, he eventually resigned from the advertising firm to join Ross's enterprise full time. At last he had discovered a way to make a living by writing what he wanted and when and where he wanted to write it. Like everyone else in the first years of the magazine, White wrote whatever was needed, from captions for drawings to movie and drama reviews, from verse to "Comment" and "Talk of the Town" copy, those short pieces of news, gossip, and editorial opinion that filled the magazine's opening pages. His colleagues, fellow contributors, and friends included some of the most important names in twentieth-century American journalism, art, and literature, including, among many others over many years, James Thurber, Ralph Ingersoll, Peter Arno, Charles Addams, Rea Irvin (whose Regency dandy, "Eustace Tilly," appeared on the cover of the first issue and on each subsequent anniversary issue), Katharine S. White, George S. Kaufman, Clarence Day,

S. J. Perelman, Dorothy Parker, Ogden Nash, Phyllis McGinley, Marc Connelly, Alexander Woollcott, Frank Sullivan, Clifton Fadiman, Sam Behrman, Heywood Broun, Ring Lardner, John O'Hara, Brendan Gill, Edmund Wilson, Lewis Mumford, Vladimir Nabokov, and John Updike.

Ross's smart, sophisticated metropolitan weekly was tottering precariously when he hired Katharine Angell in the summer of 1925. "I can't imagine what would have happened to the magazine if she hadn't turned up," White wrote later of the woman who was to become his wife. Refined, cordial but reserved, patient but sturdy in her opinions, a product of Miss Winsor's School for Girls and Bryn Mawr, Katharine Angell was everything Harold Ross was not. (According to all accounts, Ross was clumsy and ungainly, unpolished and profane, and largely uneducated—a man of uncouth habits and uninformed opinions who nevertheless possessed the vision, taste, and genius to impose his will on a disorderly new magazine and transform it into one of the most admired and influential publishing ventures in all of American letters.) As White later indicated, Katharine Angell "complemented [Ross] in a way that, in retrospect, seems to me to have been indispensable to the survival of the magazine" (*Letters*, 74). They came together—and White joined the two of them at this juncture—in their passion for clarity, for humor, for what Ross called "journalistic integrity." Ross and Katharine Angell soon discovered that "there was practically no purpose to which words could be put that White was unable to master" (Elledge, 122). In 1927, according to Elledge, White published 24 "Talk of the Town" pieces, 30 "casuals" (short, usually humorous anecdotal paragraphs), 15 pieces of light verse, four theater reviews, numerous taglines for "Newsbreaks" and captions for pictures, and 10 full-page advertisements for a *New Yorker* subscription campaign.

During 1927 White met James Thurber and introduced him to Ross, who promptly hired him at the *New Yorker*. In the early years of this important friendship White helped Thurber discipline his writing; he also discovered Thurber as an artist. According to Brendan Gill in *Here at the New Yorker*, "It was White, indeed, who helped to form Thurber and to ensure that his contributions to the magazine were substantial ones."[12] White retrieved Thurber's crumpled doodles from the wastebasket, often provided them with captions, and argued their merits tirelessly with Ross, later inking in and coloring a Thurber drawing that he persuaded Ross to run as a *New Yorker* cover, the first of many to follow.

While his friendship with Thurber was developing in 1927, White found himself increasingly attracted to Katharine Angell, by then the

New Yorker's fiction editor. White's interest in this unhappily married mother of two, who was technically his boss and also seven years his senior, was initially expressed in an understandably indirect and tentative way—through a poem, "Notes from a Desk Calender," edited by Mrs. Angell, published in the *New Yorker* early in 1928, and followed by other thinly disguised love poems in that magazine and in Franklin Pierce Adams's "The Conning Tower." Later in 1928 White and Katharine Angell rendezvoused in Paris, where she had gone with her family on holiday. After an interlude in St. Tropez and Corsica, White and Katharine Angell returned to New York determined to be sensible. At the beginning of 1929 White was debating in his journal whether or not to quit his job, as he had so often done in early youth, and leave town without telling anyone where he was heading. By February 1929 Katharine Angell had separated from her husband, and in May, despite familial pressures exerted on her to remain in what she considered an abusive marriage, she left New York for the three months in Reno, Nevada, that were required to obtain a divorce. (She insisted throughout her life that her relationship with White had nothing to do with her decision to divorce a man whom she had married while very young, who had developed very different ideas of marriage from those she cherished, and with whom she had discovered she had little in common.) Hoping White would visit her in Reno, she was disappointed when he opted instead to return to the boy life of Camp Otter in Ontario, Canada, and to buy a share in the camp where he had served as a counselor in his college days.

By September 1929 both White and Katharine Angell were back at work at the *New Yorker*. Earlier in the year White had published a book of poems, *The Lady Is Cold*, and in November, *Is Sex Necessary?*, a spoof of popular sex manuals and psychosexual jargon. Co-authored with Thurber and published nine days after the stock market crash, the work featured some of the first drawings by Thurber. On 13 November 1929 White appeared at Katharine Angell's apartment to take up again the old issue of whether or not they should marry. They married that afternoon and were back in their offices on time the next morning. A day or so later Katharine White received by inter-office memo a Rea Irvin cartoon of a man deep in thought, the original caption changed by her new husband (a man notoriously wary of entanglements that would compromise his freedom) to read, "E. B. White slowly accustomed himself to the idea that he had made the most beautiful decision of his life" (*Letters*, 89). Katharine White confided to a friend that "if it lasts only a year, it will be worth it" (quoted in Elledge, 173). Their son Joel was born on 21

December 1930, providing White with the "mixed pride and oppression of fatherhood in the very base of my spine" (*Letters,* 103).

The first six years of White's marriage proved to be among the happiest and most productive of his life. The *New Yorker* was prospering, gaining in subscriptions and in literary attention and acquiring more and more accomplished artists and writers on staff and as contributors. Both Whites were professionally engaged and handsomely paid. Katharine White as fiction editor was forging a distinctive and influential *New Yorker* narrative style. E. B. White's contributions continued to ensure the success of the magazine and in large part determined its essential tone and character.

During the summer of 1931 the Whites rented a house in Blue Hill, Maine, where they returned for the next several summers until they bought the large salt-marsh farmhouse and connected barn at Allen Cove outside of Brooklin, Maine, in the fall of 1933. There White was to produce *Charlotte's Web* and *The Trumpet of the Swan* as well as the essays upon which his reputation now firmly rests.

"The Slow Blood of Our Discontent"

Toward the end of 1933, White, then 34, was apparently depressed by his failure to write anything other than his weekly pieces for the *New Yorker*, those "few rather precise little paragraphs, into which we pour the slow blood of our discontent."[13] In mid-January 1934 he repaired to Camden, South Carolina, to work on what he hoped would be something more important, but there he remained unfocused, frittering his time away and returning in only five days. Six weeks later he was in Florida recuperating from the flu, one of the illnesses—most of them hypochondriacal—that he was to suffer in 1934, a year of discontent filled with fears, illnesses, and brief attempts at escape from a life made unsatisfactory by what he felt was the modest scale of his success at the *New Yorker*. This growing unease in his personal and professional life was exacerbated by the mounting world tensions that Ralph Ingersoll, a former colleague at the *New Yorker*, accused White of irresponsibly ignoring in writings that skirted the important social issues of concern to citizens facing the Great Depression and the impending world disasters then escalating in Europe. Ingersoll described White as "shy, frightened of life, often melancholy, always hypochondriac" and scolded him for reflecting these narrow qualities in his "gossamer writing" that was "so carefully swathed in whimsey" while the world tottered around him.[14]

In 1935 White's father died, Katharine had a miscarriage, Thurber left the staff of the *New Yorker*, and White lost his substantial investment in Camp Otter, that place where he had tried so hard to recapture his lost boyhood. In that year also, Ross summarily rejected White's request to write henceforth in the first person singular rather than in the editorial "we" and turned down his request to write his own column in the magazine. White was, however, cheered by the largely appreciative reviews occasioned by the publication in October 1934 of *Every Day Is Saturday*, a selection of his *New Yorker* "Notes and Comment" pieces from 1928 to 1934. In this work he had confirmed the general speculation that he was indeed the author of these anonymously published paragraphs, all of which employed the masking editorial "we" that he had come to feel a burden on his freedom as a writer: "It is almost impossible to write anything decent using the editorial 'we,' unless you are the Dionne family," he wrote to Gus Lobrano in 1934. "Anonymity, plus the 'we,' give a writer a cloak of dishonesty" (*Letters,* 121).

Though he continued to produce his full share of "Notes and Comment" paragraphs through 1936 and early 1937, White was eager for a break from his duties and deadlines at the *New Yorker*. Accordingly, by the end of May 1937, he had decided to take a year's leave, not only from the magazine but also from his family. In a letter of 31 May 1937 he gave his wife three reasons for taking what he called "my year of grace": he was quitting his job, he wrote, "partly because I am not satisfied with the use I am making of my talents . . . ; partly because I am not having fun working at my job—and am in a rut there; partly because I long to recapture something which everyone loses when he agrees to perform certain creative miracles on specified dates for a particular sum" (*Letters,* 154). Katharine White could not have been happy with this abdication of job and familial duties, but she knew well the premium her husband put on independence, the focus on the creative self unencumbered, the recapturing of a creative youthful spontaneity, the Thoreauvian return to a simplicity difficult to maintain in New York City. It was understood that during this year White was to devote his energies to completing a long, autobiographical poem, though he insisted that he had no real plans and was simply invoking "man's ancient privilege of going and coming in a whimsical, rather than a reasonable, manner" (*Letters,* 154). After leaving New York, White went on a 12-day cruise in Maine waters and pilgrimages to the scenes of his youth, ignoring *New Yorker* pleas to return to writing "Notes and Comment" and Thurber's admonitions that "this is not a time for writers to escape to their sailboats and their farms" (quoted in Elledge, 205).

White's "year off" actually extended only from August 1937 to April 1938. He felt he had made "an unholy mess" of it (*Letters,* 170). Though he had little to show for these eight months in actual work accomplished, he had made some crucial life decisions. By 1 March 1938 he had persuaded a reluctant Katharine to give up what she apparently considered the best job held by any woman to live in Maine full time and serve the *New Yorker* as long-distance, part-time fiction editor. White had also decided to give up his anonymous weekly *New Yorker* paragraphs in order to write a monthly signed column for *Harper's,* though a forlorn Ross persuaded him to continue to contribute occasional pieces to the *New Yorker* on his own schedule and at a handsome increase in pay. For the next four and a half years, from 1937 to 1941, White's primary allegiance was to *Harper's,* and the signed works he produced in his "One Man's Meat" column were masterpieces of the informal essay, some of the best works in that medium in all of American letters. Though uncertain as to the appropriateness of their retreat to a farm in the face of an escalating world crisis, the Whites were relatively happy in Maine and highly productive, editing together *A Subtreasury of American Humor* (1941) and seeing White's volume of poems *The Fox of Peapack* (1938) and his collection of satirical sketches *Quo Vadimus?* (1939) through the press.

In 1942 White published a collection of the *Harper's* columns in *One Man's Meat,* generally considered his best book of essays. In his foreword to that collection White connected his writings to what he saw the war as being all about: "Individualism and the first person singular are closely related to freedom, and are what the fight is about." In addition to its large sales at home, *One Man's Meat* was published in an Armed Services Edition of 150,000 copies and translated into French and German for an additional 100,000 copies to be marketed overseas.

The occasional pieces White was publishing in the *New Yorker* during the years of his commitment to *Harper's* more than satisfied Ross in style and content but not in quantity. Ross cajoled White to return to his magazine, but what Ross could not accomplish on his own the outbreak of hostilities in Europe accomplished for him: White acceded to Ross's argument that he could make a greater contribution in this time of national emergency by covering the war in "Notes and Comment" for the *New Yorker* than he could in Maine writing his monthly column for *Harper's.* Accordingly, White gave up "One Man's Meat" in March 1943, a significant career departure since he considered the essays for this column his best hope for critical acceptance as a serious author rather than as a journalist devoted merely to the topical and the passing event. Becoming again a staff editorialist for the *New Yorker* would necessitate a move back to New York—a move much desired by his wife, who was eager to return to full-time editing at the magazine. Granted a large increase in salary and bonus incentives, sensitive to his wife's professional needs, and, most important, convinced that he could use "Notes and Comment" to contribute to the war effort and to advocate an effective world government in lieu of the squabbling nationalism responsible for the ongoing butchery in Europe and the Pacific, White returned in fall 1943 to full-time work at the *New Yorker* and to living in the city.

In April 1945 he traveled to San Francisco as the *New Yorker's* correspondent at the conference called to establish the United Nations, and in the fall of 1946 he published *The Wild Flag*, a collection of his editorials and articles on world government. In this work, as he wrote to his brother Stanley, "I make my debut as a THINKER," which White equated with "stepping up on the guillotine platform wearing a faint smile" (*Letters,* 277). White was keenly aware that advocacy and political involvement were not his suits as a writer, as he demonstrated in a "Notes and Comment" piece written in 1945 for the twentieth anniversary of the magazine: "we feel like a man who left his house to go to a Punch-and-Judy show and, by some error in direction, wandered into 'Hamlet.'"[15] On the dust jacket of *The Wild Flag* White, or an advertising agent whose copy White surely approved, noted that the author "feels ill-at-ease writing editorials on massive themes" and that he regards himself as "a clown of average ability whose signals got crossed and who found himself out on the wire with the Wallendas."[16] Despite White's frustration at what he considered the postwar failure of his bright hopes for a "supranational" world government and his discomfort at having become embroiled as a political thinker and an advocate of causes, his popularity as a writer had increased enormously, and his involvement with *Harper's* and the *New Yorker* from 1938 to 1946 had netted these publications substantial increases in subscribers.

"To Improve the Nick of Time"

White came to the writing of children's books relatively late in life and, according to Scott Elledge, with a sense of failure at not having yet produced a work that would validate him as a serious author rather than as merely a journalist writing of the topical and therefore ephemeral. In late 1944, while enduring bouts of severe depression and "head trouble," White, then 45, was completing the manuscript of *Stuart Little*, his first children's book. The novel, with illustrations by Garth Williams, was published in October 1945 and had already sold more than 42,000 copies before the end of the month, helped, apparently, by strong reviews in major periodicals and New York newspapers. By January 1977 *Stuart Little* had sold over two and a half million copies and had been translated into more than 20 languages.

Despite the outstanding success of his first work for children, White's depression and various psychosomatic illnesses persisted. During 1946 his output for the *New Yorker* amounted to only about half of the previous year's production, and he suffered bouts of anxiety over the publication of *The Wild Flag*. In 1947 Ross finally approved White's request, repeated over the years, to write a signed column for the *New Yorker*, though White produced only two pieces before giving up the project, perhaps at the advice of a psychiatrist he was then seeing. Both "The Second Tree from the Corner" and "Death of a Pig" were written at this time, essays recounting episodes in which, as Elledge interprets them, "a sick man is temporarily relieved of his anxiety" (270).

The following year, 1948, saw White considerably buoyed by a return of his usual productivity in writing *New Yorker* editorials and by the honorary degrees conferred on him by Yale, Dartmouth, and the University of Maine that spring. In January 1949 White wrote his brother Stanley of his "decision to give up the responsibility of the *New Yorker*'s editorial page," preferring to apply himself "to more irregular and peaceable pursuits for a while, to work patiently instead of rapidly," and, in a quotation from Thoreau, "to improve the nick of time" (*Letters,* 305).

In short, White opted for the freedom to write where, when, and what he wished. He may have used this unscheduled time in 1949 to work on what was to become *Charlotte's Web*, though the first draft was written in his boathouse in Maine, apparently during the spring and summer of 1950. White prided himself on the scientific accuracy of his descriptions of Charlotte, as well as on Garth Williams's illustrations for the book.

The contract with Harper for the publication of *Charlotte's Web* was not signed until March 1952. During the period between the book's first-draft completion and its publication, he had substantially increased his contributions to the *New Yorker* and was rethinking and rewriting *Charlotte's Web*. In December 1951 Ross, suffering from lung cancer, died suddenly in Boston on the operating table, and White wrote his obituary for the *New Yorker*. Ross was succeeded by the magazine's "fact editor," William Shawn, for whom the Whites threw a party attended by almost 140 people.

These events served to distract White from his usual prepublication jitters. He need not have worried. From its publication date of 15 October 1952 to the present, *Charlotte's Web* has been an enormous success. Only seven years before, *Stuart Little* had sold more than 100,000 copies in its first year. Excellent reviews by the likes of David McCord, Bennett Cerf, Richard Armour, Eudora Welty, and P. L. Travers proclaimed the book a classic and helped to boost its sales far beyond the expectation of author or publisher. According to Elledge, more than six million copies of *Charlotte's Web* had been sold by 1984. Even if White had written nothing else besides *Charlotte's Web*, his contribution to children's literature would have been immense and his reputation secure.

The Whites decided to remain in New York until Katharine's sixty-fifth birthday and subsequent retirement in 1957. Though White himself apparently chafed at remaining in New York tied to his *New Yorker* deadlines, he did not wish to separate his wife from a job she found every satisfaction in, as he had done in 1938. In January 1954 he published *The Second Tree from the Corner*, a "clipbook" of works first published in the *New Yorker*. He remained in Maine from April to October, producing more for the *New Yorker* in that year than he would ever produce again. In June 1954 he accepted honorary degrees from Harvard University and Colby College and agreed to submit an essay to the *Yale Review* marking the centennial of the publication of *Walden*, the work most influential in his own life and career.

After a brief excursion to England in June 1955, White stopped contributing to "Notes and Comment," and Katharine gave notice that she intended to stop working full time for the magazine after February 1956, a year earlier than her sixty-fifth birthday when she had originally intended to retire. With, however, the death in February 1956 of Gus Lobrano, the fiction editor who had succeeded Katharine when she resigned the position in 1938, she was asked to stay on for two more years, and she accepted.

During this time—and before and after—the Whites continuously worried over "a joint ill health," which, according to their longtime colleague Brendan Gill, "many of their friends have been inclined to regard as imaginary." In *Here at the New Yorker*, a work that incensed the Whites, Gill commented that "it was always wonderful to behold the intuitive adjustments by which one of them got well in time for the other to get sick. . . . Certainly they have been the strongest and most productive unhealthy couple that I have ever encountered" (293).

In May 1957 Katharine White informed William Shawn that she was resigning as fiction editor on the magazine, and she and White began to make plans for a permanent resettlement in Maine. They were to have 20 more years together at their North Brooklin farmhouse on Allen Cove. According to Elledge, the move to Maine meant "coming home" to White: "it meant, not retirement, but increased activity—more time for the business of living" (323). No longer fretted by deadlines, he nevertheless intended to continue writing, sandwiching this now-lucrative occupation between farm duties that he considered more rewarding. Katharine, too, soon accommodated herself to the slower pace of her retirement, though she continued to edit for the *New Yorker* on a part-time basis.

Soon after moving to Maine, White began to revise *The Elements of Style*, a 43-page pamphlet that formed the nucleus of William Strunk, Jr.'s writing courses that White had taken at Cornell. This revision amounted to a rewrite, complete with new material and examples, as well as a 3,500-word essay entitled "An Approach to Style," in which White argued that the primary duty of any writer is to write to please the self, to attempt to disclose one's own thoughts to oneself: "The beginner should approach style warily," he wrote, "realizing that it is himself he is approaching, no other."[17] When certain preliminary reviews from teachers of college composition suggested that White's manuscript should be less prescriptive and should accommodate itself to majority usage, White opted that this work "of a dead precisionist and a half-dead disciple of his" should be published as is or not at all. He refused to adjust "the unadjustable Mr. Strunk to the modern liberal of the English Department, the anything-goes fellow" (*Letters,* 454–55). *The Elements of Style* was published as is in 1959 and sold more than 200,000 copies in the first year; by 1982, three years after the third edition of a book White had earlier characterized as "small, concise, opinionated, non-comprehensive—a squeaky voice from the past," it had sold close to six million copies and was in use in thousands of college English courses in the United States (*Letters,* 453).

In 1960 White received the Gold Medal for Essays and Criticism awarded by the National Institute of Arts and Letters. At the first of the following year Katharine White reluctantly severed her editorial ties with the magazine she had worked for for more than 35 years and into which she had poured so much of her energies. White quipped that on her retirement she looked "as though she were entering Leavenworth" (*Letters,* 474). Her achievement at the *New Yorker* was considerable. Brendan Gill, though he seems to have had few cordial feelings for her, indicated that "she had helped to invent the magazine as a whole" and that "her influence extended far beyond [the fiction] department" because "she took care to make her weight felt at every turn." "Thanks in part to her," he stated in his usual two-handed commentary, the *New Yorker* "would be not simply a funny magazine; we would be a magazine as serious, and as ambitious, as she was, and we would be much the better for it" (290). Within a few weeks of her retirement, her health began to fail, though she was to live, a semi-invalid, until 1977.

The year 1961 was to be one of losses. Thurber died in November, ending a long, important, though often strained friendship. The careers of White and Thurber had been closely intertwined from the early days of the *New Yorker*. Brendan Gill noted that together "they had done more than anybody else to set the tone of *The New Yorker*"—"a certain gentle and playful acuteness of sensibility" that Ross could not himself supply but that "he was quick to sense the need for . . . and to champion it when he came upon it in White's and Thurber's writing." In their works "Ross found an attitude around which to construct a magazine" (Gill, 287). Gill credits the triumvirate of Thurber and the Whites with the enormous—and unexpected—success of Ross's enterprise.

The fall of 1962 saw the widely and favorably reviewed publication of White's *The Points of My Compass*, a collection of essays written for the *New Yorker* during the preceding seven years. There followed a fallow period during which White, attentive to his wife in her time of deteriorating health, wrote comparatively little. Katharine was unable to continue writing her annual articles on gardening for the *New Yorker* as she had discontinued writing the *New Yorker*'s annual review of children's books some years earlier. In January 1963, while spending a month in Florida, White's health broke down: he was diagnosed by a doctor with a duodenal ulcer and by himself with a "total collapse," "what in happier days we used to call a 'nervous breakdown'" (*Letters,* 498). His health improved on his return to Maine in February, however, and in July he was awarded the Presidential Medal of Freedom by President Kennedy, but Katharine's ill health prevented his journeying to Washington to receive the medal in person.

The years from 1960 to 1965 were thus challenging ones for the Whites, beleaguered as they were by ill health and by the tensions, especially in Katharine's case, of adjusting to advancing age and the gradual relinquishing of pursuits that had been satisfying for so long. By the end of 1965, however, White was writing several *New Yorker* essays, and Katharine, temporarily in improved health, had begun another gardening essay. But such creative periods did not last long: through much of 1967 and 1968 White was complaining of persistent dizziness and consulting doctors as to its cause. There were varying diagnoses, including White's: "My own suspicion," he wrote Roger Angell, his stepson, "is that I am dizzy for all the old reliable reasons, inability to write being one" (*Letters,* 564).

In 1968 White was writing his third children's book, *The Trumpet of the Swan,* which he had begun sometime earlier. An impetus to complete it was provided by Katharine's continued ill health and by his recurrent fears that he himself would die soon, leaving her unprovided for. After almost three months in a hospital in early 1969, Katharine emerged an invalid attended by nurses and sleeping at home in a hospital bed. When White presented the manuscript of *The Trumpet of the Swan* to his publisher in November 1969, both he and Katharine were in such ill health that he did not think they would live to see its publication if he let the manuscript sit idle for a year before rewriting it, as he had done with *Charlotte's Web.* White, disappointed in the work, came to regret what he considered its premature publication. Part of his regret was that because of the early publication deadline, Garth Williams could not do the illustrations. Williams was one of many to whom he expressed his disappointment in *The Trumpet of the Swan*: "I'm not entirely happy about the text of the book—I am old and wordy, and the book seems to show it" (*Letters,* 592). Despite White's reservations, *The Trumpet of the Swan* was a best-seller, and, though White was correct in recognizing its weaknesses, it remains a thoroughly engaging work, justifiably earning for itself a continued wide readership.

In 1969 White turned 70, an age he found difficult to credit since he maintained a mental image of himself as "a lad of about 19" (quoted in Elledge, 350). This youthful inner vision of himself was corroborated externally by Brendan Gill, who described the 75-year-old White as "invincibly boyish-seeming," as a man unable to "lose his youthfulness by the tiresome necessary accident of growing old" (294). Though Gill found White's youthfulness "intrinsic and inexpungeable," White himself found his aging mind less than cooperative in his attempts to write, deploring its "bagful of nasty tricks, one of which is to tuck names and words away in crannies where they are not immediately available"

(*Letters,* 629). Nevertheless, in 1971 he wrote two "Letters from the East," and in 1972 he and Katharine helped Dorothy Lobrano Guth select and edit his letters. This volume took four years to compile and came as close as White would ever come to writing a full autobiography, his headings and footnotes to certain sections of the collected letters constituting brief autobiographical essays meant to orient the reader to the major life events chronicled in the letters. It proved an odious task for him, though he kept at it because he felt he needed the money. On its publication in November 1976 *The Letters of E. B. White* sold more than 55,000 copies by Christmas, and White took great pleasure in the letters he received from readers, many of them old friends and acquaintances who had joyfully relived their experiences with him through their reading.

The 1970s brought White several important honors. In 1971, for example, he accepted the National Medal for Literature, though he did not attend the presentation ceremonies at Lincoln Center. In 1974 he was inducted in absentia into the American Academy of Arts and Letters, and in 1978 he was awarded a "special citation" by the Pulitzer Prize advisory board in recognition of his lifetime achievement in American journalism and letters. Thus the literary world was not of White's opinion that he was "the Hall Porter of American Letters," as he called himself in a letter to Harriet Walden of 3 September 1971 (*Letters,* 625).

On 20 July 1977 Katharine White died of congestive heart failure several months short of her eighty-fifth birthday. White was by her side, but he did not attend the simple graveside service he had written for her. During the several months following her death, he answered hundreds of letters of condolence, writing lovingly of her and warmly of their nearly 48 years of marriage. To a longtime colleague on the *New Yorker* staff, White wrote, "I don't know what I ever did to deserve a wife with Katharine's qualities, but I have always had a lot of luck, and she was the most notable example." To another *New Yorker* writer he lamented that "I have lost the one thing that seemed to make any sense in my life, and I feel like a child lost at Coney Island" (Elledge, 354). As a final tribute to her, White edited and published her *New Yorker* gardening essays in *Onward and Upward in the Garden* (1979).

Though he had selected the works to be included in the *Essays of E. B. White,* he delayed publication of the volume until 1977 so as not to precede his *Letters.* His editor at Harper & Row, Corona Machemer, had helped him to edit the *Essays,* during which time they became close friends. She helped him also to compile and edit the *Poems and Sketches of E. B. White*, accompanying him in spring 1980 on a working trip to Sarasota, Florida, where they sifted through the enormous number of his fugitive pieces in order to decide which ones to include. The volume was published in 1981, and with it White felt his literary affairs had been successfully concluded. His friendship with Machemer continued, and he celebrated his eighty-first birthday canoeing with her on Great Pond, the Belgrade lake where he and his family had spent those happy Augusts nearly 70 years before. For several years following, Corona Machemer was able to detach herself from her editorial duties in New York to join White for a few days' holiday on the lakes they both knew so well from childhood.

White's last years were serene. In his eighty-third year he wrote a new preface for a third edition of *One Man's Meat*, in which he told of his intention to continue in the Maine farmhouse among scenes and settings well known and loved and among the barnyard creatures that he had for so long befriended. Though he ceased writing for publication, correspondence with many friends, acquaintances, and admirers persisted into his final years. Advancing age brought with it increasing infirmities, a gradual diminution. On 1 October 1985 he died quietly in his eighty-sixth year, of Alzheimer's disease.

One of the last of the many quotations from Thoreau with which White had salted his works and correspondence appeared in a letter to a 17-year-old student who had written him for advice in facing a future she found daunting. "At seventeen," White wrote, "the future is apt to seem formidable, even depressing. You should see the pages of my journal circa 1916." He encouraged her to "advance confidently" with the understanding that "a person's real duty in life is to save his dream." White concluded this generous letter with a quotation from Thoreau's *Walden*: "If one advances confidently in the direction of his dreams, and endeavors to live the life which he has imagined, he will meet with a success unexpected in common hours" (*Letters,* 650). Thoreau's assertion serves equally well as advice for the young and as an apt coda for White's own long life and distinguished career.

Chapter Two
"Headed in the Right Direction":
Stuart Little

The Genesis of the Novel

Stuart Little, the two-inch-tall mouse-boy, was born of a memory, a dream, and a necessity. According to Scott Elledge, White's biographer, White had been fascinated with mice since boyhood when he had built a little house, "complete with a gymnasium," for a pet mouse to whom he taught "many fine tricks." This remembered mouse, according to Elledge, was "the original Stuart Little" (Elledge, 16).

White himself chronicles Stuart's creation in an account published in the *New York Times* on 6 March 1966, the eve of Stuart's debut in a televised version of the book. On a journey by train to Virginia in the late 1920s, White indulged himself in a springtime hike up and down the Shenandoah Valley before boarding the train again for New York. Drowsy after his exertions, he fell asleep in a rhythmically rocking upper berth and there dreamed of "a small character who had the features of a mouse, was nicely dressed, courageous, and questing." This proved no ephemeral dream; White, on awakening, made a few notes about "this mouse-child" to hold Stuart in memory against a time when he might find a use for him. Stuart was, according to White, "the only fictional figure ever to have honored and disturbed my sleep."[1]

As uncle to 18 nephews and nieces, White was occasionally asked by them to weave an extemporaneous story, a task he shied away from because he found it difficult to create stories on demand and dreaded the resulting disappointment in his expectant child auditors. Answering the need to invent spontaneously, White's "dream mouse," by then named Stuart, was pressed into service. White kept the several episodes he wrote of Stuart's adventures in a desk drawer and would pull them out to read when a story request surfaced, adding to the tale as the years passed. According to his account in the *New York Times*, White reviewed the dozen or so accumulated episodes in 1938 as he was preparing to leave New York for the Maine farmhouse and, on the encouragement of his wife, submitted them to several publishers, who apparently expressed little interest in them. White then moved to Maine, taking his manuscript with him, delaying for the moment any further plans to present Stuart before the public.

In winter 1944–45 White was back in New York in a furnished apartment, again working for the *New Yorker* after discontinuing his "One Man's Meat" column for *Harper's*. His feelings of dissatisfaction at not yet having produced, at least in his own estimation, any work of enduring value and at having to leave the Maine farm resulted in a "nervous crack-up" that made him feel certain he was about to die. Apparently White resorted to writing about mice whenever he experienced these stressful conditions of what he termed "head trouble": "Instead of bats in the belfry," wrote Elledge, White "had a mouse in his mind" (252). In a poem written in February 1944, for example, White noted that "Ever at home are the mice in hiding, / Dust and trash, and the truth abiding," and in the summer of that troubled year he was complaining of "mice in the subconscious and spurs in the cervical spine." In October he wrote a poem titled "Vermin," which begins,

> The mouse of Thought infests my head,
> He knows my cupboard and the crumb.
>   Vermin! I despise vermin. . . .
> I've seen him several times lately.
> He is too quick for me,
> I see only his tail. (quoted in Elledge, 251–52)

White's hypochondriacal belief in his imminent death prompted him to find a way of providing for Katharine; thus he turned to the manuscript of *Stuart Little*, whose tail he had seen again, disappearing into his cupboard. Encouraged by his editor at Harper, White completed the work in just eight weeks, and *Stuart Little* went to press in 1945, nearly 20 years after Stuart had walked into White's dream "all complete, with his hat, his cane, and his brisk manner" (*Letters*, 193).

According to Peter F. Neumeyer in his study of the manuscripts of *Stuart Little*, this white-heat composition resulted in "a sort of loosely constructed, high-spirited lark," a juvenile novel that is "the most inspired, the most surprising, the freshest, the funniest of White's books." *Stuart Little*, he concludes, "is the rapid, asymmetrical product of slow and unsystematic subconscious accretion, written down pell mell. It evidences . . . the joy, the genius of the rough sketch—fresh, fluent, unsmudged by compulsive erasure or the soot of a library lamp."[2]

Born the second son of Mr. and Mrs. Frederick C. Little, Stuart is only two inches tall and looks like a mouse. His diminutive size allows him to retrieve a ring from a drain, to push Ping-Pong balls from under furniture, and to unstick a piano key during the playing of a lively rendition of the "Scarf Dance," all the time keeping a vigilant eye on Snowbell, the treacherous family cat. After an adventurous voyage on the lagoon in Central Park where he sails the *Wasp* to victory against the *Lillian B. Womrath*, Stuart meets Margalo, a wren, or perhaps a "wall-eyed vireo," rescued from the cold by Stuart's mother. Margalo in turn rescues Stuart from certain death in a garbage scow being towed for dumping into the ocean. The two of them return to Stuart's home, but Margalo almost immediately departs to escape a plot against her devised by Snowbell and his Angora friend. Stuart goes on quest to find her, stopping en route to serve one day as a substitute grade-school teacher and later to court a diminutive young lady in the idyllic New England town of Ames' Crossing. When this courtship comes to naught, Stuart continues on his journey, and the work concludes with the questing hero heading north in pursuit of his dream.

The plot design for the work is essentially episodic, and the book as a whole is "a series of self-contained incidents, designed to be read to a child (or by a child) whenever the occasion arises," as Gerald Weales notes in "The Designs of E. B. White."[3] In his revision of *The Elements of Style*, White added a new rule to Professor Strunk's original number: rule 12 advises writers to choose "a suitable design and hold to it," though, in his insistent avoidance of pedantic rigidity, White admits that sometimes "the best design is no design" and that even when a clear design governs, the flexible and adept writer "will in part follow this design" and "in part deviate from it, according to his skill, his needs, and the unexpected events that accompany the act of composition" (*Style,* 15). This seems exactly what White does in his first juvenile novel. According to Weales, "Deviation is the art of *Stuart Little*," largely because of the way the story grew, episode by episode, but also because the story is part picaresque adventure story and part Grail romance (408). White called the work "my innocent tale of the quest for beauty" ("The Librarian Said," 19).

As Weales notes, in quest literature "the search is only the string on which the beads of incident hang" (408). This combination of picaresque plot and quest romance determines the loose construction of the work as a whole. Thus the first 10 chapters of *Stuart Little* are essentially picaresque incidents, each chapter so self-contained that it can be detached and read out of sequence with no diminution of understanding or enjoyment. With chapter 11 the quest actually begins, but even this quest is interrupted by adventures peripheral to Stuart's pursuit of Margalo—namely, the day spent as a substitute teacher and the frustrating date with tiny Harriet Ames. Thus White's design for *Stuart Little* is loose, even seemingly random at times, providing Neumeyer with his accurate impression of the novel as evincing all the freshness of a "rough sketch." The novel's 15 loosely connected episodes are united in the end by their focus on the plucky protagonist of the book who faces the world with bravery, resourcefulness, and genial good humor.

Stuart's Strange Birth:
The Miniaturization of a Hero

The first part of *Stuart Little*—that dealing with Stuart's domestic misadventures—is by far the longest segment of the work. Chapters 1–10 give full rein to White's Lilliputian fascination with the miniature and diminutive placed in the foreground against a full-scale world.

Chapter 1 begins with the now-famous (and once controversial) opening sentences: "When Mrs. Frederick C. Little's second son arrived, everybody noticed that he was not much bigger than a mouse. The truth of the matter was, the baby looked very much like a mouse in every way."[4] White insisted that Stuart was not an actual mouse but a boy who happened to look a good deal *like* a mouse, being only two inches high and possessing "a mouse's sharp nose, a mouse's tail, a mouse's whiskers, and the pleasant, shy manner of a mouse" (2). In a letter to his Harper editor Ursula Nordstrom (14 November 1945), White objected to several publisher's ads for the book referring to Stuart as a "mouse": "This is inaccurate," he wrote, "and probably better be abandoned. Nowhere in the book (I think I am right about this) is Stuart described as a mouse. He is a small guy who *looks* very much like a mouse, but he obviously is not a mouse. He is a second son" (*Letters,* 270). In this letter White suggested that the Harper advertisements might use any or all of the following terms for describing Stuart: "being, creature, party, customer, fellow, person" but not "mouse." The fact is, however, that Stuart is indeed called a mouse within the first several pages of chapter 1, a feature White himself acknowledged as an error: "He should not have been" (*Letters,* 270).

White's distinction between man and mouse is certainly blurred throughout the book, and his numerous and insistent disclaimers that Stuart was actually a boy who only looked like a mouse were far from convincing or effective. Even today the Harper paperback edition of

Stuart Little continues to describe the work in boldface print on the back cover as "the famous story of a most unusual mouse" and features a blurb describing Stuart as "a mouse in the family of the Frederick C. Littles." Peter Neumeyer demonstrates that this confusion in the onto-genetic nature of Stuart results from White's rapid composition of the final version of the work: "White wrote with such haste that he did not even bother, in manuscript, to be consistent about the biological nature of Stuart, even though the point would eventually become extremely important to him" (597).

Today one may be tempted to wonder why White was at such pains to make the disclaimers concerning Stuart's nature: certainly readers, particularly juvenile ones, are adroit enough to recognize the work as a whimsical fantasy, as true primarily to the inner lives of readers rather than to the external realities of the observable world. The motive for White's insistence on Stuart's being a boy lies, undoubtedly, in certain negative critical reactions to the book offered by its first readers. On its publication the work was assailed by some as a tasteless venture into the monstrous and unnatural in its grotesque depiction of the birth of a mouse to a human mother. This was apparently one of the criticisms lev-eled in a 14-page letter addressed to Katharine White by the influential Anne Carroll Moore, then recently retired children's librarian at the New York Public Library. Having earlier encouraged White to write a work for children, she was so disturbed by *Stuart Little*, which she read in man-uscript, that she insisted the work "mustn't be published" (*Letters,* 267). Twenty years after the work's publication and its enormous popular suc-cess, White recalled that *Stuart Little* violated the taboo against "mon-strosity" in children's books with its "highly questionable" account of Stuart's birth, an account that would have been "bad," White admitted, "if it were stated in any other than a matter-of-fact way" (*Letters,* 532).

This controversy around Stuart's birth lingered for some time. Frances Clarke Sayers, Moore's successor at the New York Public Library, was also troubled by "the birth of Stuart to human parents, in this day when even the youngest child knows the facts of life."[5] The critic Edmund Wilson wrote of his dissatisfaction that White had not developed the issue of Stuart's monstrous birth by writing a novel in the vein of Kafka's *Metamorphosis.* Even Harold Ross stormed into White's *New Yorker* office after having read the first chapter, strongly objecting to Stuart's being "born" into the Little family in the first place: "God damn it, White," he fulminated, "you should have had him adopted" (Neumeyer 1983b, 340, 342). White relied on a semantic solution to diffuse some of these early reader difficulties: in subsequent editions of the work, he replaced the word "born" in the first sentence with the word "arrived." Writing in the *New York Times* in 1966, White indicated that of the many thousands of letters from readers that he had received since the publication of *Stuart Little*, "only two . . . questioned the odd fact of Stuart's arrival in this world and the propriety of an American family's having a boy that looked like a mouse." "After twenty years," he added, wryly, "I am beginning to relax," largely because "children can sail easily over the fence that separates reality from make-believe. . . . A fence that can throw a librarian is as nothing to a child" ("The Librarian Said," 19).

These initial dissatisfactions with Stuart's nature and genesis are occasionally echoed by contemporary critics, though most modern readers seem to enter with little difficulty or resistance into the work's fantastic and infectious humor from its opening pages on. This acceptance of Stuart's ambiguous nature results, perhaps, from White's blithe obliteration of any crucial distinctions between man and mouse. Indeed, in a sentence like the fourth one in chapter 1, White blurs any sense of separation by declaring, whimsically and matter-of-factly, that before Stuart was many days old, "he was not only looking like a mouse but acting like one, too—wearing a gray hat and carrying a small cane" (2). About this issue White had the last word: in an interview conducted nearly 50 years after he had written the first chapter of *Stuart Little*, he noted that Stuart's birth into the Little family "would have been completely unacceptable had I entertained any monstrous ideas about the matter, or had I introduced it gradually and in detail. It all happens in the first sentence and without the slightest suggestion of anything untoward or disagreeable. You have to make the leap boldly, if you are going to jump at all." Even children of the 1970s, whom White noted "are better informed about mammalian birth," seem for the most part to accept Stuart's arrival "without question, which is the happy approach."[6]

Stuart's controversial entry into the realm of children's fiction is not without precedent. Indeed, he belongs to a distinguished tradition of diminutive characters in literature for juveniles, his forebears including Tom Thumb, Gulliver in Brobdingnag, the Lilliputians, Thumbelina (or, as she is sometimes called, "Inchelina"), and Alice at various intervals during her sojourn down the rabbit hole. Though the possibility of direct influence between these well-known works and *Stuart Little* seems slim (since White claimed not to have read much children's literature—either classic or modern), it is clear that White's work shares many features with others in the tradition to which *Stuart Little* clearly belongs. All of these works evince a fascination with the diminutive and the miniature. In chapter 1, for example, Stuart, two inches tall, is described as sleeping in a tiny bed fashioned by his father out of "four clothes-pins and a cigarette box" and as being weighed each morning by his mother "on a small scale which was really meant for weighing letters"—a scale indicating that Stuart "could have been sent by first class mail for three cents" anywhere in the country, except that his parents "preferred to keep him rather than send him away" (2–3).

This delight in the diminutive also characterizes Andersen's story of Thumbelina, its tiny heroine being given a walnut-shell cradle with a rose-leaf counterpane and also a tulip-petal boat that she propels through a bowl of water using two white horsehairs for oars. Tom Thumb, too takes the air in a walnut-shell coach drawn by four blue-flies on wheels made of buttons. In featuring the minuscule, these works, among which *Stuart Little* takes its place, appeal to young people who are themselves frequently reminded of their small statures in a world largely geared to the full grown, who are themselves intensely aware of the problems, perils, and occasional pleasures of living like a pygmy in a land of giants.

Another similarity between Tom Thumb and Stuart Little is that they are both essentially mature at birth. Tom Thumb as a baby, we are told, had "at the first minute it tooke life, the full and largest bignesse that euer it grew to."[7] Stuart, too, is presented as being able to walk "as soon as he was born," his mother observing immediately that "the infant clothes she had provided were unsuitable" and making for him instead "a fine little blue worsted suit with patch pockets in which he could keep his handkerchief, his money, and his keys" (3). Stuart is thus from birth a miniature grown-up, having, as we are told Tom Thumb also has, "a desperate little spirit" and a "small bignesse" that does not quail at the often stern face life turns toward him. This convention of having Stuart born full grown provides White's audience with a fantasy particularly satisfying to child readers who are introduced to a character as new to the world as they are but who, unlike them, is able to live in the world fully and to negotiate his often difficult way in that world without the many limitations consonant with childhood. Stuart is a child and an adult simultaneously, a being who captures at once what children are and the adulthood toward which they are tending. To be at once what one is and what one will become, to be both naive and experienced,

simultaneously surprised by the world and completely capable of handling whatever it throws in one's way is, perhaps, the most alluring of all
fantasies.

Another advantage of Stuart's immediate postnatal maturity is a certain cleanness and simplicity of plot. The work is not a maturation story,
as so many works for children naturally are. Instead, it is an adventure
story and quest romance, and the fact of Stuart's original postpartum
competence allows the adventures to begin immediately, though, not
surprisingly, Stuart's initial adventures are confined to the domestic
arena. Chapter 1 early on establishes that Stuart, because of his small
stature and his willingness to help out, is often called upon to do favors
for his mother, father, and brother George, with whom he lives in a
sunny New York apartment near a park. When, for example, Stuart's
mother loses her ring down the drain as she cleans the bathtub, Stuart's
father suggests that Stuart be sent down the drain after it. Stuart agrees,
and then, though apparently only a few days old, orchestrates the entire
operation, first having the foresight to change into work clothes and
then devising the plan whereby his father will hoist him out on the third
tug of the string by which he is lowered into the dark sliminess of the
drain. No one thinks anything of asking Stuart to perform such dirty
and often dangerous tasks or expresses any surprise at his wonderful
ingenuity in accomplishing them. Stuart is, indeed, stoic upon completion of this task; he does not complain or even describe the hardships or
attendant unpleasantnesses of his descent into the slime and stench of
the drains. "It was all right," he demurs when his father asks him how it
was down there, but the truth is that he has to ditch his slimy clothes
and scour himself in the bath, sprinkling himself with his mother's violet water "before he felt himself again" (6).

Chapter 1, then, is characterized by an ambivalent, bifocal view of
Stuart. The close-up, microscopic vision is of a plucky, endearing little
fellow of great heart and capacious spirit, whose clothes, furniture, and
possessions are attractively small. His is a miniature existence, amusing
to contemplate. The doctor to whom Stuart is taken shortly after his
birth, for example, is "delighted with Stuart" (3), as is the reader,
because of his Lilliputian size and his tiny hat, cane, and blue-worsted
suit with the patch pockets. According to Malcolm Cowley, White
achieves this close-up view of Stuart by looking "through the wrong
end of a telescope" or, to change the figure, by taking "his readers down
the rabbit hole and [showing] them the bottle that Alice found there."[8]
But instead of looking through a tiny door into a lovely, enclosed gar-

den as the miniaturized Alice does, Stuart looks out from his diminutive realm of clothes-pin beds and paper-clip ice skates into the full-sized world and finds it menacing, however undaunted he remains in the face of it.

When the perspective changes and Stuart is viewed through the right end of the telescope, the reader is presented with a less comfortable vision of the two-inch mouse-boy and his singular plight. In this view of the tiny Stuart silhouetted against the backdrop of the full-sized world, his situation is presented as essentially perilous, filled with dangers and incipient disasters. From this vantage point, Stuart occupies a threatening world that looms menacingly over him on all sides—an essentially inhospitable world in which he can never be comfortably at home. Chapter 1, then, presents a double perspective, a series of disturbing shifts between the agreeable and the grotesque, the appealing and the pathological, for Stuart is both of these, depending on the perspective from which the reader views him. White leads the reader to adopt these alternate perspectives throughout this chapter and, indeed, throughout the first 10 or so chapters of the work. The effect on readers of this double perspective is curious, allowing them, as Marion Glastonbury noted in an early assessment of White's works for juveniles, "to identify simultaneously with underdog and top dog." Part of the humor of the book and much of its underlying pathos evolves from a central incongruity, resulting, as Glastonbury points out, from "the difference between the hero's picture of the figure he is cutting and our own."[9] The text and illustrations in *Stuart Little* everywhere cooperate to render this double perspective and this central incongruity of point of view.

White was particularly fortunate when Ursula Nordstrom secured Garth Williams as illustrator for *Stuart Little*, having rejected seven previous illustrators whose sample drawings all depicted Stuart as disappointingly Disney-ish or dressed in what she and White both concluded was inappropriate (because too contemporary) attire. According to Nordstrom, Williams had not illustrated an entire book before; nevertheless, he seemed completely attuned to the spirit and intention of this first work of White for children: Williams's illustrations are near perfect delineators of the bifocal perspective presented in the text.[10] The pictures alternate in their depiction of an often nattily dressed Stuart in close-up with those in which he is a mere dot, all but lost in the larger world that surrounds him. Thus the pictures veer from the microscopic to the telescopic, from the endearing close-up to the menacing, threatening long view of Stuart dwarfed by an alien Brobdingnagian world.

In the frontispiece, for example, Williams presents the newly arrived Stuart confronting his family. Stuart stands with hat and cane, one arm akimbo, a tiny figure all but lost on a table top while his full-sized parents and brother George contemplate him. Mr. Little is clearly speculative, perhaps even skeptical, his face partially eclipsed by a hand covering his mouth, given over to a sad pondering over this bizarre second-born son. Next to his father stands George, a dubious, even superior look on his face, his left arm encircling his mother's waist. Mrs. Little's expression can best be described as bemused and loving, the only one whose face does not register strong reservations concerning this latest addition to their family. Stuart is clearly on display before them and is not *of* them; that he is a grotesque anomaly is nowhere made more clear than in this initial illustration.

The illustration following this frontispiece heads the first chapter and switches perspective to the microscopic view of Stuart in close-up—dapper, even a bit of a dandy, insouciant and in control. It is a comforting and amusing illustration. The following illustration shows Stuart sleeping in his snug little bed, made of four clothes-pins and a cigarette box, secure in a world his own size (2), but this illustration is followed by two others depicting Stuart radically diminished, now a mere dot in the picture plane, being examined by the doctor (3) and then being lowered into the bathtub drain on a string by his comparatively enormous father (5). The last illustration of chapter 1 returns to the microscopic view and reveals Stuart dousing himself with his mother's violet water (6). Like the text, the illustrations, almost exactly balanced in number between the two perspectives, interchange charming, intimate views of the miniature Stuart comfortably at home in a diminutive world with frequently alarming views of Stuart dwarfed and alienated in the larger environment, against which he seems almost to disappear from sight among the oversized items that threaten to overwhelm him.

Domestic Misadventures

This double perspective is reinforced in chapter 2 in both text and illustrations. In the first paragraph of this chapter, entitled "Home Problems," Stuart is presented as "helpful" to his family but, because of his size, is excluded from family activities and normal family life. Because he is so small, for example, his involvement in the family Ping-Pong games is limited to retrieving balls that skitter into corners and under furniture and radiators. It was "a great sight," the narrator tells us, to see

Stuart emerge from under a hot radiator, "pushing a Ping-Pong ball with all his might, the perspiration rolling down his cheeks" (7). The first illustration in the chapter depicts a perspiring Stuart, like Sisyphus, throwing his whole weight behind an enormous Ping-Pong ball, obviously straining. These exertions are apparently expected and continuous, accepted matter-of-factly by his family at play, indulging in a game Stuart is excluded from.

This ambivalence of perspective—the presentation of a diminutive character in a full-sized world, the shifts between the amusing and the menacing, the charming and the dangerous—continues in the second episode of the chapter when Stuart agrees to a proposal that he enter the sounding chamber of the family's grand piano to push up a sticking key the second it is played in George's spirited renditions of the "Scarf Dance." "This was no easy job for Stuart," we are told, because "he had to crouch down between the felt hammers so that he wouldn't get hit on the head" (8). Though the narrator avows that Stuart liked the excitement of dodging the crashing keys, he admits that Stuart often emerged "quite deaf" from the terrific noise, and "it would be some little time before he really felt normal again" (9). Williams's illustrations show a dwarfed Stuart precariously unsticking an enormous hammer in the darkness of the sounding chamber as others crash around him (8), this illustration being succeeded by one depicting the emergence from the piano of a deafened Stuart holding his right ear (9).

The chapter concludes with the reflections of Stuart's parents, who, we are told, "had never quite recovered from the shock and surprise of having a mouse in the family" (9). Some of the "many problems" his family faces because of Stuart's tininess include self-editing their own conversations so as to avoid the word "mouse," censoring such juvenile classics as "Three Blind Mice" and "'Twas the Night Before Christmas," and fretting over the mouse hole in the pantry for fear that Stuart would be curious enough to enter it one day. The concerns of Mr. and Mrs. Little are motivated by a desire to spare Stuart's feelings, but their "problems" assume an ironic disproportion in comparison to Stuart's own.

Stuart's problems continue in the next several chapters. Not only is Stuart relied upon to perform less-than-pleasant domestic chores, but his daily living in the house is a hardship. The New York apartment, it soon becomes clear, is not a true home for Stuart. No wonder he is an early riser, one who enjoys "the quiet rooms with the books standing still on the shelves, the pale light coming in through the windows, and the fresh smell of day" (13). Perhaps Stuart likes this early morning peacefulness because there is no one to make the usual requests of him and the ordinary perils of the day seem quiescent.

Chapter 3 provides quotidian details of Stuart's rising and his subsequent exercises and ablutions; the chapter capitalizes on that fascination with the miniature which characterizes the work as a whole. In the bathroom Stuart, much like a handicapped person, must negotiate a myriad of rigged-up contrivances for turning on the lights and the taps. He must, for example, throw his entire weight on a long string to light the room, and he has to hit the faucet several blows with a tiny wooden hammer swung three times around his head in order to get a thin stream of water flowing so he can wash his face and brush his teeth with a doll's cake of soap and toothbrush. Williams's three illustrations for the chapter are faithful visual interpretations of the plot events and again play upon the double perspective: the full-page initial illustration (12) for the chapter shows Stuart touching his toes (and looking for all the world like a real mouse on all four legs, his mouse-tail straight up in the air), in George's rumpled, Cornell-pennoned room, dwarfed by messy dresser, unmade bed, and Brobdingnagian brother. The second illustration is a close-up of Stuart looking like a monk in a belfry as he tugs at the light cord in his bathroom (14), and the final illustration shows Stuart wielding his hammer against an enormous hot-water faucet, the "plink, plink, plink" of his hammer-on-metal awakening the sleeping family, telling them "that Stuart was trying to brush his teeth" and indicating that Stuart's struggle to live in an inimical full-sized world has begun yet again (16).

That full-sized world is overtly menacing in chapter 4 where Stuart confronts the family cat, Snowbell. Indicating, perhaps, Stuart's animal as well as human nature, he can converse as fluently with the hostile Snowbell as he can with the human members of his family. Stuart begins the new morning by looking into Snowbell's teeth, "sharp as needles," bared in a competition initiated by Snowbell to prove whose teeth are larger (18). Stuart refuses to be intimidated by Snowbell's menacing teeth, however. Williams's adroit drawing shows Stuart fronting Snowbell's toothsome ferocity with an admirable nonchalance, picking his own teeth with a straw and leaning cavalierly on his cane, unimpressed. Conceding that his own teeth, though completely serviceable, are smaller than Snowbell's, Stuart argues that his stomach muscles are firmer than the cat's, jumping up to chin himself on the windowshade pull ring. To his chagrin, the shade flaps up, trapping Stuart in it—a fresh calamity to inaugurate Stuart's new day. Snowbell, whose treachery is now obvious, ignores the pleas for help of a bruised Stuart and instead deposits Stuart's hat and cane by the mouse hole in the pantry to thwart any would-be rescuers. Snowbell, we are told, "was not fond of Stuart and it didn't bother him at all that Stuart was all wrapped up in a window shade, crying and hurt and unable to get out" (20). This chapter, then, and its illustrations show Stuart's environment, heretofore presented as potentially perilous, to be actively hostile in the form of the scheming Snowbell. As a result of Snowbell's ruse with Stuart's hat and cane, the Littles fear that Stuart has become a mouse in fact and has gotten lost in the passages winding behind the pantry wall.

Stuart's rescue in chapter 5 resonates with the humorous and the macabre. The Littles entertain various strategies for rescuing Stuart, from calling to him down the hole to calling the incredulous police to report their two-inch son missing, from ripping up the pantry floorboards to spooning applesauce down the hole in case Stuart should be hungry. Having given up hope, George rushes about the apartment pulling the shades down in "respect for the dead," dropping Stuart onto the window sill (25). The double perspective is fully operative in the chapter's conclusion: though Stuart's plight was serious (he emerges shaken, weak, and hungry), it is at the same time humorous: when asked how he got rolled up in the blind, Stuart replies that "it was simply an accident that might happen to anybody" (25). Well, not quite. Only to Stuart. The chapter closes with the reader feeling that peculiar mix of sympathy for and amusement at Stuart's situation that characterizes the tone of the entire book.

Such mixtures of reactions give texture to this work, for adult readers especially. Child readers, perhaps less capable of experiencing direct empathy because of their natural egocentrism and often embued with a blither response to the world generally, may not be as aware as many adult readers are of the sober side to Stuart's plight. Such juvenile readers may allow amusement to crowd out the seriousness at times descending on a reader who considers the situation of a being not at home in his surroundings, whose every moment is filled with the possibility of calamity. For younger readers, the bifocal perspective may be closer to monocular. They may not clue into that double perspective everywhere so marked in the work, not least of all in chapter 6, which indicates a subtle change of direction in the chronicle of Stuart's experiences. In this chapter, the first of Stuart's nondomestic adventures, he gets his initial taste for the wide world—a taste for adventure and travel that never leaves him.

The chapter opens with episodes similar to those featured in the previous chapters, and the double perspective is still operative. Stuart in sailor suit sets out for a walk, "full of the joy of life and the fear of dogs," a phrase that perfectly captures the double perspective everywhere played out in the early part of the novel, that dual view of joy and fear, of self-sufficiency and necessary caution in a world dangerous and menacing (26). Stuart, enjoying his walk mightily, must nevertheless climb onto the coattails of doormen or roll himself into newspapers at the approach of any dog, and he must cling to the cuff of a fellow passenger's pants in order to board a city bus. Once Stuart is settled in his seat, the bus conductor hassles him about his fare, though a dime is far too large for Stuart to negotiate, let alone carry. In the city, as in his own home, then, Stuart is still dwarfed and threatened. Halfway into this chapter, however, Stuart comes into a competence unalloyed with fear and menace when he arrives in the great world of Central Park and stops at the sailboat pond. There he persuades the owner of a large black schooner, the *Wasp*, to allow him to sail against the racing sloop *Lillian B. Womrath*. Here Stuart is in his element: the dual perspective vanishes for all intents and purposes, and Stuart, "so proud and happy" to be in command of a ship just his size on an enclosed ocean, lets go of the wheel of the *Wasp* for a second "and did a little dance on the sloping deck," unaware of his near collision with the wreck of a tramp steamer drifting by (35).

As usual, Williams's illustrations are fit accompaniments to Stuart's transformation as accounted for in the text. The early illustrations in the chapter once again show Stuart dwarfed and vulnerable in a world of gargantuan size. The chapter's second illustration (27), for example, shows a doorman standing under an awning, a dog down the street from him. Stuart, however, apparently hiding in the doorman's coattails, cannot be seen. He can be seen—but barely—in the next illustration, where he is depicted as clinging to the pants cuff of a man boarding a crowded bus, his hanging tail being the only give-away as to his identity (28). These illustrations serve once again to emphasize Stuart's plight in a world scaled differently from him and his heroic refusal to be defeated by that world. In the last illustration for the chapter, however, Williams returns to the microscopic view, showing an exuberant Stuart commanding a ship in an ocean just the right size for him, sailing blithely by dangers that, in this diminutive world, no longer have power to harm him (35).

Chapter 7 is an important chapter. Here Stuart is utterly divorced from the domestic arena for the first time, being in command of the *Wasp* for the duration of the chapter. Stuart's involvement with the ship on the inland ocean of the sailing pond in Central Park is not without its attendant dangers and incipient disasters, but the difference between the hazards in this chapter and those presented in previous chapters is significant: chapter 7's dangers—large waves, flotsam in the water, an approaching storm, a collision—are those endemic to sailing. They do not present extraordinary obstacles, such as Stuart's being rolled up in a window shade or having to hide out from dogs on the city streets—hazards resulting from his being underscaled in a normal world. Stuart *can* confront his sailing difficulties, largely because he is sailing a miniature ship on a miniature sea and is, for the first time, operating in a world appropriately scaled for him. He can thus overcome all obstacles because they are not insurmountable. Indeed, he overcomes his challenges through his own vigorous action and adroit sailing. No wonder, then, that Stuart can proclaim, "I am happy aboard the *Wasp*—happier than I have ever been before in all my life" (37). This is, in fact, the first time he has lived fully in a world scaled appropriately—and his success in that world is obviously heartening and revelatory.

Sailing the *Wasp*, Stuart feels the freedom and exhilaration of the sea, of the open air, of a life unbounded by the traumas of the domestic. As the warm west wind blows across the pond, billowing the sails and tossing spray onto the decks, Stuart announces with delight that "this is the life for me!" (38). The race is an exciting one, especially after the large policeman is inadvertently pushed into the pond, creating a tidal wave that upsets numerous boats, causing their owners "to scream with delight and consternation" (39). This wave washes Stuart overboard; undaunted, he swims back to the cheers of the bystanders and resumes piloting the *Wasp*. When the barometer falls suddenly and a storm gathers, we are told that to Stuart the world "seemed cold and ominous," though we are confident that this is a world Stuart can master (41).

Hazards accumulate quickly: the floating paper bag looms like a cave, and a collision with the *Lillian B. Womrath* follows the *Wasp*'s entanglement with the flotsam. Stuart's adroit execution of orders from the ship's owner saves the situation, and Stuart sails the *Wasp* "straight and true" across the finish line, being applauded ashore and praised for his "fine seamanship and daring" (45). Everyone—except the water-logged policeman—shakes hands with Stuart, marking his first unqualified success in the great world, stimulating his taste for adventure and accomplishment in the world arena, and planting in his mind the suspicion that his home in the Little apartment may no longer be his true home after all. Indeed, when he returns home that night, his response to his brother's queries as to what he has been doing that day is evasive: "Oh, knocking around town," he replies, indicating both a characteristic modesty concerning his exploits as well as a hesitation to tarnish the day's triumphs by immersing them in the domestic sphere from which those triumphs are so alien (46).

In this chapter, then, the double perspective of the earlier chapters is fine-tuned into a monocular vision. Stuart is heroic in a miniaturized world that he can negotiate inventively, bravely, and successfully. The illustrations register this single vision. A beautifully executed two-page illustration, which flows in a serpentine curve between pages 36 and 37, begins the chapter with a rush of people gathering from all over the park to see the race. A large crowd rings the pond. This initial illustration in the chapter is interesting because it depicts human adults as miniaturized, flocking to see miniature boats sailing a diminutive sea, one of those boats being under the command of a mouse-sailor. Indeed, the men running from all directions over the hills to gather at pondside are depicted as being the same size as Stuart when he is depicted as alien in the full-sized world in earlier illustrations. This reversal in scale is consonant with what the chapter accomplishes—the first glimpse of Stuart operative in a world at last appropriate to his own size. A later illustration shows Stuart roiling in the wave washing over the deck of the *Wasp*. To this illustration is added a pendant showing Stuart regaining his ship and hauling himself up its sides, the ship's scale congenial to Stuart's own small size (40). The focal illustration of the chapter occupies a full page and shows the *Wasp* entering the mouth of the cavelike paper bag floating in the pond. Stuart runs forward in an attempt to avert the disaster while the *Womrath* plows into the ship astern (42). Though diminutive, Stuart is at least in the same size gradient as a human on a full-sized schooner would be.

The following illustration is a close-up of Stuart cutting away the entrammeling paper bag, capably remedying the situation, efficient in this world which frees him to act effectively (44). The succeeding illustration depicts Stuart, once again dwarfed by full-sized men and boys, being congratulated after his plucky success. This illustration ushers us back to the full-sized world and Stuart back to quotidian life, discouraging views of which the next chapter is quick to provide (45).

Margalo: The Call to Adventure

Chapter 8 focuses us again on Stuart's problematic smallness and the
domestic calamities attendant upon this fact. The full-sized Littles are no
more comfortable in their home than Stuart is, being "in constant fear"
of losing Stuart or of sitting or stepping on him. The chapter opens with
Stuart, now seven years old, becoming trapped in the refrigerator when
he slips into it to find a piece of cheese while his mother has the door
open. Stuart remains in the cold and the dark for a half hour, stumbling
into a saucer of syrupy prunes and beating his arms together to keep
from perishing in the cold. Upon being rescued, Stuart asks for "a nip of
brandy" but is served hot broth instead and is put to bed where his bad
cold soon progresses into bronchitis. The brief respite from domestic
infelicity provided by the previous chapter is now clearly over.

Stuart's chilly misadventure in the refrigerator is exactly paralleled
midway in this chapter by Mrs. Little's finding a small bird lying on the
windowsill as if dead, stunned by the cold. But Margalo, as this bird is
called, soon revives on being placed near the radiator. On her subsequent
rambles about the house she meets Stuart. The similarities between
them are immediately evident: they both have sore throats from their
experiences in the cold; they both have an uneasy relationship with
Snowbell the cat. Margalo serves in this chapter to call Stuart to a different kind of life. Similar to him in many ways, she has little to do with
the domestic, which she enters only for this brief period of her recupera-
tion. But the Littles' apartment is not her home, as she makes clear in
her musical account to Stuart of her origins: "I come from fields once tall
with wheat, from pastures deep in fern and thistle; I come from vales of
meadowsweet, and I love to whistle" (51). On hearing this, Stuart "sat
bolt upright in bed" and insisted on hearing her account again immediately because what she tells him is what his heart wants to hear. The
boat race, Stuart skimming along in the open air on a wide sea, had for
the moment satisfied his longing for freedom from the domestic; now
Margalo's song of freedom in vales, pastures, and fields reminds Stuart
again of the burden of his unsuitable home in the New York apartment,
a home Margalo denigrates with qualified praise: "It's a nice place, for a
city location" (53).

Appropriately, Margalo eschews all other nesting options in the apartment, preferring a Boston fern on a bookshelf by an open window in the
living room, that roost most reminiscent of the fern and meadowsweet
she has just sung to Stuart about. No wonder Stuart begs Margalo to

repeat what she has just said about the wheat, fern, and thistle. Stuart falls in love with Margalo, quite simply, quietly, and completely, heaving tender sighs when he thinks of her. With the introduction of Margalo, Stuart's more-or-less random adventures begin to take on a degree of focus, unity, and coherence, which, after a few more episodes like the ones in earlier chapters, will ultimately lead to the quest chronicled in the latter chapters of the book.

Meanwhile, Stuart's domestic calamities befall Margalo too. Stuart must save her from Snowbell, whose "two gleaming yellow eyes" peer up at her from behind a sofa (55). Stuart's heroism is proved once again: sick as he is and frightened, but ever "a brave mouse, even when he had a sore throat," he shoots one of his miniature arrows into Snowbell's ear (55). The scene here is cinematic, White obviously playing against reader awareness of scenes and dialogue from *Robin Hood* and other swash-buckler films of the day. "This is the finest thing I have ever done," says Stuart before letting fly the arrow responsible for routing Snowbell. His benediction to Margalo before retiring—"Sleep dwell upon thine eyes, peace in thy breast"—is a remnant of "a speech he had heard in the movies," but the kiss he throws toward Margalo's sleeping form seems to come from his own heart (54).

The illustrations for the chapter are once again apt accompaniments to the text. The dual perspective that characterized previous chapters is featured fully in this one as a diminutive Stuart dances in the dark refrigerator on a covered butter dish (48) and as a tiny Margalo hops up an imposing stairway (50). The close-up illustration of Stuart in his clothespin bed recuperating from bronchitis, his paper-clip skates scattered over the floor (49), returns the perspective of the viewer to a comfortable scale as does the depiction of the colloquy of Margalo and Stuart as Margalo takes her temperature (52). These close-up views locate these miniature characters in a world they fill out and belong to, while the long-shot drawings alienate them in an enormous space they cannot hope to occupy with any degree of security or comfort. The chapter ends with a particularly fine visual realization of the dangers plaguing both Margalo and Stuart in the Littles' apartment. In this picture, Stuart crouches, an arrow nocked in his bow, and takes aim at a particularly ferocious Snowbell, his teeth bared, eyes glinting, and ears flattened as he stares up greedily at Margalo asleep in her fern, head buried beneath her wings. The answer to these dangers, for both Stewart and Margalo, is the freedom promised by the open casement at upper-center of this evocative drawing (56).

Stuart wisely withholds from Margalo any information concerning Snowbell's frustrated designs on her. Had she known of these dangers, she would have flown away immediately. But chapter 9 begins with the news that Margalo, liking the Littles' apartment so well and fearing the cold, has decided to stay for a time rather than flying through that open window to her true home, the open country of field and meadow that she sings of in her first meeting with Stuart. More probably, she likes Stuart enough to remain in a sphere alien to her.

It is fortunate for Stuart that Margalo remains, for this chapter introduces the most serious of all of Stuart's mishaps in the domestic arena. When Stuart sets out to find an ice pond to skate on, an Irish terrier causes him to seek refuge in a garbage can where he hides "in a grove of celery" (57). When two men from the Department of Sanitation dump the can into a garbage truck, "Stuart landed on his head, buried two feet deep in wet slippery garbage. All around him was garbage, smelling strong. Under him, over him, on all four sides of him—garbage. Just an enormous world of garbage and trash and smell" (58). The scene is one of existential tragicomedy, the diminutive hero buried in "an enormous world of garbage." Stuart even feels nausea, a parody, perhaps, of Jean-Paul Sartre's famous reaction to such a world: "I bet I'm going to be sick at my stomach before I get out of this," he says to himself (59). But getting out of this is not easy: the garbage truck dumps its load into a scow on the East River and Stuart's predicament changes from comic and parodic to uncomfortably serious as he hits his head on falling and lies unconscious for an hour as though dead. When Stuart recovers consciousness, he contemplates his own death in an existential way: he decides to face death bravely and "die like a man," though he regrets the stains and stench of his last moments (61).

When Stuart gives over any hope of survival, he grows sentimental, remembering his family and his love for them and for his home, how especially pleasant it was when he was up in the early morning by himself with the light just coming in through the curtains. These memories bring on sobbing, and the reader—who does not, of course, doubt for a moment that Stuart will be saved—is nevertheless strangely worked upon: the situation is too real somehow, too serious, unrelieved, except for White's implied parody of Sartrean existentialism.

Margalo proves the deus ex machina, the miracle who alights on a Brussels sprout to save Stuart, and her appearance buoys the sinking story and makes it soar again. "Anything is better than death," she assures Stuart, who again worries about being indecorously nauseous as he ascends into the air holding onto Margalo's feet (63). When they return to the apartment, Stuart's family greets him matter of factly: his mother kisses him and orders him into the bath, his brother takes his soiled clothes to the cleaners, and his father demands to know the details of their adventure over the ocean, sighing that someday he hoped to break free of his routine "to see all those fine things" (66).

Chapter 9, "A Narrow Escape," thus chronicles the culmination of Stuart's misadventures in the familial, domestic, and urban arenas. This is, appropriately, his worst experience in a life hedged round by disasters. The illustrations in the chapter serve to heighten the sense of danger to Stuart and his existential loneliness in the world. The first illustration shows Stuart hiding in a thicket of celery stalks close to the top of the garbage can: he looks a sojourner in the woods, a hiker on a woodland trail (57). The following illustration shows him tumbled upside down in a tangle of food scraps as the can is emptied into the truck and as Stuart's world is literally turned topsy-turvy (58).

The following two illustrations serve to emphasize Stuart's existential insignificance in an essentially indifferent world. The garbage truck is rendered from a great distance and is thus tiny: a minuscule man carries on his back a barely perceptible garbage can bearing Stuart (59). This and the following illustration emphasize Stuart's essential paltriness in the world's balance. Again, the garbage truck and scow below are presented from a distant perspective. Somewhere in that blur of garbage cascading from the truck to the scow is Stuart, his tragedy insignificant in a world of waste (60). It is a sobering vision: whereas the text affords us a close-up view of Stuart's condition and grants him a certain nobility of stature—an admirable if comic stoicism—the illustrations draw us away from the immediacy and particularity of his plight to the essential meaninglessness and paltriness of his place in the universe.

The following illustration (62) shows Stuart plucked from the void, lifted out of the abyss by Margalo's salvific powers of love and self-sacrifice. Stuart and Margalo fly over the city, which looks, in the next illustration, like a tiny model of itself (63). Mouse-boy and bird are no longer lost in the abyss; they ride above it and preside over it in an empyrean of fresh air and open space. This, as they will both come to recognize soon, is where they belong. But until they realize this, there remains the comparative haven of the Littles' apartment, the open casement of which is figured prominently in the chapter's penultimate illustration (65). A depiction of Margalo's reward of a seed cake as large and plump as she is concludes a series of chapter illustrations perfectly adapted to the tenor of the text they accompany (66).

Margalo's rescue of Stuart prefigures Charlotte's more ingenious rescues of Wilbur in *Charlotte's Web*. Margalo is thus the prototype of the saving female character to be perfected in White's next and greatest work for children. Even before this rescue, which essentially evens the debt Margalo owes Stuart for earlier rescuing her from Snowbell, Stuart has become thoroughly enamored of Margalo because of the sweetness of her song in praise of open fields and clear skies, because she is a light and beautiful traveler in air, a singer of paeans to the countryside and to freedom in the great natural world. Chapter 10 marks a break in the progression of the novel, for in this chapter Stuart, for the first time, does not himself make an appearance. This chapter chronicles Stuart's loss of his guiding spirit and Margalo's gain of her true sphere—this loss and gain brought on by Snowbell's treachery with the "beautiful young Angora" who has escaped from her cage in a pet shop to live on her own in a park near Stuart's home.

In an amusing interchange the Angora expresses incredulity that Snowbell can live in an apartment "with a bird and a mouse" and not "do anything about it," and Snowbell confesses to being an emotional wreck "because I'm always holding myself in" (68–69). The plan devised by the two cats, whereby the Angora will steal into the apartment and eat Margalo, is overheard by a roosting pigeon who sends Margalo an anonymous warning couched in phrases meant to echo, even parody, penny dreadfuls and dime-store novels: "BEWARE OF A STRANGE CAT WHO WILL COME BY NIGHT," signed by "A WELL WISHER" (71). As a result a frightened Margalo hops onto the open casement just before dark to fly north into the springtime dusk, as her heart tells her to "when spring comes to the land" (71). Thus this sweet singer of meadows and fields, this evanescent creature of air, grace, and soft feathers, leaves in springtime, without a word to anyone, but with serious repercussions for Stuart, in whose heart the image and memory of her have taken such strong hold.

This shortest of chapters almost exactly midway in the work provides a pivot on which the plot swings. The first half of the book has focused on Stuart's plucky determination to accommodate to a world out of scale for him, to one that persistently threatens him in the familial, domestic, and urban spheres. His adjustments to this world are only moderately successful; they prove humorous because they are so ingenious, but they are not ultimately very satisfactory. With the exception of chapter 7's great sailboat race, where Stuart lives freely in the open landscape and where he excels in a world appropriate to his size, the remainder of the chapters show Stuart adjusting, often painfully, to a world where he is not at home. Chapter 10 propels Stuart into a search for Margalo and, indeed, a search for a life more rewarding, a world more accommodating, and a place in that world more fulfilling than he has yet experienced. The remaining half of the book details the quest Stuart soon embarks on away from his family and outside of the city.

The illustrations for chapter 10 are ingenious: the first depicts the cats' colloquy in the dark. The text intrudes into the illustration plane and separates the depiction of the cats from the listening pigeon figured above, its head barely perceptible in the covering leaves (68). This figuration of text and picture is an adroit fusion: while attending to the text, readers have ever in peripheral vision the depiction of the discoursing cats and the listening pigeon, text and image coalescing into a full participatory verbal-visual experience. The final illustration provides a fit accompaniment to the exhilaration Margalo experiences upon venturing out from the dangers of the apartment to the freedom of the open springtime world (71). The illustration plays adroitly with perspective: in the foreground is the dark and shadowy apartment, in the center of which is the open casement through which we glimpse light, the open skies, the freedom and expansiveness of the great world. In the center of this open space flies Margalo, wings extended in a gesture of embrace and joyful acceptance.

The Quest

Filled with delightful non sequiturs, amusing dialogue, and preposterous events, chapter 11 chronicles the beginning of Stuart's quest. Stuart, of course, is heartbroken at Margalo's disappearance and rejects all the explanations for it offered by his family, especially the possibility that Margalo has flown to meet a husband. Stuart's decision to leave home is casually arrived at, and the plan is to run away without telling anybody. His primary motivation to "go out into the world" is to "look for Margalo," but while he is on quest he also decides that "I might as well seek my fortune, too" (73). His packing does not take long, but before he leaves home, he takes a strand of his mother's hair from her comb to remember her by and feels a fleeting nostalgia for the home he is leaving.

Stuart is, in essence, answering the call to adventure. Like all heroes on answering the call to journey forth, he feels the tug of the familiar and the safe. He also feels the hesitation, uncertainty, even fear that comes from leaving home, no matter how limiting or unsatisfactory, for the great world with its uncertainties, trials, and dangers. As Stuart stands musing in the street before his house, he contemplates his destiny. "The world was a big place," we are told, and Stuart does not know where to begin the quest, which direction in which to head (75). Like all heroes on the romance-quest, he seeks advice from an older helper. As Merlin is to King Arthur, as Gandalf is to Bilbo Baggins, so Dr. Carey, the "surgeon-dentist" whose schooner *Wasp* Stuart had sailed to victory, is to Stuart.

Stuart's visit to Dr. Carey results in some delightful nonsense. Instead of one advisor, Stuart receives two, the second being Edward Clydesdale, a patient of Dr. Carey's. This second oracle speaks in a special language that must be interpreted, much as the language of the Delphic Oracle must be translated. Edward Clydesdale is in the dentist's chair enduring a tooth extraction, his mouth stuffed with wads of gauze. Dr. Carey encourages Stuart to listen to Mr. Clydesdale's advice: "Oftentimes," says Dr. Carey, "people with decayed teeth have sound ideas" (77). Dr. Carey translates Mr. Clydesdale's distorted speech, and the two sages concur that Stuart should head north.

Heroes setting out on quest are usually given magical gifts to initiate their journeys or to aid them in their trials. Arthur receives Excalibur, for example, and Jack is given the magical beans; Joan of Arc receives her voices, and Vasilisa the Beautiful has her magical doll. Stuart is no exception, though his magical gift is peculiarly appropriate for a twentieth-century American heroic quester. Dr. Carey offers Stuart a car, "a tiny automobile, about six inches long—the most perfect miniature automobile Stuart had ever seen" (78). The car is a magic one in that at the push of a button it becomes invisible, a vehicular advantage that soon proves the cause of considerable difficulty. Like all heroes, Stuart must learn the powers of the gift he receives at the outset of his journey. The remainder of chapter 11 is devoted to the fantastic adventure of Stuart and the invisible car, how when Stuart goes to press the button to make the car visible again he inadvertently pushes the starter button, causing the invisible car to career around Dr. Carey's office, caroming off the hearth broom, the wastebasket, and other more damaging (because immovable) objects before running out of gas. White's prose account of Dr. Carey's attempts to capture the invisible runaway car demonstrates a virtuoso control of breathless pace, quick rhythm, and frantic tone—a style filled with exclamation points and comic-book brevity of utterance. When at last the car runs out of gas, Dr. Carey presses the visibility button, only to reveal a car crumpled and shattered, Stuart dissolving into tears at the sight of it. It has been an inauspicious beginning of the journey, and "Stuart was already homesick," certain that the journey was hopeless and that he had lost Margalo forever (82).

The Garth Williams illustrations for the chapter are particularly adept. He perfectly captures, in a full-page illustration, the isolation, uncertainty, and loneliness of the hero departing from the known and venturing on his journey into the great world of potential and possibility. Appropriately, the illustration depicts a diminutive Stuart, his shadow long behind him, dwarfed by a meticulously detailed street leading into the distance (74). Williams admirably captures the hesitation, the fear, the sense of being overwhelmed that Stuart and other heroes feel in confronting the great world completely on their own, for the first time unmediated by family, home, and friends. The illustration depicting the oracular Mr. Clydesdale is also adroit (76). He is central in the illustration, his mouth open, his eyes shut, seemingly in a trance, while Dr. Carey hovers over him, interpreting for a listening Stuart perched on the dentist tray among the implements. The final four illustrations revolve around the automobile, the first one depicting it in all its Lilliputian grandeur (78). The second illustration shows the collision of the invisible car with a dented metal wastebasket (80), and the third, the most ingenious of all, depicts Dr. Carey on his hands and knees being directed in his chase by Stuart, poised on the top of a table (81). The last illustration captures perfectly Stuart's deflated spirits at the end of the chapter: he weeps over a car clearly totaled as judged by even the most conservative of insurance adjustors (82).

Chapter 12, "The Schoolroom," is essentially didactic. White puts into it a jumble of his opinions about education, writing, the important things in life, and political issues concerning world government. Appropriately (if preposterously), White makes Stuart a substitute teacher, a guise consonant with White's humorously didactic intent in the chapter, and Stuart as pedagogue apparently becomes White's mouthpiece. Stuart's venture into the classroom also represents a side-step away from the quest, a seduction into adult responsibilities that can anchor one to a place, a job, or a family, and can thus replace the uncertainties and essential fluidity of the quest with stability and routine. To the great disappointment of the scholars in his class, Stuart does not stop in the classroom for long, taking up again the quest at chapter's end.

The chapter begins with Stuart's outfitting himself for his long journey, charging his purchases at a doll's shop while Dr. Carey oversees the repair of the miniature car. After leaving New York early in the morning, Stuart drives by a man sitting by the side of the road deep in thought. His stop to question the man begins the highest bit of whimsy in the entire work. The man turns out to be the superintendent of schools in the town and his problem is that he cannot find a substitute for a Miss Gunderson, who is absent from her post in Number Seven school suffering from an attack of "rhinestones," an ailment that Stuart transforms into a further parodic affliction resulting from Miss Gunderson's confusion over her own self-administered vitamin therapy. "There's nobody in this town who knows anything," laments the superintendent, and there are "no spare teachers" (85). Stuart's offer to substitute catapults him into the classroom, but not before he changes into professional attire: "a pepper-and-salt jacket, old striped trousers, a Windsor tie, and spectacles" (86).

Stuart's entrance into the classroom provides an occasion for White to display his attitudes toward education. On being asked by the superintendent if he feels he can maintain discipline among the scholars, Stuart argues that making schoolwork interesting in and of itself takes care of discipline, a pedagogical principle of sound common sense. Stuart has a tendency to interest the children at the expense of their schoolwork, however, blithely dismissing arithmetic from the day's curriculum, for example. Moving on to spelling, Stuart serves as puppet for White's ventriloquism: "A misspelled word is an abomination in the sight of everyone" (90), Stuart pronounces in a phrase worthy of the author of *The Elements of Style.* Spelling as a subject is dismissed with Stuart's injunction that scholars should provide themselves with a *Webster's Collegiate Dictionary* and consult it whenever the slightest doubt about spelling correctness presents itself. The third subject of the day, writing, is dismissed with impatience: "Don't you children know how to write yet?" he asks (91). The next subject, social studies, Stuart dismisses with contempt: "Never heard of them" (91).

Instead of following the school protocol, Stuart proposes that the class simply talk about something together. Stuart has gotten to this point in the first 10 minutes of the school day, and his dismissal of routine suggests his (and White's) apparent opposition to the artificial boundaries and divisions endemic in the multiple-subject elementary school curriculum, the lack of connection or interrelation among the disciplines, and the consequent lack of motivation or application on the part of students who are spoon-fed information and skills in doses measurable in quantity and in duration. Stuart's approach is synthetic rather than analytic and involves active concentration and participation as opposed to passive reception of instruction. He begins the instructional component of the class with the question, "How many of you know what's important?" (92).

Yet Stuart remains very much in control of the classroom, guiding his young charges into profitable areas and topics for discussion. Stuart's classroom is clearly student-centered rather than content-focused, yet Stuart maneuvers the children into rich and productive areas of investigation and discovery, declining student suggestions that the class talk about the feel of hand-held snakes wrapping themselves around the wrist, about "sin and vice," or about the fat woman at the circus. After rejecting these suggestions, Stuart prompts his students to talk about a hypothetical "Chairman of the World." According to Stuart, "The world gets into a lot of trouble because it has no chairman," an assertion echoing White's own convictions that a world government would best obviate a repeat of the global disasters of a just-completed World War II (92). White's commitment to work for a centralized world government was reflected in the numerous *New Yorker* editorials he had been writing for some time and that he gathered into a book entitled *The Wild Flag* (1946). Indeed, shortly after completing *Stuart Little*, White journeyed to San Francisco to report for the *New Yorker* on the founding of the United Nations. These concerns are clearly echoed in this chapter of *Stuart Little* and form part of the direct didacticism White indulged in in this schoolroom chapter.

When Stuart offers to be Chairman of the World himself, he is told that he is too small—a reason he rejects immediately, indicating that a Chairman of the World would not be required to impose world government mandates by force but by cooperation. The true requirement for such a chairman is not that he or she can use force effectively but that he or she knows what is truly important.

When Stuart asks Henry Rackmeyer, a student in class, what is important, Henry responds, "A shaft of sunlight at the end of a dark afternoon, a note in music, and the way the back of a baby's neck smells if its mother keeps it tidy" (92).

Clearly Henry is a poet, as is Margalo, and his answer pleases both Stuart and the reader. These metonymic images connoting renewed hope, the grace and harmony of music and the arts, and the regeneration and renewal of birth and springtime are, for White, persistent themes and pleasures in that they provide the poetry, the spirit in an otherwise prosaic life. But Stuart cautions that Henry has forgotten one important thing, which Mary Bendix hastens to supply—ice cream with chocolate sauce on it, a further metonym for the pleasures of the body and of the physical world to complement Henry Rackmeyer's impressive list of poetic, spiritual gifts.

After Stuart and the class establish the important things in life, Stuart directs the students to establish laws for the smooth operation of this world. The children offer a plethora of suggestions, which Stuart accepts or rejects, indicating which are merely advice and not laws and which are laws but faulty because unfair or impractical. Two laws emerge: "Nix on swiping anything" and "Absolutely no being mean" (93–94). Stuart tests these laws by having Harry Jamieson snatch Katharine Stableford's pillow stuffed with sweet balsam—a pillow very precious to her because given her the previous summer by her first boyfriend. When Harry retreats to his desk with the stolen pillow, Stuart as Chairman of the World invokes the two rules operative in the set derived by the students, and all his classmates crowd around Harry, forcing him by their presence to return the pillow to Katharine. In short, Stuart provides a graphic demonstration of how world government would work, how the cooperation of nations would curb the wayward actions of criminal states and pressure them nonviolently to conform to a world order governed by cooperative international laws.

The problem with this solution to international anarchy stems from the weaknesses endemic in the human heart. Interestingly enough, Stuart begins to covet Katharine's sweet-smelling pillow, reflecting that it would make a perfect bed for him. He must quell this covetous streak in himself lest he plunge the class and its lesson in effective world government into chaos and cynicism. His effort to curb his desires is only narrowly successful, demonstrating White's clear perceptions of the very real difficulties of implementing such a world order and ensuring its success. But Stuart *does* control his impulses and returns the pillow to Katharine with a benediction, indicating that this plan for world government can indeed work, despite the challenges afforded it by a human nature attended by covetousness, greed, and self-interest.

Stuart leaves Miss Gunderson's class with a final addition to the list of important things established earlier. "Summertime is important," he adds, just like the shaft of sunlight, the note of music, and the smell of the back of a baby's neck. "Never forget your summertimes, my dears," he tells the students wistfully (98). Treasure freedom in the green and golden world of childhood, he means, and take that separate space of unstructured time and freedom intact into the harried world of adulthood, for that too is important—perhaps most important of all. So Stuart departs from Miss Gunderson's classroom, much to the regret of his students, who wished they could have a substitute every day. The call of the quest is too strong in Stuart to allow him to stay: he refuses an occupation, a place, and adult responsibility in order to remain true to the northerly direction of his search for Margalo.

Asked in an interview published in 1974 whether this depiction of a schoolroom was in reaction to the way he himself was educated, White admitted that he was educated in a time when schoolrooms "were dull and unimaginative, when discipline was firm, and when not much effort was made to give scholars free rein." Perhaps, he continued, if the schoolroom in *Stuart Little* is "on the disorderly side," it is "a subconscious attempt on my part to raise a rumpus and break the monotony" (*Pied Pipers*, 129). He insisted, however, that no matter how monotonous his own schooling was at times, it resulted in his knowing how to read, write, and spell—a knowledge too many modern children, educated in more "interesting" classrooms, sorely lack. Thus White makes it clear that his satirical depiction of Stuart in the classroom is only partially tongue-in-cheek, that though it criticizes the contemporary classroom for its dullness, it is not meant to deflate the importance of careful instruction in the basics of literacy. Better dullness in the classroom, he implies, than illiteracy in the child scholars.

The illustrations for this chapter differ markedly from those in earlier chapters. Though Stuart's size is still at grotesque variance from the size of the world around him, and the double perspective is thus still operative, there is no longer that ominous atmosphere of a looming and threatening world. Stuart is no longer menaced by his environment; indeed, he is usually presented as in control of it, as an active and dynamic, if diminutive, figure negotiating the world successfully and adroitly. The opening illustration, for example, shows Stuart approving the fit of his new clothes in a pier glass among the appropriately sized packages, valise, and chairs at the doll shop (83). In the chapter's second illustration Stuart stops his tiny car by the side of the road to inquire of the sad superintendent what he might do to help him out of his difficulties. Though tiny in relation to the large man sitting dejectedly on the curb, it is Stuart who is powerful and in control, who can offer comfort and assistance (85).

In the third and fourth illustrations, each on facing pages, Stuart is presented on the left-hand page in all his professorial splendor while a group of gossiping scholars is figured on the right-hand page (86–87). Williams presents this group of students in the distance, their size nearly exactly equal to Stuart's size in the illustration facing this one. The double illustrations on the next two pages play on the same equality (88–89). Though Stuart is depicted as smaller than the students in the illustration on the right page, he is nevertheless portrayed as standing up to the seated students who respectfully raise their hands in answering his questions. Stuart stands in the foreground, arms akimbo, very much in control of the classroom and the students. The illustration of Stuart on p. 92, a close-up, balances in size the depiction of Harry's theft of the pillow from Katharine on p. 95, and Stuart's denunciation of Harry on p. 97 causes Harry to recoil, even though Stuart is depicted as only slightly taller than one of Harry's fingers is long. This illustration, unlike many coming earlier in the work, shows Stuart firmly in control of his life, a potent force rather than a sad grotesque constantly buffeted by a Brobdingnagian world. The chapter's last illustration depicts Stuart driving away from the schoolhouse in his minute automobile, the students crowding onto the porch to wish him a warm and exuberant farewell, sorry to see him go (99). Thus Stuart resists this call to stability, to a profession and a settled life, and remains true to his quest for Margalo.

Harriet Ames: The Real vs. the Ideal

Stuart's second temptation to abandon his journey, detailed in chapter 13, is even greater than the earlier temptation afforded by his substitute teaching. As Stuart enters the idyllic New England town of Ames' Crossing, he recognizes its beauties, and he soon meets Harriet Ames, like him a scant two inches tall and, unlike him, human in features, beautiful, affluent, and socially prominent. The chapter opens with a virtuoso sentence, rich in poetry and parallelism, describing Ames' Crossing: "the loveliest town of all," the "most peaceful and beautiful spot [Stuart] had found in all his travels," a place "he would gladly spend the rest of his life in" except for the fact "that something deep inside him made him want to find Margalo" (100–101). He describes Margalo to a storekeeper as "perfectly beautiful," a "remarkable bird," but the storekeeper does not really answer Stuart's inquiries as to whether or not he has seen a bird answering to Margalo's description (103). Instead, he directs Stuart to a meeting with Harriet Ames. An unpleasant sexism creeps into the chapter when Stuart asks the store-keeper for a description of Harriet, surmising that she must be "fair, fat, and forty" (104). The storekeeper describes her as young, pretty, and "one of the best dressed girls in this town"—a girl whose prominent family originated from a ferryman in the Revolutionary War who carried anybody across the stream—British soldiers or American—as long as he got his toll (104). Stuart declines to meet her, describing himself as a "will o' the wisp," as "always looking for Margalo" (104).

As Stuart drives out of Ames' Crossing, however, he reflects again on its being "the finest town he had ever known" and he swerves sharply off the main street, deciding to stay awhile, camping out by the stream (105). After spying Harriet in the post office—and suffering a paralyz-ing bout of shyness—he writes her a letter in which he confesses that his "only drawback is that I look something like a mouse," even though "nicely proportioned" and "muscular beyond my years" (109). Stuart is a bit of a poet himself, asking Harriet to meet him for a canoe ride on the stream at sundown "when the petty annoyances of the day are behind us and the river seems to flow more quietly in the long shadows of the wil-lows." He conjures for her the atmosphere of "tranquil spring evenings" designed "by special architects for the enjoyment of boatmen" (110).

This invitation is offered, however, without Stuart's having the means to fulfill it. He buys a souvenir birchbark canoe stamped with "Summer Memories" on the side and, though a bit humiliated by them, accepts two cardboard ice cream spoons as paddles, hoping not to meet "an American Indian while I had one of *these* things in my hand" (111). This chapter ends, then, in the midst of the episode, the closure of which is provided in chapter 14. The illustrations for chapter 13 are some of the finest in the book. The first depicts Stuart arriving at the general store on the outskirts of Ames' Crossing featured in the distance framed in trees and situated across a bridge, its lovely buildings composing a har-mony of nature and human habitation (101). In this illustration Ames' Crossing looks to be the haven at the end of Stuart's long pilgrimage, a place seductive enough to tempt Stuart away from his quest. The subse-quent moonlit picture of Stuart sleeping on the river bank against an idyllic setting of trees and houses confirms the Edenic quality of the first illustration and provides a visual confirmation of Stuart's verbal assess-ment of the beauties of the town and its seductiveness (105).

Other illustrations in the chapter hint, however, that this town will not really suit Stuart. The double perspective of earlier pictures is again employed here in illustrations depicting Stuart dipping sarsaparilla out of a cup that he cannot lift and that is placed on a lower step so that he can lean precariously over and dip his cap in it (102). Another ominous illustration shows Stuart held by his tail by the storekeeper, who dips him into a bottle of ink so that he can fill his fountain pen (109). These vaguely menacing illustrations depicting a miniature Stuart inconvenienced by a perilous larger world are, however, countered by close-ups of Stuart hiding behind the public inkwell in the post office spying on a person exactly his height (106–107) and by the final depiction of Stuart carrying an appropriately sized canoe over his head in portage to the river (112). Harriet is depicted as pretty, slender, with a pleasing figure, her depiction having been a point of contention between Williams and White, who thought Harriet was not as appealing in Williams's illustration as she should have been and who sent Williams a cut-out picture of a model from a mail-order catalog as a guide to how Harriet should really look. It is, of course, important that Harriet be beautiful, as she represents Stuart's greatest temptation to abandon his idealistic quest and to pursue instead a realistic accommodation with the world.

Chapter 14 is a continuation of the episode begun in the previous chapter, which ends so hopefully with the possibility of Stuart's truly connecting with another who shares his peculiar and diminutive fate in a world that is by all reckoning much too large for him. But what begins so promisingly soon ends disastrously, indicating that Ames' Crossing, despite its beauty and its calm, despite its miniature princess, is no true home for Stuart. The disastrous outcome to Stuart's romantic dream is equally determined by situation and by Stuart's own rigidity in the face of disappointment and unfulfilled expectations.

Stuart sets himself up for disappointment. From the first he is dissatisfied with the souvenir canoe because it does not conform exactly to his ideal. He spends hours caulking it with spruce gum, weighting it with stones, making a backrest and a pillow for Harriet, and grousing over the paper ice cream spoons he was given for paddles. Stuart thinks of nothing but his date with Harriet, imagining every detail, picturing to himself "every minute of their evening together" (116). The romantic pictures his imagination provides him are highly idealized: he sees himself as insouciant and dashing, as swimming boldly around the lily pad on which Harriet sits admiring his prowess. The actual and the imagined, however, fail to coincide, as is so often true in life. Everything that

can go wrong does go wrong: the day is chilly and gray; Stuart has a
headache; the afternoon spent awaiting Harriet's arrival is wearisome
because he is so nervous; he must keep changing his shirt because he
perspires profusely. The canoe is wrecked, and all his careful preparations
of the day before are undone by vandals. Stuart is utterly dashed.

Harriet, however, is more adaptable, more buoyant. She answers
Stuart's concern over the weather with a matter of fact acceptance of circumstances: "if it rains, it rains," she says (119). She urges Stuart to tidy
up the wrecked canoe and take her for a canoe ride anyway, but the disconsolate Stuart cannot rally himself, so absorbed is he in the romantic
dream he has spent 24 hours concocting. Every ameliorative suggestion
that Harriet makes is summarily rejected, including her final invitation
to dinner at her house and a dance that evening at the country club.

This abortive date poses an interesting contrast between Harriet and
Stuart. Harriet is adaptable, a realist. She makes the best of situations, is
flexible in dealing with the whims of chance. Indeed, she comes from a
long line of realists, her ancestor, the ferryman at Ames' Crossing during
Revolutionary days, having carried anybody across the stream—"he
didn't care whether they were British soldiers or American soldiers, as
long as they paid their fare." We are told that the Ameses "have always
had plenty of money," apparently because they followed this pragmatic
and accommodating approach to life established for them by their ferryman forebear (104).

Stuart, on the other hand, is an idealist who cannot exchange ideal
pictures for ones more in accord with the way things are. Paradoxically,
this inflexibility is at once his greatest strength and his greatest weakness. It leads him to give up the possibility of establishing himself in the
most beautiful town he has ever seen with a woman who has every
attribute of size, family background, and personal attractiveness that
should suit him. The idealism that makes him restless, however, that
spoils for him any accommodation with the demands of Ames' Crossing
and the real world, also holds him steady and true to the quest. With
chapter 14 we come to recognize that Margalo is not simply a small bird
Stuart happens to fancy. She crosses from literal to figurative, from actual to mythic presence. She comes to signify that quest for the ineffable
and perfect, that search for the something more in life than settledness,
security, and comfort, that journey toward the fulfilling ideal that is ultimately unattainable in this life. And Stuart himself becomes mythic—
the wanderer, the quester, ever in search of something beyond the
satisfactions of a well-ordered, safe, predictable tenancy in time. Stuart

becomes, in short, Galahad to Margalo's Holy Grail. Thus Stuart comes to recognize that Harriet Ames and all she represents, as attractive as she is in so many respects, is not, at last, what it is he seeks. Chapter 14 concludes with Stuart sitting by the stream "alone with his broken dreams and his damaged canoe" (124).

The illustrations for the chapter indicate clearly the real satisfactions that a life with Harriet would afford Stuart. For one of the few times in the book, the illustrations show Stuart essentially in unity and harmony with an environment that neither dwarfs nor overwhelms him. There is a consistently monocular vision in the pictures for this chapter: the illustrations do not divert our vision between a world alternately amicable and hostile to Stuart, alternately in-scale and out-of-scale, as do the illustrations in most of the previous chapters. The first three illustrations depict Stuart's readying the canoe for the next day's date and preparing a light supper for himself of dandelion milk and deviled ham (114, 115). These illustrations depict those practical arrangements that allow for the daydreaming indulgence of the fourth illustration (116), which features an imagined Harriet sitting primly on a lily pad, the canoe moored near her, and Stuart displaying for her admiration his swimming prowess.

The following illustration depicts Stuart's carefully practiced, nonchalant pose as Harriet approaches him down the path (119), but the next four illustrations (120, 121, 123), showing his anxiety, frustration, and grief at the collapse of his idealized vision, prepare for and explain the concluding illustration (124) of Harriet walking back down the path she had earlier walked up, her gift of a box of peppermints untasted. Interestingly enough, however, the book's cover demonstrates Stuart expertly rowing this same canoe, blazoned with "Summer Memories" and ballasted with rocks, the sky blue, the weather warm, all in a springtime atmosphere buoyant and brimming with life. This cover illustration depicts the way the canoe ride was supposed to be, the canoe ride of dream and not of reality. This, perhaps, is why Stuart is depicted as rowing the boat alone. This dream-vision picture does not admit the practical, realistic Harriet Ames.

An Open-Ended Conclusion

The final chapter in *Stuart Little* is pure lyricism, though it opens with the sure pragmatics of Stuart refueling his tiny car and checking the oil. Once out of Ames' Crossing, Stuart, who is "glad to be on the move again" (126), comes to a fork in the road, one veering westward, the

other continuing north. At this juncture he meets a Thoreauvian repairman for the telephone company, a transcendentalist who looks forward
to climbing his poles, realizing that he climbs heavenward while repair-
ing those telephone lines that connect human beings, allowing them to
transcend space and time. This repairman, who bridges the vertical and
horizontal, the near and the far, understands intuitively Stuart's quest
and promises to help, taking notes on Margalo's physical description and
on the song she sings about her origins in wheat fields, pastures, and
vales of meadowsweet, promising to drop Stuart a line if ever he meets
her in his daily climb heavenward, up where birds congregate to sing on
the wires. This repairman is comfortable in the universe, approving of
Stuart's decision to head north but indicating that "south-west is a fine
direction, too" and that "an easterly course" promises interesting experiences as well. But, according to this celestial repairman, "there's something about north" that "sets it apart from all other directions" so that a
person heading north "is not making any mistakes" (129).

   In the repairman's approbation, Stuart finds a confirmation of the
quest: "I rather expect," he says, "that from now on I shall be traveling
north until the end of my days" (129). The repairman is given one of the
most hauntingly beautiful passages in the entire work when he tells
Stuart of the wonderful places he has seen while following a broken telephone line north, of transcendent moments spent in pastures, in spruce
woods, on freight platforms, and by the shores of fresh lakes, all of which
resounds with the images and cadences of *Walden*. "A person who is looking for something," the repairman concludes, "doesn't travel very
fast"—a sentiment Stuart concurs with before heading down the road
"into the great land that stretched before him." Though the way seems
long to Stuart, "he somehow felt he was headed in the right direction"
(131).

   White's book, then, concludes open-endedly with an indication that
Stuart now understands the nature of his quest and can set out purpose-
fully on it. The lack of any definitive or obvious closure in White's conclusion prompted one of Anne Carroll Moore's strictures against the
book—a criticism echoed over the years by a number of child as well as
adult readers of *Stuart Little*. In his letters, White repeatedly defended
his choice of leaving the book open-ended. Numerous children wrote to
White asking him if Stuart ever found Margalo or ever got home again.
White indicated that he did not answer these questions in the book
because "Stuart's journey symbolizes the continuing journey that everybody takes—in search of what is perfect and unattainable." Admitting

that this was perhaps "too elusive an idea to put into a book for children," he "put it in anyway," thus refusing to condescend to children or to falsify his own vision of life itself as essentially a quest (*Letters,* 406).

Almost 20 years later White was justifying his decision to keep open the ending of his first children's book to yet another generation of child readers. White wrote to a youthful correspondent on 4 February 1974 that "many of us in this world go through life looking for something that seems beautiful and good—often something we can't quite name." For Stuart, he continued, Margalo represents this ideal: "Whether he ever found her or not, or whether he ever got home or not, is less important than the adventure itself." If, he concluded, "the book made you cry, that's because you are aware of the sadness and richness of life's involvements and of the quest for beauty" (*Letters,* 652). As White added in an interview published in 1974, Stuart's story "is the story of a quest— specifically, the quest for beauty. Life is essentially inconclusive, in most respects, and a 'happy' ending would have been out of key with the story of Stuart's search." Occasionally, White noted, a child-reader "perceives this and writes me a letter of approbation" (*Pied Pipers,* 129).

Thus White was clearly aware that closing the work with Stuart still on his quest was unusual in books for juveniles with their penchant for tying plot incidents into definitive conclusions. White was not to repeat this indefinite conclusion, which is so significant a part of his first work for children. Indeed, both *Charlotte's Web* and *The Trumpet of the Swan* have clear-cut conclusions. But in taking a risk with the plot of *Stuart Little,* in waiving conventional closure expected in usual quest romances for children, and in presenting an adult perspective on life itself, White produced a richer and certainly more memorable book.

Critical Reception

Anne Carroll Moore's dislike of *Stuart Little*—which she saw as "nonaffirmative, inconclusive, unfit for children," and harmful to its author if published—and her attempts to prevent the book's publication initiated a tradition of controversy about the book. Critical reactions to *Stuart Little* have varied from disapprobation to unqualified admiration since the book was published in 1945, though generally it has been well received.

Reviewing the book for the *New York Times Book Review* of 28 October 1945, Malcolm Cowley indicated that though Stuart "is a very engaging hero" and *Stuart Little* "an entertaining book, whether for children or their parents," he nonetheless found the work "a little disappointing," perhaps "because I had been expecting that E. B. White would write nothing less than a children's classic." Cowley clearly does not accord the work that high status, observing that "the parts of *Stuart Little* are greater than the whole, and the book doesn't hold to the same mood or move in a straight line." In addition, Cowley complains of "loose ends in the story" that leave readers confused, for example, about the prowlings of the gray Angora cat through the Littles' apartment in search of Margalo the night she flees or, more important, about the outcome of Stuart's quest. Cowley concludes that White "has a tendency to write amusing scenes instead of telling a story" and closes his review by calling *Stuart Little* "one of the best children's books published this year," though acknowledging that this "is very modest praise for a writer of his talent" (7).

The reviewer for the *Saturday Review of Literature* for 10 November 1945 shared Cowley's reservations about the book, concluding that "as a character Stuart is not convincing and his adventures end inconclusively."[11] A month later the *Saturday Review* published a longer, more positive review by Rosemary Carr Benét. Comparing the book to *Alice in Wonderland, The Wind in the Willows,* and works by Milne and Disney, Benét noted that the "humorous, wise quality found in E. B. White's other work is reflected here in miniature," and that there is a welcome "matter-of factness about all Stuart's adventures that keeps them from being too whimsical and that gives them substance and charm," making this work suitable "for all ages, all shapes and sizes of readers who like the light fantastic tone."[12] The reviewer for the *Horn Book* (November 1945) agreed with Benét as to Stuart's audience: "This is an endearing book for young and old, full of wit and wisdom and amusement, and Garth Williams' drawings make a perfect accompaniment."[13] The reviews are generally unanimous in their positive assessments of Williams's illustrations.

The early reviewers repeatedly saw the book as appropriate for both adult and child readers. The reviewer for *Time*, for example, called the work "a tale of few laughs and many smiles. Adults may read into it any meanings they like. Children will read and reread it for fun."[14] The reviewer for *Kirkus*, however, proclaimed *Stuart Little* "pseudo-fantasy, synthetic, and lacking the tenderness that makes a story such as *The Wind in the Willows* wholly the children's own. Undertones and overtones of this story of a mouse in a human family are unjuvenile on all counts."[15] This library reviewing service thus echoed Moore's assessment of the manuscript, which may account for the hesitance of some librarians to order the book for their juvenile collections. As White noted in 1966, Stuart "got into the shelves of the Library all right, but I think he had to gnaw his way in" ("The Librarian Said," 19).

Though sales for *Stuart Little* have continued steady since its publication, literary critics largely ignored the book—as they did with so much of children's literature—until the early 1970s. In his brief article on "The Designs of E. B. White," for example, Gerald Weales offered the first close examination of the work's structure, observing that the plot of *Stuart Little* is essentially episodic and noting that the book is "a series of self-contained incidents" and that these incidents "need not be taken in sequence" (408).

In an interview published in 1974 by Justin Wintle and Emma Fisher, White once again defended Stuart's arrival in a human family from charges that such a birth was "nauseous" or "monstrous," arguing that "the whole business is so fantastical as to rule out any anatomical embarrassment" (*Pied Pipers*, 129). In a Twayne book on E. B. White, published in 1974 by Edward C. Sampson (son of Martin Sampson, one of White's professors at Cornell and convener of the Manuscript Club), no mention is made of this perennial issue in discussions of *Stuart Little*. Sampson notes that *Stuart Little* is free of the didacticism of so much contemporary children's literature, though it does deal with "loyalty, honesty, love, sadness, and happiness"—the themes of all great children's works.[16] Sampson does, however, see the structure of *Stuart Little* as a "weakness" notably absent in White's other two works for children. Sampson's assessment offers, "with a clear awareness of the dangers," a biographical reading of the work, citing White/Stuart's mutual love of sailing; their joint wanderlust, so notable in White's postcollegiate journey across the continent; and their ambivalence in matters of dating and romance in general in their early years (98). According to Sampson, White made Stuart "the embodiment not just of his own early restlessness but of the restlessness and the yearning that come at some point in many people's lives" (99–100). Scott Elledge also offers a detailed biographical reading of the work, suggesting many more corollaries between Stuart and White, their adventures and perspectives, than does Sampson.

During the late 1970s *Stuart Little* received a number of negative assessments. In *Animal Land: The Creatures of Children's Fiction*, for example, Margaret Blount calls *Stuart Little* a "sad, moving fantasy about the human-animal gulf," a "melancholy" work featuring the story of "a human soul in mouse form" that ends with "inevitable failure." The book, Blount continues, is about Stuart's "tragic dilemma," a "unique tale of a social misfit" "inappropriate for children in its implications."[17] According to Blount, this "sad, haunting—some critics have called it sinister—book tells the story of an outcast who must always remain so," being accepted in neither the human nor animal worlds (244). In *Fairy Tales and After: From Snow White to E. B. White* (1978) Roger Sale was considerably more dismissive of *Stuart Little* than was the more deliberative Margaret Blount. According to Sale, *Stuart Little* is not "even good enough to be called a distinguished or considerable failure," and White seemed "terribly bored during many of its episodes."[18]

The 1980s saw three commentaries on White written by Peter F. Neumeyer. In his entry on White for *Twentieth-Century Children's Writers* Neumeyer suggests that *Stuart Little* is "unobtrusively symbolic and suggestive of larger significances" and that this account of "the jaunty, plucky, diminutive hero in often hazardous pursuit of an ideal is recognized, even if only subliminally as . . . a book in the heroic mode, written in our unheroic times" (1983a, 817). In the same year (1983) Neumeyer's fuller assessment of White appeared in the *Dictionary of Literary Biography* volume on *American Writers for Children, 1900–1960*. Again, Neumeyer emphasizes the epic (though diminutive) conclusion of the work when he argues that this ending with Stuart driving north into the great world of promise "may make the reader think of the end of Milton's *Paradise Lost*—the challenge of the brave new world to Adam and Eve as they venture out on their own responsibility—a parallel that White acknowledges" (1983b, 338).

Neumeyer demonstrates White's adroit use of "rhetorical contrast" throughout this work, noting that parody is "one of the main devices by which White achieves his effects" in *Stuart Little*. Neumeyer points out White's comical stylistic juxtapositions of the high-flown with the banal and his humorous parodies of W. C. Fields and Harry Truman, Robert Louis Stevenson and R. M. Ballantyne, Henry Fielding and Mark Twain (Neumeyer 1983b, 338). Neumeyer's excellent commentaries on *Stuart Little* continued in 1988 with his published examination of the manuscripts of the work in the E. B. White Papers at Cornell. Though the work evolved over years in White's thinking, manuscript evidence shows the finished version to have been written "with the utmost rapidity and with apparently no research," though this method of composition accounts for the work's many strengths (Manuscripts, 593). Neumeyer concludes his investigation of the manuscripts of *Stuart Little* with his own judgment that this work is the most inspired and the funniest of White's books. For Neumeyer, *Stuart Little* evinces the joy and the genius of the rough sketch in all its freshness and fluency.

Scott Elledge's 1984 biography of White devotes a complete chapter to *Stuart Little*, detailing the origins of the work, describing its long generation and evolution, and offering an interpretation of this first of White's works for children. Elledge's conclusion concerning *Stuart Little* provides a perfect coda for any serious reading and consideration of this moving work: what happens to Stuart, Elledge argues, is "pretty much what happens to us all, and the tear we may brush from the corner of our eye as we close the book is a tear for ourselves. What the story leaves us with, however, is not a sense of frustration but a memory of things that give us courage equal to the insults of fate: the contents of the repairman's catalogue . . . and the memory of little Stuart, whose jaunty pluck, passion for independence, and devotion to an ineffable dream make him strong enough to endure" (260–61).

Chapter Three

"A Paean to Life; A Hymn to the Barn": *Charlotte's Web*

The contrasts between *Stuart Little* (1945), White's first book for children, and *Charlotte's Web* (1952), his second, could not be more pronounced. *Stuart Little* features a diminutive mouse-boy whose full maturation occurs within a matter of days. Accordingly, Stuart's distinguishing characteristic is his independence and self-sufficiency. Stalwart, even at times cocky, Stuart makes his way in the world through all the ordinary difficulties encountered in daily living as well as through the extraordinary trials confronting him because of his freakish smallness in a looming world dramatically out of scale for him. Much of the plot of *Stuart Little* is set in New York City, with all its urban confusion, dangers, and often unexpected delights. The work is episodic, featuring an often radical disconnection among characters and events in the plot. Stuart himself remains essentially a loner, connecting only with Margalo, whose early departure leads him on a quest for her that is never fulfilled. At the end of the work Stuart is alone, heading north on an apparently endless search for Margalo, that representative of beauty, of ultimate meaning, that incarnation of the ineffable something that makes life rich, full, complete.

By contrast, *Charlotte's Web* opens with new life nascent and dependent. The setting is rural; indeed, on one level the entire work is a pastoral celebration of the joys and beauties of the rural life—of the barn, the farm, and the whole wheeling seasonal world of nature and the open countryside. Wilbur is a baby pig among a host of springtime farm babies, and his gradual maturation is the focus for a large part of the plot. From the first, Wilbur, in his extreme dependence, is cared for by nurturant protectors who rarely leave him to his own devices, and he soon finds himself in a web of complex communal interrelationships in Zuckerman's barn, being reciprocally interconnected with a girl, a spider, a rat, numerous geese and sheep, and eventually the neighboring human community at large. The plot of the novel is carefully interwoven, a complex intermingling of scenes and characters and events. Indeed, the novel is about connection and loss, dependence and gradual maturation, longing and fulfillment. *Charlotte's Web*, unlike *Stuart Little*, concludes with full fruition and the satisfaction of each character's deepest longings.

The Genesis of the Novel

Unlike *Stuart Little*, which grew out of a dream and the practical expediency of satisfying nieces and nephews clamoring for a story, *Charlotte's Web* grew out of White's leisurely observations of and close connections with the barnyard animals he fed daily on his farm in Maine. In her edition of White's collected letters, Dorothy Lobrano Guth noted that *Charlotte's Web* is "a book that could never have been written by anyone lacking an emotional involvement in the lives of domestic animals" (*Letters,* 149). Apparently White began to make tentative plans for the work as early as the beginning months of 1949 after having given up responsibility for the *New Yorker's* editorial page. Though the exact dates of White's first attempts to produce a manuscript are uncertain, the circumstances that led him to write the work are well known. White admits to having been disturbed by the fate of most farm livestock, including his own, which are eventually "murdered by their benefactors." "I have kept several pigs," White noted,

> starting them in spring as weanlings and carrying trays to them all through the summer and fall. The relationship bothered me. Day by day I became better acquainted with my pig, and he with me, and the fact that the whole adventure pointed toward an eventual piece of double-dealing on my part lent an eerie quality to the thing. I do not like to betray a person or a creature. . . . It used to be clear to me, slopping a pig, that as far as the pig was concerned I could not be counted on, and this, as I say, troubled me. Anyway, the theme of *Charlotte's Web* is that a pig shall be saved, and I have an idea that somewhere deep inside me there was a wish to that effect. (quoted in Elledge, 290)

Though the story was apparently initiated by White's secret guilt and wish to preserve his own livestock, it was helped along, according to Scott Elledge, by his close reading of Don Marquis's *archy and mehitabel*, for which White wrote an introduction during the summer of 1949. From this work White apparently developed his central understanding of the character of Charlotte, whom he modeled on Mehitabel. Mehit-abel, White noted, was "always the lady, *toujours gai*" (quoted in Elledge, 292). Marquis's work also featured "warty bliggens," a toad who assumed that the entire cosmos revolved around him—an assumption shared, according to Marquis, by human beings who tend to place them-selves at the center of the universe as well. *Charlotte's Web* thematically counters this pre-Copernican human assumption by focusing on the farmyard and relegating humans to a shared existence with all other creatures in a universe richly teeming with interdependent and indepen-dently valuable species. These two features of *archy and mehitabel*, accord-ing to Elledge, were significant catalysts in the writing of *Charlotte's Web*.

White seems to have written much of the first draft of *Charlotte's Web* between April and October 1950 in the boathouse of the Maine farm. The immediate instigation for the work, according to White's letter of 10 April 1953, was his musings concerning "a way to save a pig's life." The solution came to him after weeks of "watching a large spider in the backhouse" (*Letters*, 375). White observed this spider, whom he named Charlotte, "at her weaving and at her trapping" and "even managed to be present when she constructed her egg sac and deposited her eggs" (*Letters*, 633). White consulted Willis J. Gertsch of the American Museum of Natural History as to this spider's species (*Aranea cavatica*) and read Gertsch's *American Spiders* as well as other similar works to inform himself more thoroughly of the gray spider's characteristics and behavior. According to Elledge, White was proud of the scholarly accu-racy of the emerging text of *Charlotte's Web* and insisted that Garth Williams's illustrations be pictorially accurate in every detail, especially in his representations of Charlotte. To ensure this accuracy, White sent Williams a copy of Gertsch's book on spiders and adamantly declined to have Charlotte given anything even remotely suggesting a humanized face.

White completed the first draft of his manuscript on 19 January 1951 but "put it away for a while to ripen (let the body heat go out of it)," as he wrote to his Harper editor Ursula Nordstrom on 1 March. The book "doesn't satisfy me the way it is," he continued, "and I think even-tually I shall rewrite it pretty much, in order to shift the emphasis and make other reforms" (*Letters*, 331). It had taken White "two years to write the story" and another year to make the revisions, but, as he put it, the year he took to recast the story "was a year well spent" (*Letters*, 644). That White labored over this work is evidenced by the nine successive drafts labeled "A" through "I" deposited with his papers in the Cornell

University Library. The most intensive revisions centered on the novel's beginning, White quipping that he "had as much difficulty getting off the ground" with *Charlotte's Web* "as did the Wright brothers."[1]

Peter F. Neumeyer's examination of the manuscripts of *Charlotte's Web* reveals White's experiments with no less than four conceptually different beginnings before arriving at the dramatic opening where Fern confronts her ax-bearing father and intercedes for Wilbur, the runt pig. These four early experiments included beginning the book by introducing Charlotte, by introducing Wilbur, by singing the praises and the beauties of the barn, and, last, by having John Arable pull his boots on preparatory to going out to the pigpen in the night to discover the birth of 11 piglets to a sow with only 10 teats. The present opening—the beginning in medias res, with Fern confronting her father—provides the dramatic action White needed to entice the reader into the novel and to introduce the girl who provides the way for the reader into the world of the barn. Fern, though absent in the first versions of the work, grew significantly in thematic importance in subsequent revisions.

White signed the contract for *Charlotte's Web* in March 1952. At the outset, the Harper staff was confident that the book would fare well, though they apparently had no premonitions as to its eventual astounding success. The initial run of 50,000 copies sold out almost immediately after the 15 October 1952 publication date. Indeed, the book far outsold every title on the Harper list in the pre-Christmas season and began its long history of perennial reprintings. Widely and favorably reviewed, the book has now sold well over six million copies and is consistently ranked first or second by educators and librarians asked to name the ten best works for children written in America. It has been translated into more than 20 languages and outsells such great juvenile classics as *Alice in Wonderland*, *The Wind in the Willows*, *Winnie-the-Pooh*, and the Mary Poppins books. The work's enormous and enduring popularity stems from White's undisguised love of life and the physical world—a love transparent throughout *Charlotte's Web*: "All that I hope to say in books," he wrote to a youthful reader of the work, "all that I ever hope to say, is that I love the world. I guess you can find that in there, if you dig around" (quoted in Elledge, 300–301).

The book's resonance and popularity also undoubtedly stem from its roots in one of the oldest literary conventions of Western civilization, a tradition spanning three millennia and traceable from the Greek poems or idylls of Theocratus through the Latin and English eclogues of Virgil and Spenser to the eighteenth-century *Pastorals* of Pope and "The

Seasons" by James Thomson. The connection between *Charlotte's Web* and the pastoral tradition has been clearly established by Peter F. Neumeyer, who demonstrates how crucial that link is in any reading of the work. "This seemingly slight children's story," Neumeyer notes, "flows in the mainstream of Western literary tradition, drawing for its names, themes, even its plot, from rich classical backgrounds."[2] White called *Charlotte's Web* "pastoral, seasonal," essentially "a hymn to the barn" (*Letters,* 481). The forward progression of the plot is retarded by what Neumeyer calls "lyrical intermezzos" or pastoral reflections on the beauties of the rural countryside and the changing seasons. During these intermezzos the plot is suspended, and time stands still, as in White's paean to early summer that interrupts chapter 6 and suspends the forward progression of the plot in order to list the various birds of summer and their melodies, including the song sparrow, "who knows how brief and lovely life is" and who sings of summer's "sweet, sweet, sweet interlude."[3]

As Neumeyer demonstrates, such passages as this connect with the pastoral tradition in at least two ways. First, they celebrate the seasons and the serenity and beauty of rural life, and, second, they often connect with the sweetly sad insistence in pastoral on the inevitability of death, even in Arcadia. Thus White's celebration of the pastoral and the rural in *Charlotte's Web* is everywhere conditioned by the melancholy undertone of the presence of death. *Et in Arcadia ego,* the pastoral poets insist: even into the Arcadian paradise death finds entry, though from death comes life and new birth. From winter comes spring and renewed fruition, a truth celebrated by traditional pastoralists and certainly by White in *Charlotte's Web.* White's most direct allusions to this ancient pastoral literary tradition are evident in his naming the farmer who presides over Wilbur's barn "Homer" and in his having Dr. Dorian serve, as Neumeyer reads him, as an "understanding choral interpreter of the relationship of nature's beasts to the natural child, and to the lapsarian adults" (Neumeyer 1979, 74). Dr. Dorian's name itself is derived from the ancient early inhabitants of Arcadia.

Elledge, too, points out the pastoral nature of *Charlotte's Web.* Calling the work "an eclogue that takes its readers back to an early vision of an arcadia," Elledge notes the Wordsworthian, Blakean, and Proustian influences: "As we grow older we lose the vision, but not beyond recall; in the vision of innocence is contained the wisdom of experience; the act of remembrance of things past affirms their value, affirms our value, and creates a sense of man freed from the clutches of time" (305). Readers are so moved by White's nostalgic description of the pastoral world in *Charlotte's Web* because they no longer inhabit such a world and consequently hallow its memory, having lost the original. In loving and longing for this lost pastoral innocence, readers, according to Elledge, "are persuaded of its truth and perhaps of its perpetuity" (305). White thus connects *Charlotte's Web* to one of the oldest of Western literary traditions and taps the archetypal themes that have fueled literature from time immemorial.

The Plot: An Interwoven Design

The lyrical, pastoral intermezzos interspersed in the text form part of the beautifully sustained fretwork of themes and devices overlaid on the novel's classically simple plot. The novel begins on an Edenic spring morning with eight-year-old Fern interceding with her father for the life of a runt in a litter of pigs born the night before. On being given the piglet to raise, Fern christens him Wilbur, rears him on a bottle, and transforms him into her baby until at the age of five weeks, Wilbur is sold to Fern's uncle and goes to live in the Zuckerman barn. Fern visits Wilbur there daily and records his interactions with other barnyard animals, including sheep, geese, a rat named Templeton, and Charlotte, a large gray spider whose web occupies the upper corner of a doorway. After Wilbur dissolves into frantic tears on hearing from the old sheep that Farmer Zuckerman is fattening him up only to slaughter him in the winter, Charlotte promises to save him. Her salvific strategy is ingenious: she spells out in her web the words that eventually come to describe Wilbur, who lives up to her woven encomia.

Wilbur's maturation is ongoing during the story, as is Fern's. As Fern eventually turns her attentions to the great world beyond the barn, Wilbur grows famous because of Charlotte's wondrous web-weaving. Wilbur triumphs at the county fair in the fall, bringing much attention to the stage-struck Zuckermans and thereby assuring Wilbur of a secure and happy life as Charlotte's life rounds to its appointed seasonal close. As a final gesture of love and gratitude to the solicitous, maternal Charlotte, who dies alone at the deserted fairgrounds, Wilbur carries her egg sac back to the barn where he guards her progeny until they make their appearances the following spring, when the cycle of birth and renewal begins again. The novel's cyclical plot thus turns upon the seasons and chronicles the great archetypal cycles of birth, maturation, death, and renewal.

This simple underlying cyclical plot structure provides a strong, spare frame over which White throws a fabric of rich texture and shimmering complexity. White's schematic plot for the novel provides a base for an elaborate textural overlay, a keynote for a harmony of counterbalancing rhythms. There is, first of all, a counterbalancing of the static and the cyclically progressive throughout the novel. The static elements consist of objects and things, both natural and man-made, which White almost obsessively lists so as to provide a sense of the richness of the physical world. This rich, teeming, abundant world is setting and backdrop for the great cyclical drama made up of chronological events and assorted beginnings and endings structuring the diurnal roll of time's passing. This dialectic between static phenomena and cyclical events and episodes in the external, physical world is further counterbalanced by those enduring inner realities of emotions, sympathies, and feelings that bring forth and dignify external actions and that are essentially independent of clock time. These three rhythms—the static, the progressive, and the emotionally enduring—blend in a harmonic overlay enriching the dominant base note of the plot structure.

The static overlay on the basic plot structure consists of White's careful noticing of each separate thing in the world and his celebrations of the world's richness and abundance. Perry Nodelman rightly argues that "The basic structural pattern of *Charlotte's Web* is the list."[4] The work is full of static lists suggesting "both the glorious multitudinousness and the glorious variety of everything" that exists in the world. This static listing includes catalogs of the parts of a spider's leg, the contents of Zuckerman's farm dump, the varieties of sounds made by birds joying in the beauties of early summer, the collection of creatures that Charlotte traps in her web, the disgusting litany of Templeton's gorgings at the fair, the schedule of the events of Wilbur's day, and the detailed contents of the slop pail from which Wilbur feeds. These lists of things and events are plentiful and exultant, celebrating the abundance the world offers to the five senses. Overlaying the basic plot, then, is the work's great litany of "the glory of everything."

Counterbalancing this static cataloging are the rhythmic and cyclical progressions chronicled throughout the work. The great cycle in *Charlotte's Web* is the cosmic turning of time and the stately procession of the seasons, beginning in early spring and revolving through summer, fall, and winter before concluding with a regenerative return to the season of renewal and initiation. Within this large cycle is chronicled the perennial instability of things, growing into full fruition and then declining. Wilbur the runt piglet grows into a hog of considerable girth and stature, and his physical growth is paralleled by an inner maturation as well. The springtime goslings grow into mature gabblers, the lambs into sheep, the nestling song sparrows into full choristers. Fern grows from girl to beginning adolescent, with all the losses and gains of that growth thoroughly colored for a reader. Charlotte, of course, lives her life fully and richly before declining into a death from which regeneration and renewal proceed. Thus, in addition to the constant cataloguing of individual, isolated objects and actions, the sheer cumulative weight of which accounts for the profusion and abundance of this glorious world, White overlays the basic plot with rich temporal progressions. He records sequences of renewal and maturation, decay and regeneration that counterpoint and harmonize with the static lists of farm implements and occupations, of objects that the rain falls on, and of various reactions to the sad, monotonous song of the crickets, harbingers of the end of summer.

Enriching this dialectic of the static and the cyclical in the external world are the intangible but enduring inner emotions that instigate actions and give them meaning. Wilbur's love for Charlotte, for example, participates in the cyclical and the static at the same time that it transcends them. We see him grow to love Charlotte after his initial aversion to some of her "messy" habits and her "miserable inheritance" of blood sucking (39), but once Wilbur's love matures, it remains permanent. "Wilbur never forgot Charlotte," we are told at the end of the work; "although he loved her children and grandchildren dearly, none of the new spiders ever quite took her place in his heart" (184). Wilbur's love, then, participates in the cyclical and in the static, though it ultimately transcends that dialectic. Charlotte's love for Wilbur endures beyond her death; each winter that he passes safe from the butcher's blade is her perennially renewed gift to him. Fern's initial nurturing of Wilbur will intensify into the maternal love she will show to her own children, and Wilbur's celebration of the good world endures beyond all change. Thus the internal verities counter time and its progressions and extend over the static richness of the world's objects, elevating and purifying them, as Charlotte herself wished to do as she explains to Wilbur: "By helping you, perhaps I was trying to lift up my life a trifle. Heaven knows anyone's life can stand a little of that" (164).

The static, cyclical, internal realities of love, nurturing, generosity, and celebrating—all three currents counterpoint and harmonize in a rich fretwork over the basic plot of *Charlotte's Web*. This richness of texture has also been observed by various commentators on the work, who offer differing perspectives and vocabulary to describe the same complex layering effect on the basic plot structure of the novel. Roger Sale, for example, takes White at his word that the book is "a paean to life; a hymn to the barn," but he argues that the book features two counterpointing hymns, the first being in praise of early summer days and the love of life, a love which necessarily "includes the knowledge of transience and death" (Sale, 262). This is the hymn that fills the "sweet, sweet, sweet interlude," that combination, according to Sale, of "the moment of singing, the early summer days, and all of life, and all three at once" (262). The second hymn counterpoints the first in praise of the enduring in the midst of life's fluid change, for this is a hymn whose refrain is "remember the best things, treasure them" even in the midst of the flow and flux of this so brief, so beautiful life one is immersed in (Sale, 267). This second hymn is in praise of those memories which endure because they are somehow magically exempted from time.

Peter Neumeyer also notes two distinct but interwoven levels of plot, the first telling the tale of the title character, Charlotte, and her machinations on the part of Wilbur, the runt pig she nurtures and sets out to save. This plot is complemented by the story of Fern Arable whose beginning maturation parallels, in certain ways, Wilbur's own. The intermingling of these two levels of plot and the close interdependence of the human and animal worlds makes for a complex overlay on a basically simple, straightforward story line and adds a richness of texture that comes from the work's implicit notion that humankind does not have sole dominion over earth and its creatures, that humankind is instead enmeshed, not exempt or removed from, the large web of nature, natural process, and the fullness of creation.

In addition to these two levels of plot, the human and animal stories, White schemes the work as a dialectic between reality and fantasy, which he claims to have discovered actually "make good bedfellows": "I discovered that there was no need to tamper in any way with the habits and characteristics of spiders, pigs, geese, and rats. No 'motivation' is needed if you remain true to life and true to the spirit of fantasy" (*Letters*, 613). This shading between these two "truths" everywhere characterizes *Charlotte's Web*. Truth to reality comes in the presentation of the animals *as* animals. Charlotte, for example, "does what she does," according to White, and despite her verbal web-weaving and her "magnifying herself by her devotion to another," she remains essentially "just a trapper."

Templeton, too, "starts as a rat and he ends as a rat—the perfect opportunist and a great gourmand" (*Letters,* 613).

Of course there is magic in the story, especially when communication takes place between Fern and the animals in the barn cellar. "This is truly a magical moment," notes White in describing the cross-species communication and the general admixture of reality and fantasy to which any reader of *Charlotte's Web* must be responsive. "In writing of a spider," White insists, "I did not make the spider adapt her ways to my scheme. I spent a year studying spiders before I ever started writing the book. In this, I think I found the key to the story" (*Letters,* 614). This "key," then, is being "true to Charlotte and to nature in general" while at the same time admitting fantasy and magic and the marvellous into this "hymn to the barn."

White carefully distinguished his achievement in *Charlotte's Web* from Disney's fantasy works involving human/animal interactions: "My feeling about animals is just the opposite of Disney's. He made them dance to his tune and came up with some great creations, like Donald Duck. I preferred to dance to *their* tune and came up with Charlotte and Wilbur. . . . It just comes natural to me to keep animals pure and not distort them or take advantage of them" (*Letters,* 614). White persistently defended his particular blending of reality and fantasy in *Charlotte's Web*, admitting that conversation between sheep, pigs, spiders, and rats occurs only in the realm of the fantastic but insisting that when such conversation "does finally take place, in that fabulous and pure world, it is indeed a spider who talks, indeed a pig. It is not a woman in spider's clothing, or a boy in a pig's skin" (*Letters,* 615).

This blending of reality and fantasy is for White the "key" to the book and should, he insisted, be the key to any successful motion picture adaptation, negotiations for which occurred several times before a film was finally made of *Charlotte's Web* in 1973. In unsuccessful negotiations for an earlier film, White was insistent that the work had only "a thread of fantasy" but was, for the most part, centered on "ordinary situations" and might thus be made into a movie featuring, not animation, but "live action—real girl, real barn, real creatures." Though "a good deal of the action in the book would present no problem whatever to the camera," according to White, there are scenes where animation would be required. The transition between real pig, real spider, and animated ones would occur as Fern sketches the animals for her mother as she narrates the happenings in the barn, thus centering Fern in the film, as she is in the novel, as the intermediary between reality and fantasy. Just as White did not try "to patronize an arachnid," so "a film maker might have the same good results by sticking with nature and with the barn" (*Letters,* 481–82). Though the film as envisioned by White was never made and though the 1973 animated version of *Charlotte's Web* deeply disappointed White, his discussions with various interested film directors reveal much about the novel and White's intentions and methods in interweaving reality and fantasy into the unique blend that is *Charlotte's Web.*

White's most direct statement concerning the blending of reality and fantasy in the novel comes from a 1974 interview where he pointed out that in the work "animals talk to animals, people talk to people. Fern is a listener, and a translator. This is basic to the story. It also provides a story that is much closer to reality" (*Pied Piper,* 130). Margaret Blount in *Animal Land* notes White's sure success in the interweaving of fantasy and reality. For the most part, according to Blount, White's "animals do what animals always do: eat, sleep, stand about, indulge in simple forms of play." With the exception of Wilbur's speech and his consciousness of past and future, "his thoughts flow in a natural, simple manner. He plans his day into a series of enjoyable intervals," each having to do with the boring routine of a pig's daily life—slopping, sleeping, standing still, scratching, slopping, sleeping again (Blount, 259).

According to Sonia Landes, "fantasy so alternates with reality" in *Charlotte's Web* "that the reader never really leaves home" and thus "experiences fantasy as a cognate of reality." In so closely interweaving fantasy and reality, she continues, White "risks confusing two realms that in Western discourse, at least, should be kept separate," though children "seem to have no trouble following the action from one realm to another, or understanding the theme, which is a paean to the power of love and friendship despite the hard facts of life; and they understand it better for having tracked it on [the] two levels" of fantasy and reality.[5] Indeed, the novel opens with just such an exemption from reality when Farmer Arable readily surrenders his executing ax when confronted with the vision of radical innocence presented him by his daughter Fern. The "reality" figures for Landes are human beings, like Homer Zuckerman and Dr. Dorian, who "represent the world as it is" but who are ever ready to exempt themselves from reality in hopes of participating in the fantastic, as is represented by their readiness to believe in the miracle of the web-writing and in the extraordinariness of humble Wilbur. White's animals play the parts nature provided them as well as the fantastic parts "that we have consecrated in our figures of speech." According to Landes, "this counterpoint between real and unreal, people and animals, is the heart of the story; and Fern is the bridge from one to the other" (271).

This dance between reality and fantasy, between the realistic depiction of animal habits and the fabulous rendering of their hypothetical states of rational consciousness and speech, finds its corollary in the basic situations featured in the work. *Charlotte's Web* admits unpleasant but necessary realities without blandishment: spiders need to suck the blood of flies and cockroaches to survive; farmers need to slaughter animals for food and for sale. Fantasy of situation is featured in the miraculous exemption of one quite ordinary pig from rural reality. Wilbur is allowed to live in barnyard comfort for the remainder of his days, without ever having to fear the very real and expected impact of a bullet in the brain or the cleaving of the axe. Wilbur's is an incongruous longevity representing a fantastic interruption of the real and inevitable processes on the farm. By the end of the work, however, Wilbur, though spared, is firmly entrenched once again in the real cyclical and regenerative processes of nature itself. The miracle of Wilbur's fantastic salvation is wrought by Charlotte, a creature enmeshed in nature whose life is everywhere conducted according to nature's realities.

The Opening Chapters

The counterpointing of the real and the fantastic pervades not only the plot situations of *Charlotte's Web* but also its basic structure as well. The first two chapters of the work, for example, are insistently realistic. They tell, in miniature, the complete story of the novel. They provide a realistic rendering in seed form of the initial saving and nurturing of Wilbur which will be told again in the remaining 20 chapters. In this longer, more leisurely retelling, the fantastic and the real merge and blend, counterpoint and harmonize. As Sonia Landes clearly indicates, the settings for these 20 chapters alternate between the farm, which she sees as the locus of the real world, and the barnyard, site of the fantasy occurrences. These two worlds come together for the first time in the exact middle of the book (chapter 11, "The Miracle") when the human characters are forced to contemplate the intrusion of the marvelous into the real and again toward the end of the work when the human characters gather at the fair to witness Wilbur's ultimate triumph. This adroit merging of reality and fantasy represents one of White's greatest achievements in the writing of *Charlotte's Web* and may help to explain its enduring popularity among child and adult audiences alike.

Charlotte's Web begins dramatically: "'Where's Papa going with that ax?' said Fern to her mother as they were setting the table for breakfast" (1). This sentence in essence announces the central issue in the synoptic plot of the first two chapters and the expanded treatment afforded that plot in the remainder of the book—the menacing and saving of the runt, Wilbur. It is an ominous opening and a most appropriate one: the threat of death hangs over Wilbur for the duration of the work. This axe thus proves to be Damoclean.

White is particularly adroit in his opening of the novel, though this opening caused him no end of difficulty. Being only eight, Fern does not at first understand the relationship between the axe and the news her mother tells her of the birth the night before of a litter of piglets. Rejecting her mother's euphemisms concerning the necessity "to do away with" a "runt" that is "very small and weak" and "will never amount to anything," Fern shrieks out the truth—that her father intends to "*kill* it" just "because it's smaller than the others" (1). Thus, it gradually dawns on Fern, as it does on the reader, exactly what is happening on the farm.

White is also careful to site this intended violence in an almost Edenic setting. The chapter title, "Before Breakfast," indicates a new day, a new beginning, and the birth of pigs, the presence of the young girl, the wetness of the grass, and the springtime smell of the earth provide an ironic counterpoint to the deadly intent of Farmer Arable. The runt, in all its defenselessness, is an apt image for the innocence and fragility of this new spring morning with which the novel opens, and Fern feels instinctively that any harm done the piglet will violate the Edenic world she herself is so much a part of. That the pig is a runt connects what is so far a thoroughly realistic story beginning to the openings of fairy tales, which often center on a small, young, and defenseless character, the least likely to survive but marked for an unusual destiny.

Thus the first page of the novel sets up significant contrasts between springtime renewal and violent death, between childhood innocence and adult experience, and centers Fern in an Eden for the first time threatened by the harsh realities of the fallen world. These themes are continued as the chapter unfolds. Fern confronts her father, begging him not to kill the piglet, appealing to his sense of justice, while trying to wrest the axe from his hands. When she insists that it is unfair to kill the pig and asks whether he would have countenanced killing her if she had been born small, Farmer Arable makes a distinction that Fern, in her innocence, immediately rejects: "A little girl is one thing, a little runty pig is another." Fern's answer is emphatic: "I see no difference," she protests; "This is the most terrible case of injustice I ever heard of" (3).

This answer persuades the farmer to give the piglet to Fern. Recognizing Fern's innocence, he defers to her so as to protect that innocence and prolong it. He allows her vulnerable vision of perfect justice to prevail, just this once, over his own perceptions of the world as necessarily unjust to the weak and the small. As he recognizes Fern's springtime, youthful idealism, Farmer Arable laments the loss of his own childhood vision. When Fern says she sees no difference between a little girl and a little pig in their equal claims, by right of their vulnerability, to equal protection, she situates herself in nature and in the world of idealistic innocence. Her father wishes to extend this fragile state of mind rather than disspell it, so he concedes and gives her the piglet to nurse. Her father says, sardonically, that Fern has tried "to rid the world of injustice" (5); miraculously, she has succeeded on this early spring morning. Her father's love for her allows her to remain in an Arcadian world of childhood innocence just a little longer, "a blissful world" where death is defeated, love triumphs over reason, and justice remains absolute. It is a moving and beautiful opening for the work.

Once again White was fortunate in the illustrator Harper chose for the book. Garth Williams was again engaged, and his now-classic illustrations for *Charlotte's Web* contribute significantly to the book's success. The first illustration (2) depicts Fern wrestling with her father over the axe and demonstrates Fern's impassioned and tenacious defense of her innocent worldview. Farmer Arable's face registers a startled, concerned, and loving insight into the fragility of a child's perspective. The illustration depicts a man awakened from the world of experience and granted a glimpse of the innocent world that his daughter still occupies. The illustration perfectly complements White's delicately handled opposition of adult versus child perspectives in chapter 1. The illustration of Avery (5) also demonstrates Fern's uncorrupted vision. Avery has moved beyond it, armed as he is with knife and rifle but looking none too confident or happy in the world of experience he has so recently entered.

The third illustration (6), depicting Wilbur blissfully sucking a bottle while nestled in Fern's arms, provides a graphic representation of the Edenic satisfactions Fern and Wilbur are still capable of achieving. Unconditional love, mutually given and received, nurturing, satisfaction of all appetites and desires—these elements of the Edenic world are captured in the loving and contented looks Wilbur and Fern exchange. The illustration provides an inversion of the famous scene in *Alice in*

Wonderland where Alice drops the baby-turned-pig she is nursing. Here Fern turns the pig into a baby. In addition, this illustration complements the earlier illustration of Fern wrestling with her axe-bearing father, the two illustrations showing Fern's balanced personality—aggressive *and* pacific, strong *and* nurturing, fierce in her fight for justice *and* gentle in her loving attentiveness. Wilbur's infantile orality and dependence are clearly captured in this illustration of him, amusingly reminiscent of a Renaissance Madonna and Child.

Chapter 2 reinforces and extends many of the thematic concerns of the previous chapter. The nurturing relationship between Fern and Wilbur is everywhere celebrated in this chapter. Initially Wilbur's savior and forceful advocate, Fern now becomes his protector and mother who loves him "more than anything" (8). Her primary task is to feed him, which she does four times a day. Her mother gives Wilbur a bottle at noon while Fern is at school, accounting for his fifth daily feeding. We are told that Wilbur "was never happier than when Fern was warming up a bottle for him" (8). This primary, infantile orality will characterize Wilbur for much of the novel and will have important implications at the work's close when Wilbur, as a mark of his maturation, will sacrifice his selfish fixation on food for the well-being and happiness of another.

All in all, chapter 2 focuses on the idyllic world Wilbur inhabits: "Every day was a happy day, and every night was peaceful" (11). Wilbur's days speed by in an ecstatic blur of pettings, feedings, wheelings in a doll carriage, and lazings in the mud by the children's swimming hole. Wilbur's outside home is, appropriately, under a blossoming apple tree, an emblem of Eden. Fern, too, is happy in a world where she can play at being an adult, a mother, without encountering that role's risks, heart aches, and inconveniences. At five weeks, however, the real world impinges: Fern's father, impervious to her tears this time, insists that the close ties between Fern and Wilbur be severed, that Wilbur be weaned and sold. At Mrs. Arable's sympathetic urging, however, he makes Fern a concession by selling the pig to Fern's uncle, Homer Zuckerman, so she can visit Wilbur whenever she wants.

Appropriately, both of Williams's illustrations for chapter 2 focus on Wilbur and Fern. The first (9) shows a solicitous Fern assuring herself that Wilbur's first night outside will be safe and comfortable for him, that his shelter will provide him with warmth and protection in the larger world outside the house. The second illustration (11) provides a shorthand index to all the ways Fern nurtures Wilbur. She holds the omnipresent milk bottle in her right hand, and with her left she adjusts the sun shade on the baby carriage into which she has tucked Wilbur right next to her doll. The juxtaposition of the baby doll and Wilbur reinforces Fern's innocent declaration in chapter 1 that she cannot distinguish in importance between a little girl and a piglet. For her the Edenic and innocent connection or continuum between human beings and the remainder of the earth's creatures has not yet been severed as it has been for her father, who values each differently, and for her mother, who complains about Wilbur's living in the house. Wilbur and Fern still occupy the world of innocence, and this illustration, with the loving, devoted, mutual gaze that locks everyone else out of their shared world, echoes the illustration concluding chapter 1.

These first two chapters were added during the year White devoted to rewriting the original manuscript of *Charlotte's Web*. They mark an important addition, for two reasons. First, as Perry Nodelman makes clear in "Text as Teacher: The Beginning of *Charlotte's Web*," these chapters present a realistic, highly simplified version of the fantasy retelling that constitutes the remainder of the work. White does this, according to Nodelman, so as to acclimate beginning or naive child readers and prepare them for the richer, more complex, and thus more demanding reading experience to follow. The version of the plot offered in chapters 1 and 2 demands, according to Nodelman, "a minimal literary competence from young readers" (122). The events chronicled in chapters 1 and 2 are recapitulated in the remaining 18 chapters: in both sections of the work Wilbur is saved from death by a female of a different species who nurtures him as a mother. This female saves him because she feels his death is unjust, and she uses words to counter the practical reasons motivating those who plot his death. Their nurturing relationship is threatened by "an aggressive warlike male, a real rat" (Nodelman draws a parallel between Avery and Templeton here), but "the real threat is time itself, which eventually changes both the female and the pig enough to separate them from each other" (Nodelman, 120).

In the first two chapters White makes this story accessible by keeping it in the realistic realm that children themselves occupy and by setting it in an Edenic world they intuitively recognize. In the remainder of the book, which takes place in a postlapsarian world, White explores this basic plot and these thematic concerns more subtly, with greater ambiguity, complexity, and density of texture. The first two chapters prepare the reader for the fuller, richer treatment to follow—one that makes more complex demands on the reader. The chapters also assure child readers that no matter how much Wilbur is menaced in later chapters of the book, he will, by corollary with Fern's saving him in the first chapters, be inevitably spared by the end of the book as well.

Second, chapters 1 and 2 introduce Fern, who was not present in the first versions of the book. Fern serves as the link between the animal and human worlds, between the book's realistic and fantastic strands. She is a necessary intermediary, a focusing device for central themes and issues. Her gradual recognition of a barrier between the animal and human realms provides a gauge to her maturation. As she grows older, her intense identification and unity with the animals wanes, and she shifts interest to those things and people identifiably human. This shift is an indicator of the passage of time in the novel and the changes this occasions.

Wilbur in the Barn: The World of Experience

The Edenic paradise of the first two chapters ends when Wilbur moves to the manure pile in Homer Zuckerman's barn in chapter 3. As has been noted, White tried many openings for *Charlotte's Web* before settling on the one featuring Fern. Most of the trial openings began with chapter 3's "hymn to the barn," the barn being a symbol for White of the world's richness and of life's dense and wondrous texture. Accordingly, this chapter opens with a series of complex lists, a page and a half of pure description in opposition to the spare, linear, straightforward prose of the first two chapters. For the first time, the story focuses on something other than the interactions of Fern and Wilbur. White catalogs the rich admixture of smells infused in the barn, the total effect being "a sort of peaceful smell—as though nothing bad could happen ever again in the world" (13). This catalog is followed by a list of the barn's various compartments and by an inventory of the implements stored in the barn: "ladders, grindstones, pitch forks, monkey wrenches, scythes, lawn mowers, snow shovels, ax handles, milk pails, water buckets, empty grain sacks, and rusty rat traps" (14).

The world of the barn so lovingly described here is the closest one can come to Arcadia, but this Edenic realm differs markedly from that depicted in the previous two chapters. First, though Fern comes every day to visit, she is essentially distanced from Wilbur because she is forbidden to enter his pen or to take him out of it. She is restricted to the role of observer: she looks on at Wilbur from afar, sitting for hours during the long afternoons simply watching and listening in White's wonderful evocation of the long silences and empty spaces of childhood. That she retains that bond with animals so carefully set up in chapter 1 is made clear by the animal acceptance of her presence in the barn: "All the animals trusted her, she was so quiet and friendly" (15).

But the real intimacy between her and Wilbur has effectively ended. Nowhere is this better indicated than in Williams's two-page illustration depicting one of Fern's visits to Wilbur. On the left page (14) Wilbur's face is buried in his food trough, picking up again on Wilbur's infantile orality and greed. But in this gorging Fern no longer feeds him, as the illustrations of chapters 1 and 2 invariably depict her as doing, and their interlocked and loving gazes in those earlier illustrations are broken for the first time here, where their eyes do not meet. Fern is depicted on the opposite page, separated from Wilbur by a wide book gutter and a fence demarking the boundary of Wilbur's pen. This illustration is graphically prophetic: the separation of Wilbur and Fern will grow wider as both mature during the unfolding of the story.

Other changes in tone between the first two chapters and this one are marked. Wilbur, for instance, soon finds himself lonely and bored in the barn, feelings alien to him in the earlier chapters, even though there he waits long hours with nothing to do until Fern returns from school. Wilbur also crosses the line from natural piglet to a kind of talking pig found only in fantasy—a pig granted human emotions and seemingly a human consciousness: "I'm less than two months old and I'm tired of living," he complains (16). Wilbur has clearly exited the innocence of infancy and has entered the more complex world of experience. Thus the barn, paradoxically described in such blissful terms, becomes a prison to him, suggesting that Wilbur has himself changed, has left the prelapsarian world of the earlier chapters for a more challenging, more ambiguous engagement with life.

The effects of life's ambiguity and complexity on Wilbur are nowhere better shown than in his escape attempt from the boredom of the barn. His open lament about his boredom is met with the goose's invitation (in triplicate) to push aside the loose board of his pen and "come on out!" When he follows the goose's advice and squeezes through the fence, he feels strange "with nothing between him and the big world" (17). Wilbur is paralyzed by the sudden influx of choices that his new freedom presents him: "Where do you think I'd better go?" he asks the goose (17). The goose counsels anarchy, telling Wilbur to run, skip, dance, jump, prance, and "root up everything!" This freedom presents Wilbur with an existential dilemma as he becomes aware of the joys and pains of freedom, the happiness it brings and the worry and trouble attendant upon it. For Wilbur's brief flirtation with freedom in the apple orchard, the trade-off is pain and confusion. When the Zuckermans, their hired man, Lurvy, and the spaniel come for him, Wilbur again feels paralysis, not knowing what to do or where to run. "If this is what it's like to be free," Wilbur concludes, "I believe I'd rather be penned up in my own yard" (19).

Surrounded, Wilbur begins to cry for Fern, wishing she were there "to take him in her arms and comfort him" as she had done in the idyllic interlude of the first two chapters (22). Wilbur's solution to the pleasures and awful burdens of freedom and to the confusion and turmoil that his liberty presents him with is to trade that liberty for a pail of slops. He ignores the honking of the goose, who warns him that "an hour of freedom is worth a barrel of slops" (23). This episode in Wilbur's life and his consequent decision to return to the pigpen is significant for a number of reasons. First, and most obviously, it shows him as basically immature and unready to face the world, with all its possibilities and its stern obligations. Second, it demonstrates Wilbur's dawning awareness that life is quite different from the life he has so far lived. The Arcadian simplicity and security of his innocent infant life in the first two chapters gives way to a fuller understanding of life's existential loneliness and the confusion and turmoil often attendant upon self-assertion in the world of experience. Third, the episode reinforces the earlier portrayal of Wilbur as fixated primarily on oral gratification. For Wilbur, the pail of slops is worth everything, and for the appeasement of his appetites he will sacrifice the world, even though his dependent orality and his voluntary return to the pen practically ensure his death at a later date, so far unbeknownst to him.

The illustration for the chase of Wilbur is again a two-page spread with the Zuckermans, complete with slop pail, on the upper left page looking on at the tangled confusion: Lurvy grabs the spaniel as Wilbur darts out of the chaos on the lower right page. This depiction of turmoil consists of an orchestrated tangle of limbs and forms in the lower plane topped by the staggered chorus of animals—goose, rooster, sheep, lamb, and horse—each shouting different, and contradictory, directions at the confused Wilbur. These illustrations offer incomparable interactions with the text, demanding as careful a reading as the text itself requires. Williams does more with his illustrations than simply duplicate in a visual medium various plot incidents. His illustrations effectively interpret the text, bringing to it nuances and thematic implications with a spatial immediacy often more powerful than the slower incremental unfolding of these nuances in the temporal sequence of the text itself.

The security and comfort Wilbur regains by the trading of his freedom for the oral satisfactions of the slop pail do not, however, solve the existential problem that prompted his escape in the first place. Chapter 4, entitled "Loneliness," opens with a catalog of the things and places the next day's dreary rain falls upon. This catalog is followed by the hour-by-hour itinerary of Wilbur's day, a listing of planned events itself punctuated three times by the lists of the contents of Wilbur's food trough. Those lists, everywhere present in the work, show again the richness and variety of this world and everything in it, but for Wilbur at this point the world is an impoverished place. Forced to give up his plans by the incessant rain, Wilbur sees only desolation, abandonment, and loneliness. So severe is his dejection that it even supersedes his oral greed: he does not touch his morning feeding, needing love and friendship more than food and earning for himself a dose of physic in the form of sulfur and molasses.

Wilbur's overtures of friendship to three fellow occupants of the barn meet with rejection, and their reasons for rejecting him read like a catalog of causes why friendships fail. The goose, sitting on her eggs, is simply too busy to play with Wilbur; her duty toward her future brood precludes any claims of friendship Wilbur can exert. The lamb is simply a snob, contemptuous and overbearing, and Templeton the rat is exclusively self-absorbed, a "realist" concerned only with "eating, gnawing, spying, and hiding" (29).

Wilbur's misery escalates in the chapter. After his triple rejection, he has to witness Templeton eat his breakfast. He has to suffer the indignities of Lurvy's doctoring him, and he has to experience the constricting boredom and loneliness intensified by the gloomy day. The disasters and sadnesses of this day in the world of experience culminate in Wilbur's existential prostration in the manure pile, sobbing because he is "friendless, dejected, and hungry" (30). "This was certainly the worst day of his life" (31), notes the omniscient narrator in an aside very different from the assessments of Wilbur's blissful life in the earlier two chapters. At this climax of sorrow and dejection, at the point when Wilbur doubts he can "endure the awful loneliness any more," just at the moment when utter darkness "settled over everything" in a cosmic reflection of Wilbur's despair, a small, thin, but pleasant voice announces itself from the realm of shadows, assuring Wilbur that he would have a friend in the morning (31). Wilbur's great darkness is, then, illuminated by a slender ray of hope, and Wilbur can at last sleep. Thus the book paints the dark side of life in the world of experience and does not spare its young readers a glimpse of that world's ennui, boredom, and alienation.

Enter Charlotte; Enter Templeton

Charlotte's introduction is masterfully handled. No parent reading to a child at bedtime would be allowed to suspend the story at the conclusion of chapter 4. Nor does White satisfy reader expectations immediately in chapter 5; instead, he chooses to sustain these expectations for the first several pages, where he describes the long, tedious night Wilbur suffers through. Wilbur awakens a dozen times from a restless sleep, the last time just before dawn. Like Stuart Little, Wilbur likes this time the best of all for its promise of a new day, especially *this* new day, when his friend will be revealed.

At dawn, Wilbur, innocent, impatient, and sweetly naive, repeats his bulletin to the barnyard twice: "Attention, please! . . . Will the party who addressed me at bedtime last night kindly make himself or herself known by giving an appropriate sign or signal" (34). In his effort to impress, he chooses formal diction and a gender-inclusive recognition, linguistically ahead of his time, that the party he is addressing may be either male or female. When Charlotte finally responds, some time later, she chooses the same formal linguistic register to address him. Her "Salutations!" is now famous in children's literature, as is her initial comparison in size to a gumdrop (thus obviating in this saccharine simile the usual unpleasant associations most of us make with spiders) and her name, Charlotte A. (for "Aranea") Cavatica—a name rendering her personal, genus, and species nomenclature.

Charlotte's self-introduction consists of a scientifically accurate lecture on her personal tastes as well as those shared by spiders in general. The reader learns, for example, that spiders are nearsighted, focusing only on the events occurring in their webs, and that they trap insects, wrap them in their webs, anesthetize them, and then drink their blood. "I love blood," says Charlotte (39), and Wilbur, shocked out of his innocence, comes to recognize that friendships in the world of experience are not the trouble-free affairs they are in the world of innocence, where Fern is his only exemplar of friendship so far. "Please don't say things like that!" (39), Wilbur pleads, but Charlotte will not retreat. She knows that friendship must presuppose a knowledge and acceptance of a friend's character, blemishes as well as virtues. And though Charlotte concedes that her family heritage as a trapper is, in Wilbur's words, "a miserable inheritance" (39), she nevertheless insists on the cleverness of her livelihood. To Wilbur's charge of cruelty, she hastens to remind him that no one brings *her* a pail of slops several times a day or attends to her needs but herself, and she informs him that the positive benefits of her bloodthirsty life-style are insect control, something Wilbur at last recognizes as a beneficial consequence of habits he continues to deplore.

The goose, listening to this conversation, comments on Wilbur's innocence: "There are a lot of things Wilbur doesn't know about life," she reflects; "He's really a very innocent little pig" (40). What Wilbur does not know is how the food chain works in the world of experience. He is appalled that a creature like Charlotte must kill to survive, and, as the goose reflects, he is completely ignorant of his own position in the food chain—a position she reveals to child readers at this point in the novel. The chapter concludes with Wilbur's reflections on the difficulties of making friends in the postlapsarian world to which he is struggling to adapt. "What a gamble friendship is," he says as he relfects on how "fierce, brutal, scheming, bloodthirsty" Charlotte is (41). Again, Wilbur is made to confront the complexities and ambivalences of life in the world, and White assures the reader directly in the last sentence that Charlotte's difficult and unpleasant qualities that Wilbur enumerates are balanced by her beauty and cleverness and, more important, by her "kind heart" and by her ability to remain "loyal and true to the very end" despite her "bold and cruel exterior" (41).

The illustrations for this chapter serve the text well. The first (36) depicts Wilbur standing on his hind legs to get a better glimpse of Charlotte, whose web stretches across the upper left corner of the barn doorway. Interestingly, Wilbur does not look out into the great world of depicted orchards and pastures where the geese gambol freely and the cows and sheep graze at their will. That vista of relative freedom is of little interest to him now that he has a friend whose sphere of operation is restricted to the barn. Wilbur turns his back on the great world and faces into the barn, which is to be his home as well as Charlotte's. He seems reconciled to the pigpen after his one attempt at freedom. The second illustration (38) accompanies Charlotte's introductory lecture on arachnids and depicts, close up, the encasing of the fly in the threads extruded from her spinnerets. As in the text where Charlotte does not spare Wilbur the more unpleasant details of her livelihood, so with this illustration Williams provides, in an immediate way, the very action that horrifies Wilbur as he hears Charlotte describe it. This is quite purposeful: Williams, like White, seems intent on presenting arachnid characteristics up front, with complete frankness and honesty.

Chapter 6, "Summer Days," is a "sweet interlude" in the book, a paean to the "brief and lovely" period of early summer. In his earlier work for children White had Stuart-qua-teacher counsel the schoolchildren never to forget their summers, and Stuart's canoe had been christened "Summer Memories." The jubilant hymn of chapter 6 begins with the assertion that on a farm, early summer days are "the happiest and fairest days of the year" (42). There follows a catalog of summer joys, from lilac and apple blossoms to the mowing and gathering of sweet-smelling hay into the barn, from the jubilee of songbirds to the fields abundant with things "for a child to eat and drink and suck and chew" (43). "Everywhere you look is life," the narrator asserts, from "the little ball of spit on the weed stalk," with its little green worm inside, to the bright orange eggs of the potato bug hidden on the underside of leaves (43–44).

Fern, now out of school, comes daily to sit with the animals, who "treated her as an equal" (42)—a reminder that she is still in that stage of innocence where animal and human nature are continuous, where the existential loneliness of the human heart in the wilderness of the world is not yet recognized. Though Fern has moved beyond that intimacy of initial identification with Wilbur chronicled in the early chapters, she nevertheless retains a primal childhood innocence. Witness now rather than actor, she observes all as the sheep lie calmly at her feet.

On such early summer days miracles abound. The miracle focused on in this chapter is the hatching of seven of the goose's eight eggs—an event marking the high point of the season. "There is nothing (to me) more delightful than the details surrounding a batch of goose eggs," White wrote in June 1967 (Letters, 553), and nearly 15 years later he sent a class of sixth graders in Los Angeles "one of the most beautiful and miraculous things in the world—an egg" laid by his goose Felicity (Letters, 647). Charlotte is the first to notice the arrival of the goslings and employs her most formal language to make the announcement: "I am sure," she says, "that every one of us here will be gratified to learn that after four weeks of unremitting effort and patience on the part of our friend the goose, she now has something to show for it. The goslings have arrived. May I offer my sincere congratulations!" (44).

Amid the general congratulations offered by the animals of the barnyard, Templeton the rat creeps into the circle like the spurned fairy at

Sleeping Beauty's christening. He comes not to congratulate but to ask for the eighth egg, the one that did not hatch. Templeton is "not well liked, not trusted" (45), and his introduction at this point is significant. In coveting the dead egg, Templeton puts himself in opposition to the paean to life and the natural abundance and fruition of early summer that has been sung in the first half of this chapter. Templeton is the negative, the X-ray image, the dark or sinister side to the opposing exultation felt toward the natural world. The egg joins "that nasty collection" of Templeton's; he figures here as warder of the world's failures, ugliness, and disappointments. In rolling the rotten egg away, he admits that "I handle stuff like this all the time" (47). At the same time that Templeton is shrewd, calculating, base, and self-absorbed, he is also somehow endearing. He is an antihero; like W. C. Fields, he is a nasty, snarling comedian.

Life, White reminds the reader through his portrayal of Templeton, is not idyllic in all its aspects; the world of experience is, instead, ambivalent and complex. As the plot will make clear, Templeton, the dark specter, will have a crucial role to play in saving Wilbur—a role second only to Charlotte's. Nevertheless, the animals in the barnyard all "watched in disgust while the rat rolled" the dead egg away into his dark tunnel, but Charlotte alone recognizes that life embraces the beautiful and the foul, that the world's web is woven of both the desirable and the repugnant. She accepts life in all its aspects; she accepts Templeton as part of life: "A rat is a rat," she says, in simple affirmation (47). The chapter is, then, a brilliantly constructed one. It begins with a pastoral hymn to the beauties of the world in its most beautiful season. It then admits that life is but a "sweet interlude" hedged round by death. It introduces into this exulting hymn a recognition and acceptance of the sinister and the revolting. It then concludes with the goose leading her seven goslings out into the world to be counted and blessed by Farmer Zuckerman, who has the last words in the chapter: "Now isn't that lovely!" (47).

The one illustration apportioned to this chapter is beautifully orchestrated. Templeton, snarling while embracing the dead egg, occupies the foreground of the picture. Arranged in a receding perspective behind him are the gander warning Templeton to be content with the egg and to stay away from the goslings, the goose with the goslings gathered protectively beneath her, the thoughtful Fern, Wilbur peeking out from between the boards of his pen, and Charlotte hanging head down from her web. Nowhere is the opposition between light and dark, fecundity and decay, the wholesome and the repulsive made clearer than here. Williams's picture is an economical icon for the central theme of the latter half of this significant chapter.

Wilbur's Bad News

The joy of early summer chronicled in chapter 6 now gives way in chapter 7 to Wilbur's despair, though the news that plummets him into that state is delayed by initial information concerning his increasing attachment to Charlotte and his growing acceptance of her livelihood, especially how it controls the insect population at the same time that she mercifully prevents her victims from suffering. According to early passages in the chapter, Wilbur is rapidly growing stouter of girth, is eating more and more, and is consequently gaining weight. By implication also he is growing up.

Wilbur has learned many existential lessons in his maturation to date. He has learned about the exhilaration and enormous burden of freedom. He has learned about boredom and loneliness, the essential isolation of the individual. He has learned that the beauties of this life are balanced by a darker side, that Charlotte's kindness counterpoints her bloodthirstiness, that seven eggs bring forth life and one egg rots, that the radiance of early summer days can be darkened by Templeton's rolling the dead egg he covets into his disgusting underground lair. Now Wilbur learns the most disturbing thing of all—that he is fated to die at Christmastime as the result of a conspiracy embracing the Zuckermans, Lurvy, and even Fern's father, who once had spared him. This news, conveyed to him by an old sheep who loves the consternation she causes even as she verbally deplores having to bear the bad news to him, throws Wilbur into paroxyms of grief, panic, and despair. One's own mortality is, of course, always difficult to concede, but even more difficult when it is imminent, as is Wilbur's. Interestingly, on hearing the news with Wilbur, Fern is said to grow "rigid on her stool," almost as if she knows Wilbur's fate already but is disturbed that he must be confronted with it.

"I don't want to die!" screams Wilbur; "Save me, somebody! Save me!" (50). At Wilbur's plea something significant occurs: Fern is just about to jump up from her stool to come to Wilbur's aid when she hears Charlotte's authoritative voice commanding Wilbur to be quiet. At this point Charlotte assumes Fern's role as protector and nurturer. Wilbur is unaware of Fern's change in status because he is caught in existential despair: "I don't *want* to die," he moans. "I want to stay alive, right here in my comfortable manure pile with all my friends. I want to breathe the beautiful air and lie in the beautiful sun" (51). Wilbur's yearning for life gives voice to the inchoate longings of all readers aware of their own mortality. "You shall not die," says Charlotte briskly. At this point Fern has receded, and Charlotte becomes the novel's dominant force. Charlotte is confident and compelling, assuring Wilbur that she will save him and demanding that he stop acting like the child he no longer is, that he cease his hysterics in favor of more practical, more mature ways of confronting the threat that hangs over him as well as over all readers. Charlotte is here so attractive and compelling because hers is the assuring and believable voice: "I am going to save you," she promises Wilbur, and that promise, so confidently delivered, has archetypal power for the reader as well. It is the voice all mortals long to hear.

Though Fern has been replaced in chapter 7 by Charlotte in her nurturing and protecting of Wilbur, her role in the book nevertheless remains significant. In chapter 8 she proves the negotiator between animal and human realms, as is indicated in her census of the barn cellar animals, including "Wilbur and the sheep and the lambs and the goose and the gander and the goslings and Charlotte and me" (52–53). Here White again insists on the connectedness of Fern with the animals. As Fern talks with her parents over Sunday breakfast about the hatching of the goslings, she reports matter-of-factly the conversations she has overheard in her Uncle Homer's barn. Not for a moment does she feel self-conscious about her subject, nor does she seem at all aware that her parents consider her reports from the barn extraordinary. Mrs. Arable is worried about Fern and "how queerly she is acting." "I don't think it's normal. You know perfectly well animals don't talk" (54), says Mrs. Arable to her husband.

Mrs. Arable is entrenched in adulthood and has encapsulated herself in that status, being now disconnected from the animal and the natural realm. Mr. Arable is more open to that realm, defending Fern's "lively imagination" and admitting the possibility that Fern, as a child, is simply more attuned to the rhythms of nature and the conversations of animals: "Maybe our ears aren't as sharp as Fern's," he tells his wife (54). This brief chapter, then, shows the chasm that separates the adult human realm from the natural dynamics of the animal world. It also posits the need for an interpreter or a translator between these two realms. Fern, in her childhood innocence, is able to connect her adult mother with nature again, though her mother is concerned about Fern's openness to both realms. Mrs. Arable wants Fern's total absorption into the human realm and the abnegation of her instinctive, innate ties to the natural animal realm.

Fern's tie to the animals is strong indeed, as chapter 9 indicates. Fern serves as recording consciousness in this chapter, which begins one afternoon when she "heard a most interesting conversation and witnessed a strange event" (55) and concludes with Fern's leaving the barn, "her mind full of everything she had seen and heard" (65). What Fern sees and hears is typical of a usual afternoon in the barn—an afternoon without agenda, the normal course of a time of day that passes slowly and according to its own natural rhythms. The chapter begins with a continuation of the earlier entomology lesson on arachnids. Charlotte explains to Wilbur the seven sections of a spider's leg and how she goes about spinning a web. When Wilbur hears about web-spinning he is determined to try his skill at it. Charlotte and Fern, clearly maternal figures here, encourage and coach him, though they obviously know that Wilbur's enterprise is doomed to failure. Even Templeton comes out of his hole to see the fun and to tie a piece of dirty white string Wilbur borrows from him onto Wilbur's tail in lieu of web threads from a set of spinnerets. The text focuses on the love, nurturing, and maternal amusement of Fern and Charlotte for the childlike Wilbur.

Charlotte's web is an image of competence and control, an image stressing her adulthood and her ability to create her immediate environment, to weave a life for herself. Wilbur's failure to weave a web results not just from his physical incapacities but also from his immaturity, his infantile unreadiness to construct a life for himself. Charlotte, and Fern before her, have to construct that life for him through much of the novel.

After consoling Wilbur over his inevitable failure, Charlotte delivers a critique of human web-building, pointing to the Queensborough Bridge in New York City as a prime example of a web built at great expenditures of time, money, and energy for little purpose except to trot back and forth across it without catching anything, its users thinking all the while that "there is something better on the other side" (60). This passage reasserts the pastoral frame for the work as a whole. It points to the productiveness of the rural over the profitless hurry of the urban; the purposeless movement and hustle of the city is contrasted with the more sedentary purposefulness of the country. As Charlotte tells Wilbur, "I sit still a good part of the time and don't go wandering all over creation. . . . I stay put and wait for what comes. Gives me a chance to think" (61). For White, writing is like web-tending. Charlotte is herself a writer; she knows that writers must sit still and wait for what comes. Thus life itself, White implies, is happier and richer in the pastoral vein. These overheard lessons, games, and philosophical discourses, along with Charlotte's loving defense of Wilbur against a supercilious lamb's charges that Wilbur smells bad, add up to a full afternoon, not only for Wilbur but also for Fern, who, though it is suppertime, "couldn't bear to leave" (62).

Wilbur, unlike those humans criticized by Charlotte for searching restlessly and fruitlessly for something better in a different place, knows the full riches of his life and appreciates the beauty of evening as it settles over the barn. With friends, boredom and loneliness are banished, and life is good. Wilbur, we are told at the end of this long afternoon, "loved life and loved to be a part of the world on a summer evening" (62). It is this love of life that brings on the fear of losing it all: "I don't want to die," Wilbur laments. And again Wilbur hears what we all wish to hear: Charlotte says, with believable determination, "I am not going to let you die, Wilbur" (63).

So confident is Charlotte of her ultimate success in saving him that she offers Wilbur advice for living: get plenty of sleep, stop worrying, eat all your food and chew it completely, gain weight and stay well, keep fit and don't lose nerve, get plenty of rest. This is the advice a solicitous mother would offer her child. Indeed, the maternal relation between Wilbur and Charlotte is thoroughly developed in the latter part of this chapter. Wilbur knows all the dodges of any young child on being put to bed: he begs for more time; he delays bedtime by asking for more food and by requesting a drink. Before Wilbur settles down, however, there is a volley of goodnight wishes, clearly a delaying tactic, as if Wilbur is reluctant to break the connection with Charlotte, even in sleep. And so ends a typical afternoon in the barn, as Fern, the recording consciousness, slips away late to the human world where her supper awaits her.

The illustrations for this chapter allow the reader a greater tolerance for Templeton. After all, he agrees to lend Wilbur a piece of string from his storehouse so that Wilbur could attempt to spin a web. The first illustration (58) shows him tying the string onto the tail of a determined Wilbur, and the second (59), a full-page drawing, shows him laughing good-naturedly at Wilbur's folly. Wilbur, his face alight with expectation and optimism, is depicted as leaping from the top of the manure pile, unanchored string whipping out behind him as Charlotte looks on from her perfect web in the upper left corner. Charlotte and Templeton align themselves in the illustration with the leaping Wilbur between them.

This alignment foreshadows the roles they will play in Wilbur's fate, for of all the characters in the work, they—one unconditionally loving and the other bribed into cooperation—will be instrumental in saving him. This illustration shows the three central animal characters, whose fates are so closely interwoven, at play before their serious interactions commence.

Charlotte's Plan

Chapter 10 is a particularly rich one in incident and thematic development. Summer is half gone: the sweet interlude celebrated up to this point is fleeting, and, we are told, Charlotte "knew she didn't have much time" (67). This assertion is ambiguous, though it strikes an ominous tone. On one hand, it means she knew she did not have much time to devise a plan for saving Wilbur. On the other hand, it suggests that she herself does not have much time remaining in the natural cycle of her life—a meaning that prepares one for the book's conclusion. The conclusion reveals that both significances are intended.

As the chapter opens Charlotte is waiting patiently, head-down on her web, for an idea to come to her concerning a way to save Wilbur. Unlike the restless humans clambering over the Queensborough Bridge, Charlotte knows that if she waits long enough an idea will arrive, just as flies come eventually to the web. When at last an idea does announce itself, she values it for its inherent simplicity: she decides to fool Farmer Zuckerman, whose name now sounds suspiciously close to "suckerman." (White is not beyond such puns in his works. "Arable," for example, is a perfect name for a farmer, as it means "fit for cultivation." But ferreting out such puns for *all* of White's character names soon proves fruitless and frequently produces overly clever or strained significances. Some names, like "Wilbur" or "Charlotte," just *sound* right, their connotations of "lumpish" on the one hand and "gentle and refined" on the other fitting the respective characters so designated.) Charlotte slams humans when she asserts that if she can fool a bug, she can surely fool a man, because people "are not as smart as bugs" and are indeed quite gullible (67). As events prove, Charlotte knows well the psychology of humankind.

While Charlotte schemes in her web, Fern and Avery visit the Zuckerman barn. White is adept in presenting the two children. Avery, for example, carries with him a captive frog to which he pays little attention.

Fern, wearing "a crown of daisies in her hair" (68), indicating her close association with nature, is naturally attuned to the frog's sufferings in its captivity, pointing out that the frog is hot—indeed, almost dead. Avery's callous disregard for the frog's condition and his inability to even approach the level of Fern's empathy with the creatures of nature prepare the reader for Avery's planned depredations on Charlotte's web later in the chapter.

In one of the most beautiful passages in the book the children visit the barn to swing on a rope tied to a doorway beam. From the hayloft, a child straddles the knot at the end of the rope, gathers her nerve, and launches herself dizzily into the air. Significantly, this passage follows the chapter concerning Charlotte's web construction and Wilbur's abortive attempt to weave his own web. The connections are far from accidental. Charlotte, the master web-builder, is an accomplished levitator, a swinger in air. She launches forth into life and constructs a home and a means of attaining a living. At home in the air but grounded on a stable support, Charlotte is self-sufficient because she is able to weave together plan and reality, to bring into actuality an imagined structure that grants her a full and satisfying life. It is no wonder that Wilbur, too, would attempt to build a web. Unlike Charlotte, however, he does not succeed. He is too young to weave together imagination and reality. He imagines a web, but he cannot bring it into being because he is immature and ill-equipped to succeed.

Web-weaving, then, becomes a metaphor for the ability to construct a life that allows one to live authentically and fully and to satisfy one's needs for home, food, identity. Wilbur cannot do this yet. Fern and Avery are levitators as well, but their swinging remains restricted. Attached to the dooryard crossbeam, the rope they swing on remains untethered at the other end. Consequently, they swing in an arc out from the safe enclosure of the idyllic barn into the great world beyond, in and out. Childhood is itself imaged here. In childhood one is, ideally, grounded on a firm support, a place of safety and security from which one may swing out into the world for brief intervals before retreating again into the security of home. Fern and Avery launch into the sky, but they are tethered to home—a place of safety that both sends them forth and receives them back again. Childhood itself is a series of such rope swings until, in adulthood, one becomes like Charlotte, swinging out into the air, but not returning home again. In adulthood, for which Fern and Avery are practicing throughout this book, one launches forth and, once out in the world, builds one's own home and finds one's own identity and self-sufficiency. The novel is replete with such images of launching forth into the air and thereby initiating a new life.

It is no wonder, then, that "mothers for miles around worried about Zuckerman's swing" (69). They fear that children, launching themselves into air (and into life), will fall off. "But," White assures us, "no child ever did" because children "almost always hang onto things tighter than their parents think they will" (69). Mothers worry over this swing because intuitively they recognize that their children arc out into the wide world, embracing life, adventure, and possibility, and such an embrace can also bring pain and disappointment. White will eventually connect this image of the web and the swing with the Ferris wheel at the fair where Fern will launch into her future seated beside Henry Fussy.

This passage is finely crafted, thematically and stylistically, as Peter Neumeyer makes clear in his discussion of the syntax of certain sentences White employs to describe the swinging action (1983b, 346). White uses syntax to imitate the launch and return, the out and back again movements of one on a swing. The following sentence is particularly adept at matching movement with sentence construction, the rhythms of the sentence providing a mimetic echo of the swinging being described: After propelling up into the sky, the swinger "would drop down, down, down out of the sky and come sailing back into the barn almost into the hayloft, then sail out again (not quite so far this time), then in again (not quite so high), then out again, then in again, then out, then in; and then [that person would] jump off and fall down and let somebody else try it" (69).

After swinging, Fern returns to her own particular anchor, Wilbur and the other creatures of the safe and enclosing barn. Trouble dogs her to Wilbur's pen, however, in the form of Avery, whose earlier Templeton-like disregard for the frog's welfare is extended in his planned depredations against Charlotte and her web. Charlotte's narrow escape from Avery's attempt to knock her down with a stick is occasioned by Avery's clumsiness: in falling, he tips Wilbur's trough up, which comes down on Templeton's rotten goose egg. The terrible stench from the rotten egg drives the children away. Thus Charlotte's life is indirectly saved by Templeton's disgusting hoarding of the dead goose egg. This episode demonstrates that cooperation in the world between the beautiful and the ugly, the pleasant and the repulsive established earlier in chapter 6. Templeton and his actions and interests have a purpose in the right conduct of the world and perform necessary balancing functions in maintaining the world's harmony. After all, this book is a celebration of "the glory of everything," including Templeton and all he represents. Though disconsolate over the loss of the egg, Templeton nevertheless takes credit for his role in saving Charlotte's life—as he should: "It pays to save things," he admonishes; "A rat never knows when something is going to come in handy. I never throw anything away" (74). This is the first time that Templeton, as selfish and egocentric as he so clearly is, becomes the unwitting instrument of salvation and preservation of someone else. He will perform this function again in the novel. His motive will always be self-interest, but his actions will result in desirable outcomes.

This important chapter concludes with Wilbur's evening feeding. As Lurvy carries the slop pail, he smells the rotten egg and recognizes the presence of rats: "How I hate a rat!" he exclaims (74), his revulsion being generally shared. Charlotte knows the necessity and function of rats, however, and counsels Wilbur always to leave a morsel of food for Templeton. Wilbur stands *in* his trough, "drooling with hunger" as the slops run "creamily down around [his] eyes and ears" (75). White's description of the contents of the slop pail and of Wilbur's gorging are masterful. Wilbur, we are told, "gulped and sucked, and sucked and gulped, making swishing and swooshing noises, anxious to get everything at once" (75). This unrestrained effort to ingest indiscriminately characterizes the primal orality of the infant—and of Wilbur as well. But Wilbur is not himself an infant, though his orality is clearly infantile. He has, however, matured at least to the point that he can spare a whole rather than the customary half of a noodle for Templeton for his having been "useful in saving Charlotte's life" (75). The chapter concludes with Charlotte bestirring herself on her web and commencing her salvific work while the other creatures of the barn drowse contentedly.

As is fitting for such an important chapter, there are three illustrations devoted to it. The first depicts Charlotte waiting patiently on her web. At first glance, the illustration depicts her realistically. A closer examination, however, reveals that this spider is actually reposing in a very human posture: her two back legs are crossed behind her, a common position for the legs of someone lying chest-down on a floor. Her next two back legs are carelessly splayed out. Her two front legs are the most typically human in posture of them all: one arm is bent at what seems to be an elbow to support her weight against a supporting web anchor and the other is bent so as to allow her to lean her head in her palm. Her overall posture is reminiscent of someone lying on the floor daydreaming. The illustration is particularly adroit in its deference to both the realistic and fantastic strains of the work. A viewer can have it both ways in this illustration. What appears to be a naturalistic spider reposing on its web comes to be, on closer inspection, a spider recumbent in an amusingly human (and thus fantastic) posture. This duality is, of course, appropriate: though a true spider (she has just been munching on a horsefly), she also thinks and speaks. This most subtle of Williams's drawings for *Charlotte's Web* captures this duality perfectly.

The second illustration (71) depicts Fern swinging on the rope out into the world from the safe enclosure of Zuckerman's barn. This thematically significant illustration captures in a spatial design White's verbal suggestions that the swing is a metaphor for the children's trial entries into the world of possibility and adventure before their returns to the safety and security of the familial (and familiar) world. It is significant that Fern is depicted on the swing rather than Avery and that the illustration captures her *in* the barn just as she is moving out of it into the world beyond. That this world suggests life, adventure, and possibility is further emphasized by the road leading from the barn out through the yard and through a fence into the hills beyond. This road provides a visual metaphor for the path we tread as adults, once we have left the security of home, that path that leads us to an identity and a life we make our own. In this work Fern takes her first walk down that path, and the rope swing is a perfect metaphor for her tentative adventuring.

The final illustration in chapter 10 captures Avery as he tumbles over the trough, the visual plane consisting of an orchestrated pattern of jumbled legs, arms, candy box, and stick. The raised trough is descending on the egg as Templeton retreats into his tunnel. This illustration brings Templeton and Avery—rat in the natural world and metaphysical rat in the human world—together to cancel out their mutual self-absorption and greed, the characteristics that best define them in their respective spheres.

Chapter 11, "The Miracle," is, as its title implies, also a crucial chapter, occurring as it does almost midway through the book. The chapter opens on a foggy morning with tiny beads of water silvering the grass and the asparagus plants. The whole world has turned silver (as opposed to the Golden Age alluded to in the halcyon first two chapters) and is thus a fit arena for miracles. Charlotte's web, too, glistens in silver, forming "a pattern of loveliness and mystery, like a delicate veil" (77), hiding an alternate reality beyond this visible, quotidian one. In the center of this shimmering web Charlotte has woven the phrase "SOME PIG," the miracle referred to in the chapter title. Human reactions to the phenomenon are interesting and varied. Lurvy, the farmhand, discovers the miracle and falls to his knees to utter a prayer. Mr. Zuckerman is the first to call the literate web "a mysterious sign" and a miracle and to designate Wilbur as unusual. Mrs. Zuckerman, however, proves more practical, asserting that their spider, not their pig, is really unusual, but soon she too is swept up in Charlotte's trick. Charlotte had dubbed humans "gullible," but the extent of that gullibility seems to surprise even her.

The trick escalates. Soon people begin to arrive in every conceivable conveyance from miles and miles around, drawn by the miracle on Zuckerman's farm. Charlotte's web is capacious enough to entrap myriads. Zuckerman's barn becomes a place of pilgrimage journeyed to by people longing for mystery, an enchantment that assures them that the narrow boundaries they confine themselves to in this world are indeed expandable, that the world is larger, more wondrous than they have the energy or imagination to dream of. The minister in his Sunday sermon gives voice to this when he admonishes his congregation "that the words on the spider's web proved that human beings must always be on the watch for the coming of wonders" (85). So popular does Wilbur become that the Zuckermans neglect their farm duties in their excitement over the crowd attention, though Fern herself enjoys her visits to the barn much less because of this preponderance of people. Wilbur proves so popular because, though the most mundane and serviceable of farm animals, he provides the gateway to mystery. He lightens the dailiness of this routine world and provides those who labor in it a glimpse of something larger, something beyond understanding and rational light. He provides those immured in the world a freshening sense of wonder, an exhilarating estrangement from the familiar.

There is, however, a quieter miracle occurring in this chapter that the noisy, wonder-seeking humans are not attuned to. The words of Charlotte's web are miraculous, not simply because they represent a direct communication from the animal to the human world (a line of communication Fern has been attentive to since the beginning of chapter 3), but also because these words have creative power in their own right and magically affect events and things in the actual world. Charlotte's woven words have the power to call something into being that has not existed before their weaving. The miracle these words precipitate is the eventual transformation of Wilbur from runt to "SOME PIG." Charlotte's silken assessment of Wilbur here is clearly hyperbolic, more prophetic than accurately descriptive. Wilbur, who stands under the words seeming to describe him, is not in the least extraordinary at this time. He is not yet "SOME PIG" but just "some pig," *any* pig, as his typical behavior indicates.

Wilbur gorges thoughtlessly; he snoozes on the manure pile; he falls into hysterics of fear and panic when he contemplates his own death. Nothing extraordinary here. But the words themselves call something extraordinary into being. Suddenly, the Zuckermans and Lurvy perceive of Wilbur as being "an extra good" pig, "as solid as they come" (82), and Homer Zuckerman escalates Wilbur's three feedings to four a day. In short, the words create a new perception and transform Wilbur from ordinary to "SOME PIG" in the eyes of all who behold him standing beneath the woven descriptors. Even the many visitors to the farm to see Wilbur say that they have "never seen such a pig before in their lives" (84). More important, Wilbur himself perceives a need to live up to these assessments, to transform himself from ordinary to extraordinary, and this inner transformation begins to accelerate from this chapter on.

Words themselves, then, operate as true miracles in our world. They call things into being that did not exist before. They transform and create. Language is the creator of reality and is responsible for the formation of a self. Nowhere in White's works is this miracle of language as creative power given more forceful attention than in this chapter, a crucial one in *Charlotte's Web* as it provides one of the few points of convergence between people and animals, between the realms of human reality and animal fantasy interwoven throughout the text.

Williams's illustrations for this chapter are, however, more serviceable than inspired. The first offers a straightforward depiction of the web-writing in beads of dew against the dark background of early dawn. Two things are striking about this illustration. First, Charlotte is omitted from it so that the writing stands out in undisputed primary focus, just as in the text Charlotte is largely ignored by the viewers of her web. Second, the writing is prominent in the cleared-out center of the web. This illustration insists on the miracle; this writing cannot be accident or peculiar aberration or trick of lighting. The second illustration (83) depicts the throngs of people peering into the pigpen, their cars filling the pasture beyond the barn. Homer Zuckerman regales a visitor with further details of the miraculous pig he is master of. The illustration is smaller than most in the book, almost as if to emphasize the gullibility of these visitors—a gullibility Charlotte takes full advantage of.

Chapter 12 features a meeting of the barn residents, at which Charlotte asks for brainstorming help with words to weave into the web.

She accepts the goose's suggestion of "terrific," though Wilbur demurs, insisting that he is "just about average for a pig" (91). Charlotte, ever cynical about human nature, indicates that though her woven assessment of Wilbur is hyperbolic, people will nevertheless "believe almost anything they see in print" (89). This new descriptor of Wilbur again proves more prophetic than strictly accurate when ascribed, for Wilbur will become "terrific" in his own right by novel's end.

The chapter also links the destinies of Wilbur and Templeton, whose shared fates accomplish that duality White is so insistent upon as characterizing the world of experience that Wilbur is trying to make his way through with the help of his friends, that duality of admirable and disreputable, innocent and jaded, good and bad. Templeton, coaxed into bringing back magazine clippings from the dump for word suggestions, at first refuses to cooperate. His awareness that the enterprise could save Wilbur's life does not affect him: "Let him die," snarls the rat; "I should worry" (90). The old sheep must appeal to Templeton's "baser instincts, of which he has plenty" (90). Templeton is reminded that if Wilbur is butchered, his slops stop coming. Only then does Templeton realize that his prime food source originates in Wilbur's feedings. He thus agrees to cooperate, forging an interdependence between the noble and the ignominious, the generous and the base, which lies at the heart of this glorious world.

The single illustration in this brief chapter depicts the barn meeting convened by Charlotte. Interestingly, the chapter begins with a humorous roll call of all the barn animals in attendance. There is no indication whatsoever in the text that Fern may be present as well, though the illustration depicts her sitting among the sheep and geese, attentively listening to Charlotte in her web. Her presence comes as a bit of a shock, so completely absent is any mention of her in the verbal text itself. Fern is less and less a significant presence in the lives of these animals, an interesting commentary on Fern's gradual human maturation and eventual defection to the human realm. Fern's silent presence also counters an anthropocentric view of the world typical of humans: nature and these animals have viable existence independent of human presence or intervention. This illustration depicts the deflation of human self-importance; Fern sits, just one with the barn creatures, her connection with them stressed by her silence and by her height sitting down, which is comparable to the heights of the other animals she is so clearly integrated with here.

Spider Lore

Chapter 13 consists largely of spider lore. The chapter begins with an excursus on web-building and the kinds of threads and maneuvers Charlotte uses in weaving "TERRIFIC." Charlotte, we are told, "loved to weave and she was an expert at it" (92). In addition to being a joyful weaver, Charlotte is a lover of words. Thus, she accompanies her weaving with a patter similar to a square-dance caller calling the moves: "Attach! Descend! Pay out line! Whoa! Attach! Good! Up you go! . . . Over to the right! Pay out line! Attach! Now right and down and swing that loop around and around!" (94). The spider lore continues later in the chapter when Wilbur demands a bedtime story and Charlotte obliges by telling him of her cousin who nets small fish and another cousin who was an aeronaut, employing her billowy web to float her to other locations.

In addition to the spider lore, of entymological interest in and of itself, the chapter records the results of Charlotte's second weaving. Wilbur, again, stands beneath the woven assessment and tries to live up to the quality ascribed to him. The power of words to create reality is again a crucial subtext in this chapter: standing beneath the wondrous web, Wilbur *feels* terrific, "quietly swelling out his chest and swinging his snout from side to side" (96). "There isn't a pig in the whole state that is as terrific as our pig," Farmer Zuckerman declares, who believes everything he sees in print (96).

Charlotte knows that human gullibility, like most human characteristics, is fickle and must be constantly sustained. Thus she is ever seeking new words to weave into the web. Templeton's visits to the dump result in his bringing back extraordinarily inappropriate words for Charlotte's consideration: "Crunchy," for example, and "Pre-shrunk." Added to his other shortcomings is Templeton's almost complete lack of sensitivity to connotation and the suggestive power of words. Grumbling about being turned into a "messenger boy," Templeton agrees to try again, returning this time with a passage from a laundry-detergent package, inscribed "with New Radiant Action." Charlotte, ever concerned with accuracy, asks Wilbur to *act* radiant in front of her, to run and twist and jump and do back flips so as to see if his actions can in any way be called "Radiant." Radiant she decides he is: "I *feel* radiant," Wilbur assures her, before nestling back into the manure pile, testifying again to the power of words to create in reality what they signify (101).

The chapter concludes with Wilbur's requested bedtime stories, followed, in childlike succession, by his begging Charlotte for a lullaby. She
sings to him a song that epitomizes their relationship and summarizes
the primary plot motivator:

> Sleep, sleep, my love, my only,
> Deep, deep, in the dung and the dark;
> Be not afraid and be not lonely. . . .
> Rest from care my one and only,
> Deep in the dung and the dark! (104)

That motivator is love, and love will, in this work and for this once, triumph over the inexorable processes of logic that demand that a pig
raised through summer must be slaughtered in winter. At the conclusion
of this lullaby, Fern, that silent observer, gets up quietly from her stool
and makes her way home.

This chapter is punctuated by five illustrations, the first (92) func-
tioning as a visual display in the science lesson about web-weaving with
which the chapter begins. The following illustration depicts Wilbur
beneath the web, trying to live up to the sobriquet woven there.
Standing sturdily, his tail curled tightly, he confronts the barn visitors
(and the reader), trying to smile, his eyes squinting in self-deprecation.
Templeton's tour of the dump is visually chronicled in a small circular
illustration depicting him as at one with the scraps and discarded things
among which he prowls. The lines of this beautifully orchestrated illustration are complex and entangled but have a natural fluidity:
Templeton is at once drawn into and dominates the junk in which he
stands. There follows (100) another endearing illustration of Wilbur
doing "a back flip with a half twist in it" and justifying Charlotte's
ascription of "Radiant!" to him. The concluding illustration depicts for a
possibly incredulous readership the capturing of the fish in Charlotte's
cousin's stream-spanning web.

It is the tale of Charlotte's cousin and the fish that Fern regales her
disturbed mother with the next morning as they wash the breakfast
dishes together. Mrs. Arable demands that Fern face the fact that spiders
do not talk, but Fern remains adamant in her declaration that Charlotte
at least does. Mrs. Arable's incredulity is invincible, which is especially
surprising because she knows of the word-weaving in Charlotte's web.
Yet the possibility that Charlotte speaks as well as writes seems never to
occur to her. Worried, Mrs. Arable consults Dr. Dorian, whose perspec-

tive is the exact opposite of hers on every issue she raises. When, for example, she complains that Fern spends most days on a milk stool in the barn watching the animals, Dr. Dorian exclaims, "How enchanting!" When Mrs. Arable mentions the miracle of the web-writing, Dr. Dorian indicates that people have lost sight of the true miracle—that spiders can spin webs in the first place. When she worries about Fern's belief that animals converse, Dr. Dorian keeps open the possibility that they may indeed talk, though adults, being "incessant talkers," do not pay attention.

Dr. Dorian, in short, is that rare adult who is open to wonder, to the possibility that the neatly categorized physical world is punctuated by mystery and enchantment. Dr. Dorian's reaction to the world's wonder is very different from the reaction of Mrs. Arable, who at one point proclaims emphatically, "I don't like what I can't understand" (110). When, however, Dr. Dorian wistfully assures Mrs. Arable that Fern will all too soon turn her attentions away from her barn-cellar friends, Mrs. Arable is relieved. Ironically, she herself does not feel the loss at such an outcome that Dr. Dorian hints at.

The basic differences between the stolid, sensible Mrs. Arable and the more imaginative Dr. Dorian are captured by Williams in the chapter's central illustration. Mrs. Arable sits on the left page (108) on the edge of her chair, leaning forward and clutching her purse. Dr. Dorian, on the right page (109), leans well back in his chair and closes his eyes. Separated in mindsets, these two characters are separated by a wide book gutter and plentiful intervening white space as well. The illustration thus perfectly captures the variance between closed and open minds, pragmatic attitude and imaginative engagement. They come together, of course, in their mutual concern for Fern's well-being, their love for her serving as the bridge.

Dr. Dorian's wistful assurance to Mrs. Arable that Fern, in the passage of time, will leave the idyllic space of the barn and her Arcadian connection with the animals prepares the reader for the sad intermezzo of chapter 15. The crickets of the chapter's title sing "the song of summer's ending, a sad, monotonous song . . . to warn everybody that summertime cannot last forever" (113). The first half of the chapter consists of a catalog of reactions to the droning of the crickets' "rumor of sadness and change" (113). Charlotte, for example, hears that song and knows "that she hadn't much time left" (113). The song does not phase Wilbur particularly. He is busy living up to his designation as "Radiant," turning his head in the golden sun and blinking his long eyelashes at his many visitors. He also entertains them with his back flip with a half twist, earning Farmer Zuckerman's praise. Despite all the attention, we are told, Wilbur remains modest. White makes the point that Wilbur has now earned the adjectives Charlotte uses to describe him. He has *become* what she envisioned him as being. In short, her words have been directly instrumental in forging Wilbur's reality.

The chapter concludes as wistfully as it begins. Wilbur begs Charlotte to accompany him to the county fair, but Charlotte refuses to commit to going with him. Charlotte, though loving and solicitous, is not really self-sacrificing. She knows that her biological imperative to lay eggs to ensure her succession in time takes precedence over her solicitude for Wilbur. White is insistent on this point, refusing to have Charlotte promise something that would be false to her inherent nature. She does, however, promise Wilbur that she will accompany him to the fair if she can. The chapter ends, then, with strong premonitions of Charlotte's eventual death and with White's faithfulness to Charlotte's essential nature as a spider. When she must lay eggs, she must, all other concerns receding from her. This she determines at the conclusion of this chapter to make Wilbur understand.

Locus of Wonders: The County Fair

After the crickets' warning, time begins to move rapidly. Chapter 16 chronicles the preparations for the county fair made on the Zuckerman and Arable farms. The early-to-bed dreams and next-morning preparations of the humans are fully chronicled at the beginning of this chapter, especially Mrs. Zuckerman's bathing of Wilbur in buttermilk, making him "the cleanest, prettiest pig you ever saw" (121). Mrs. Arable confirms that in this state Wilbur *is* indeed "some pig." Lurvy calls him "terrific," and Fern pronounces him "very radiant" (125). This triple validation is Wilbur's private moment of triumph: he has at last become an accurate embodiment of Charlotte's woven hyperboles. Wilbur's private triumph on the farm and in the small family circle is confirmed by the ever-pragmatic Mrs. Zuckerman, who insists that Wilbur is clean at least. This triumph fades off on a sour note as Mr. Arable admits Wilbur to be wonderful but adds that he will make "some extra good ham and bacon . . . when it comes time to kill *that* pig" (126).

With this threat on Wilbur's life still so strongly present, it becomes clear that Charlotte has made the correct decision to accompany Wilbur to the fair. Charlotte requests that Templeton go with them as someone "to run errands and do general work" (122). Of course, Templeton declines. Charlotte is not particularly adroit here: she does not know how to manipulate the rat. The old sheep does, however, appealing to Templeton's self interest in describing vividly the disgusting discards and "foul remains" of a hungry fair crowd until Templeton is ablaze with eager anticipation.

After Wilbur, who faints on hearing Farmer Arable's words concerning his ham-and-bacon prospects, is at last loaded in his special crate, and Charlotte and Templeton are securely hidden, the old truck taking everyone to the fair lurches off, bearing a human and an animal cargo, each individual on the truck nursing an array of dreams and expectations. Fern's anticipations are vocalized: after she is certain Wilbur has recovered from his fainting, she turns her attention away from him. "I want to take a ride in the Ferris wheel" (128), she announces, and that announcement precipitates her turning away, not only from Wilbur but from her early childhood as well. This image of flight into the air connects to Charlotte's mature web-weaving and the immature Wilbur's abortive attempts to launch himself into life when he jumps off the top of the manure pile while trying to weave his own web. This image pattern of flight into air and launching into life thus provides a central unifying element for the book as a whole.

White has set the book up carefully in other respects as well: the fair is to be locus for wonders and miracles. It is to precipitate the fulfillment of all desires, and thus its scenes serve as climax for the work. It is appropriate, then, that the chapter begins with a catalog of the individual dreams of Fern, Avery, Lurvy, and the Zuckermans. This fulfillment of dreams is hinted at in the chapter's first illustration as well. Mr. Zuckerman's dream is that Wilbur has grown to an immense size and has won all the prizes at the fair. This dream is a naive forecast of Wilbur's real triumph; nonetheless, the accompanying illustration of an immense Wilbur dominating the fair provides an amusing commentary on Zuckerman's aggrandizing dreams as well as foreshadows Wilbur's success and the focal attention he receives later, enough attention to satisfy even Zuckerman's dream, though in a way different from his envisioning. The second illustration shows the perennially more pragmatic Mrs. Zuckerman bathing Wilbur in buttermilk. While Zuckerman dreams big, his wife attends to the practical considerations that make dreams come true.

Chapter 17 continues to build toward the climax to come. It is an important chapter in this book about maturation, primarily for the central metaphor of human maturation it presents in its early pages. The chapter begins with Fern and Avery besieging their harried parents with requests for money, for balloons and cheeseburgers and frozen custard and soda pop. New to life and just recognizing its riches and wonders, they want everything: they want to experience and taste and own and succeed. Mr. Arable, on some level, understands this and accedes to their desires for initiation, agreeing to give them money and freedom to venture off by themselves. Amidst a chorus of adult warnings and counsels ranging from the practical to the far-fetched, they are sent out onto the midway alone to face life for the first time on their own. In a beautifully crafted and moving sentence, White captures the exhilaration of that primal setting forth: "The children grabbed each other by the hand and danced off in the direction of the merry-go-round, toward the wonderful music and the wonderful adventure and the wonderful excitement, into the wonderful midway where there would be no parents to guard them and guide them, and where they could be happy and free and do as they pleased" (131).

The significance of this venturing is not lost on Mrs. Arable, deeply moved as she watches them set out alone. "They've got to grow up sometime," her husband observes wistfully, in an effort to comfort them both. This scene is important thematically: it provides both situation and specific image for one of the great issues of the book—the passage of time, the coming into fulfillment, the imperative maturing of all creatures caught up in the great natural cycle everywhere celebrated in *Charlotte's Web*.

Garth Williams devotes a full-page illustration to the passage, depicting Fern and Avery, hand-in-hand at the outset of their venturing forth into the fairgrounds and hence into life. The midway they are poised to enter is a receding congery of games and rides, a bustling conglomeration of concessions offering prizes to be won and good things to be tasted, of rides promising excitement and the exhilaration of risk and controlled danger, of booths demonstrating the world's wonders. The whole scene is dominated by the Ferris wheel, that ride that looks a bit like a web and is a wheel like the great wheel of life featured in the novel. This Ferris wheel provides the children with a lift up into the freedom of adulthood and offers a vantage point on life in all its variety and abundance. The Ferris wheel is an apt corollary to the barn swing, to the immature Wilbur's abortive web-weaving, and, finally, to Charlotte's strong, serviceable web, the image of her successful adaptation to all of life's many demands. In the front of this illustration are Fern and Avery;

over them and a bit to the left sails a loosened balloon floating free, its string dangling beneath. To the right of them walks a small boy, much younger than they. He wears a full cowboy outfit, walks away from the midway, and grasps a tethered balloon, indicative of his childhood and contrasting with the loosened balloon indicative of the greater freedom of Fern and Avery, who are leaving childhood behind as they walk toward the midway and embrace life.

The second half of the chapter intensifies the suspense as to the outcome of Wilbur's fortunes at the fair. Zuckerman's dream of a gargantuan beribboned Wilbur winning all the prizes is dashed by the pig in the very next stall, an enormous boar and, as Charlotte soon discovers in her brief interview with him, a boor as well, a spring pig like Wilbur but "too familiar, too noisy," who "cracks weak jokes" and is "not anywhere near as clean" as Wilbur "nor as pleasant" (135). Named "Uncle," he is nevertheless a natural to win the blue ribbon coveted by Farmer Zuckerman. Charlotte knows, then, that she must again intervene if Wilbur is to be saved. Her interview with Uncle is amusingly illustrated: her nimbleness on the web strand is countered by his immobile stolidity; her delicate legs and body are contrasted to his enormous snout, ears, and hairy face. Uncle may win the blue ribbon for size, but certainly not for courtliness, cleanliness, or kind personality.

The two halves of this chapter are brought together by the concluding pages detailing Charlotte's increasing fatigue. If the chapter's first half celebrates the arrival of two children at the threshold of life and their maturation into freedom and full participation, its last pages show the concluding corollary of the passage of time and the closing of a natural cycle. Charlotte has little energy. To Wilbur, she "looked rather swollen and she seemed listless" (136). The boundless energy of Fern and Avery at the start of their cycle is countered by Charlotte's fatigue at the end of hers. Her lack of energy heightens the tension: will she be well enough to pull off her most important web-weaving yet, the one that will guarantee Wilbur's final reprieve from gun, butcher knife, and smokehouse?

The tension regarding Wilbur's fate is screwed tighter in chapter 18, while the tension regarding Fern is released. Fern now assumes some of the prominence she had at the beginning of the book: long a silent presence in the novel, Fern's maturation is now closely observed and recorded in the final chapters set at the fair. The real beginning of Fern's growth into mature life is counterbalanced by the ending of Charlotte's. In the first several sentences of the chapter, Charlotte, asking Templeton to bring her back a word, announces that "I shall be writing tonight for the last time" (138). Fern, on the other hand, is just beginning her life: her surprised mother happens to look up into the starry sky to see Fern "going higher and higher into the air" (139), looking happier than she had ever looked before. Immediately, the scene shifts to Charlotte again who assures Templeton that the word he has brought her "is the last word I shall ever write" (140).

The word Templeton brings is "HUMBLE," which Charlotte agrees fits Wilbur perfectly because he is "not proud" and his stature makes him stand "near the ground." Templeton, his errand completed, slinks away into the "rat's paradise" of the fairgrounds, leaving Wilbur and Charlotte alone on what is to be their last night together. After she has woven the last word in her web, Charlotte refuses to sing a requested lullaby to Wilbur because she is too tired, but she does give him her final benediction: "You have nothing to fear, Wilbur—nothing to worry about. Maybe you'll live forever—who knows? And now, go to sleep" (142). It is a benediction everyone wants to hear, and it marks the end of Charlotte's labors on Wilbur's behalf. It hints at Wilbur's magical dispensation from certain death even as natural death begins to claim Charlotte. White's counterpointing of the realistic with the fantastic, of Charlotte's impending natural death with Wilbur's magical reprieve from death indicates clearly a thematic convergence of great importance in the novel. In this counterpointing White is able to remain true to nature and its life cycle in the presentation of Charlotte, at the same time that he grants his readers a wish-fulfilling suspension of the inevitable conclusion of that cycle in his portrayal of Wilbur.

That Charlotte can do nothing more for Wilbur she very well knows. Though generous, Charlotte is not self-sacrificial. She must obey her own biological imperatives. Hence, she answers almost curtly when Wilbur asks her if she is making something for him: "No," she says, "It's something for *me*, for a change" (143). She promises to reveal her "masterpiece" in the morning, adding to the tension White has been so carefully building. The reader anticipates Charlotte's revelation as well as the outcome of her last weaving on Wilbur's future. The chapter concludes with a resolution of Fern's story. Her summary assessment of her day at the fair confirms the maturation she has been undergoing for the duration of the work: "I had the best time I have ever had anywhere or any time in all of my whole life" (143). Fern, too, like Charlotte, but unlike Wilbur, is on the realistic life cycle, only her cycle is much longer than Charlotte's. But in Charlotte's approaching death we see, in miniature,

Fern's own longer cycle—and the natural cycle White's readers all participate in. Thus Fern and Charlotte satisfy White's desire for a realistic presentation of life processes; Wilbur will satisfy the universal desire, fantastic as it may be, that the conclusion of this inexorable life cycle will be suspended and that Wilbur will somehow be exempted from the real death that awaits Charlotte imminently and Fern—and the novel's readers—at a future date. Chapter 18 is thus an adroit interplay of tensions and resolutions, a madrigal of beginnings and endings, and the rich counterpointing is beautifully sustained.

The early morning light of chapter 19 reveals to Wilbur Charlotte's masterpiece, her "magnum opus," as she calls it—her egg sac. White describes the egg sac in connotatively positive images as "peach-colored" and as if made of cotton candy. Charlotte calls the egg sac "the finest thing I have ever made" (145), and the rest of her description of it as strong and waterproof, as containing 514 eggs constitutes a continuation of the arachnid biology lesson offered in earlier chapters.

The tone of the chapter soon shifts from ebullient pride to wistful melancholy as Charlotte reveals that she will never live to see her children. Generous to the last, she shifts a worried Wilbur's attention away from her to her newly woven web, glittering with dew. But before Wilbur can admire this new web-weaving, a bloated Templeton returns boasting of the gorge he has been on. He also increases the tension by announcing that Uncle, the huge pig in the next stall, has secured the blue ribbon and that as a result Zuckerman might take the knife to Wilbur after all. This proves the last time this threat surfaces, however, as an announcement is soon made that Wilbur is to receive a special award. The resolution of the threat so long menacing Wilbur is noisy in the human circle, as the Arables, Zuckermans, and Lurvy embrace each other in every possible combination, dancing around the celebrated pig they had come to value as celebrity rather than as provender for the winter. Wilbur is now the center of a human celebration and the focus of human joy and pride. The runt now looms large in Zuckerman's dreams; once rejected, Wilbur is now accoladed as "SOME PIG"!

The resolution of the threat to Wilbur is, however, more understated in the animal sphere than in the human. Charlotte, feeling weak, nevertheless "was sure at last that she had saved Wilbur's life, and she felt peaceful and contented" (153). Wilbur, carefully curried to receive his award, is safe at last. Interestingly, Fern skips away at this point and thus absents herself from the scene of Wilbur's triumph to ride the Ferris wheel with Henry Fussy. This abandonment of the pig in his glory has been preceded by clear signs of her growing up and turning her attention to the human world: she has put on her prettiest dress for the fair; she expresses no dismay at hearing that Uncle has won the blue ribbon; she asks for money to ride the Ferris wheel at the exact moment of Wilbur's triumph. Fern begins to grow up and leave childhood behind; she takes her first tentative steps into the real world of relationships, work, and responsibility. Wilbur, however, though he certainly matures by novel's end, remains forever in a condition resembling the golden stasis of childhood, free of adult responsibility (except to Charlotte's spiderlings), safe in the boundaries of the pigpen where his trough is never empty and where, each spring, he serves as guardian for yet another generation of Charlotte's infant progeny. The book's fantasy culminates in this dispensation for Wilbur; the book's realism finds its focus in Fern's beginning maturation at the end of the story.

The illustrations for this chapter perfectly complement the text. The first provides a depiction of Charlotte tending her suspended egg sac, a biologically accurate drawing intended to accompany the text's description of arachnid propagation. The second illustration presents a swollen Templeton splayed out in a corner of the pen, patting his bloated belly after the evening's carouse. The illustration does even more than the text to confirm that Templeton's dream of success at the fair has been amply met. The final illustration of the chapter provides a full-page exhibit of the triumph of the Arable and Zuckerman families singled out for special notice. The families are presented in the foreground embracing, Avery in front showing off by standing on his hands, the whole group set off from the admiring notice of a gathered crowd by a low wooden fence. These three illustrations, then, represent the fulfillment of dreams: Charlotte realizes her most important biological goal, propagation; Templeton's greed is at last satisfied; the Arables and Zuckermans find themselves at the center of attention among their neighbors and acquaintances.

Charlotte's Triumph

The quieter resolutions in chapter 19 are publicly celebrated in chapter 20, entitled "The Hour of Triumph." Interestingly, the title phrase applies primarily to Charlotte, even though Wilbur and his human caretakers receive the public honors while she remains in seclusion. The text makes clear that whoever else may feel triumphant, this is *Charlotte's* moment, "*her* hour of triumph" (157; my italics). From the beginning,

Charlotte's true role in the story has never been understood by the humans involved. She has waited in the wings, taken a back seat, worked undercover. Her web was woven to fool humans as well as to capture gnats. So too here: from her lonely perch on the roof of Wilbur's pen she can hear the loudspeaker braying its praise for Farmer Zuckerman and his famous pig, but this praise gives her "courage" and justifies all her scheming and night-weaving. Charlotte lives to witness the complete success of all her efforts.

The quieter resolutions of the previous chapter are now transformed into spectacle. The chapter is, however, interesting for its subtle interplay of reactions, attending in turn to each character of the book and the individual responses each character manifests. Wilbur, for example, trembles from happiness and trepidation, only to faint away, overwhelmed by the attention and the praise. Mrs. Zuckerman has an acute attack of stage fright, and Mrs. Arable disciplines her children, especially Avery, who is shamelessly showing off before the crowd. Templeton mutters disparaging comments: "What a lot of nonsense!"; "What a lot of fuss about nothing!" (156). But Templeton is called upon to play his usual role once again: though uncooperative, he proves serviceable in biting Wilbur's tail to bring him out of his faint. The moment when the judge gives Zuckerman $25 and ties a medal around Wilbur's neck proves "the greatest moment in Mr. Zuckerman's life" (160) and provides a high point in the experiences of both farm families.

The most interesting, because so poignant, response to Wilbur's public recognition is, however, Fern's. She alone does not actually witness Wilbur's success. Just before the award is presented, she secures some money from her mother so that she can offer Henry Fussy a ride on the Ferris wheel. All of Dr. Dorian's predictions come to fruition here: Fern has left the idyllic realm for the adult world of experience. She has severed, in the fullness of time, that primal connection with the animals and with natural creation that was celebrated earlier in the book. Unlike the expressed sorrow of Lewis Carroll for Alice's similar stepping over the boundary into queenhood or James Barrie's fierce resistance to that happening to Peter Pan, White chronicles Fern's beginning maturation matter-of-factly, almost incidentally. The text treats it dispassionately as an occurrence in the normal cycle of life. Its poignancy is inherent in the situation itself and must be provided by the reader. Even Mrs. Arable is too flustered by other occurrences to recognize the full import of Fern's final abandonment of Wilbur and the barnyard for Henry Fussy and the midway with its Ferris wheel and other glittering attractions.

This chapter, then, chronicles the triumph of Charlotte, responsible
for all of the events given public recognition at this fair, even though she
remains hidden, a schemer without a public presence. In her retirement
she recognizes her own role and the success of all her plans.
Appropriately, then, she is not depicted in any of the illustrations for this
chapter, which features, instead, Templeton's biting the tail of Wilbur to
bring him out of his faint and Mr. Zuckerman and Avery receiving the
cash prize while a terrific, radiant, but humble Wilbur is photographed.
The chapter is a chorus of responses, publicly played out, to all of
Charlotte's artful scheming and nights of spinning her silken solutions to
Wilbur's plight. It is an artful resolution of all the book's more public
issues.

Chapter 21, however, provides the greater, more moving resolution in
that it focuses on Wilbur's final maturation. The great questions of his
physical survival are solved in a way satisfying to all. These questions
dismissed, the question of his internal readiness for life looms large and
is dealt with in this penultimate chapter. The chapter opens with
Charlotte and Wilbur alone together. Charlotte congratulates Wilbur:
"Your future is assured," she notes; "You will live, secure and safe. . . .
Nothing can harm you now" (163). Charlotte's reason for helping
Wilbur has been twofold: as she makes clear to him, she has saved his
life out of love for him as a friend and because "I was trying to lift up my
life a trifle" from the "mess" of daily trapping and eating flies, from the
sheer physicality of providing for herself (164). What Wilbur learns here
is the power of love to ennoble and dignify life—and he learns this lesson from a great teacher.

Up to this point, Wilbur has remained essentially infantile and dependent, sucking greedily at the trough, snoozing on his manure pile while
others worked for him. He has been an emblem of childish helplessness
and oral greed, while Charlotte schemes to save him from the winter
butchering and spins through the long nights her unique solutions to his
dilemma. But now, after the triumph at the fair, something truly magic
happens: Wilbur grows up. This maturation is difficult to achieve, even
now. He first announces to Charlotte, "I would gladly give my life for
you" (164). Undoubtedly he means this in an abstract way, but such
grand pronouncements are easy to make, especially when one is reasonably certain not to be called upon to actually deliver up one's life.
Appropriately, Charlotte thanks Wilbur for his "generous sentiments."
That Wilbur's maturation is still not complete is made clear when
Charlotte announces that she will not be accompanying Wilbur back to

the barn. On hearing this news, Wilbur suffers a period of despair and infantile impotence: he throws himself down, sobbing and thrashing about with desolation. Charlotte, ever uncomfortable at histrionics, commands him to be quiet and not make a scene. Wilbur then ineffectively vows never to leave Charlotte, until she reminds him that Zuckerman would never stand for that and besides, no one would be left on the fairgrounds to feed him.

This behavior, these ideas and promises all characterize the childish Wilbur, ineffective and powerless in the face of real problems. But then the magic happens: in the midst of his panic he has an idea, and that idea is followed immediately by potent action. If Charlotte cannot return to the barn, Wilbur will ensure that her progeny in the egg sac will. All of Charlotte's silken assessments of him reach a prophetic fulfillment when he commands Templeton to climb up on the roof of his pen and haul down Charlotte's egg sac for him. When Templeton demurs, Wilbur screams at him: "Get up! . . . Stop acting like a spoiled child!" (168). That he recognizes Templeton's behavior as that of a spoiled child demonstrates how far he is distancing himself from that role which he himself has been playing since the work began.

But Templeton is not so easily motivated. Wilbur then makes Templeton a solemn promise to give the rat first "choice of everything in the trough and I won't touch a thing until you're through" (168). This promise is of crucial importance in Wilbur's maturation, for it demonstrates his final triumph over infantile orality and greed. For the first time Wilbur recognizes a higher value than gluttony and the satisfaction of his physical appetites and sacrifices them to Charlotte's needs. This moving triumph is reinforced by his gently taking the dying Charlotte's egg sac into his mouth, the only way he can bring it back safely to Zuckerman's barn.

Wilbur's mouth now serves a higher function than merely to gulp, gobble, and suck at his trough. He uses his mouth not merely for ingestion, but for preservation: "He carefully took the little bundle in his mouth and held it there on top of his tongue" (170). Wilbur, that gluttonous, greedy, childish pig, here grows up, his mouth becoming a preserving, warm enclosure—in a way, a womb. Saved from death (and from being eaten as bacon) by Charlotte, Wilbur in turn becomes a savior like Charlotte herself. Wilbur, indeed, *becomes* Charlotte: he is the child-become-parent—in this case to 514 spiderlings nestled in the cotton candy egg sac he carries safely in his mouth. Like Charlotte and Fern before her, Wilbur becomes nurturant savior, performing for Charlotte's progeny the preserving role she had earlier performed for him. Here Wilbur, like Charlotte, acts out of love and likewise succeeds in lifting up his life a trifle as Charlotte herself had aspired to do.

This scene is the crux of this beautifully wrought novel, for *Charlotte's Web* is the story of an ordinary pig who becomes special and is allowed to live in barnyard comfort forever. A maturation story, the work chronicles Wilbur's passage from helpless dependence to adult control and independent effectiveness of action. In accomplishing this passage Wilbur transforms himself from runt to "Radiant." The single illustration in this crucial chapter emphasizes Wilbur's adult effectiveness in bringing about an action for a desired end—an end that affects positively the fates of many. Williams focuses on Templeton's securing of Charlotte's egg sac at Wilbur's bidding. The illustration also prepares for the chapter's sad but inevitable ending by showing Charlotte, spent and dying, huddled into a disheveled ball an inch or so from her egg sac as Templeton snips it loose from its moorings with his bared teeth.

The farewell between Wilbur and Charlotte is a sad but satisfying one. Unable to speak because of the egg sac secure in his mouth, Wilbur winks at Charlotte as she whispers good-bye and draws on all her strength to manage a final wave of her front leg at him. She watches a new Wilbur leave for the barn, and her success at producing this new adult version of the piglet she had earlier befriended provides her only comfort as she dies alone at the deserted fairgrounds. "Charlotte died," the reader is told, and this defiantly unsentimental ending is emphasized in the chapter's last, stark sentence: "No one was with her when she died" (171). This is a necessary conclusion for Charlotte from both a biological as well as a thematic standpoint. White elected to be true to the seasonal life cycle of spiders and to bring a carefully designed plot to the conclusion made inevitable by numerous foreshadowings throughout the work. White was aware that he was violating an established taboo against dealing so starkly and realistically with death in a children's book. "Apparently," he noted in 1965, "children are not supposed to be exposed to death, but I did not pay any attention to this" (*Letters,* 531–32). Indeed, White had to resist pressures on him to change the ending from his editors and from some earlier readers as well as from later directors trying to adapt the work for the screen. White firmly opposed all attempts to persuade him to revise this ending.

The concluding chapter of *Charlotte's Web* is a bittersweet dialectic of loss and fulfillment. Wilbur, guaranteed a long life, now faces what that life consists of—its duality of contentment and sorrow, joy and pain.

Wilbur returns to the barn, "no longer worried about being killed" (172). There he was "very happy" and "grew to a great size," but he "often thought of Charlotte," a lump coming to his throat as he looked every day at the few strands of her old web still hanging in the doorway (172). His life, then, is a mixture of happiness and sadness, present contentment and wistful memories of what he had in the past and has subsequently lost.

Autumn passes, that bittersweet season of harvest fulfillment and the loss of summer and the warm earth, and with winter snows come Fern and Avery for a last appearance in the book. According to Avery, coasting in the snow "is the most fun there is" (173). Avery's ability to enjoy the gifts of the present, to take pleasure in immediate joys, is countered by Fern's yearning for the pleasures of the past. "The most fun there is," she counters, "is when the Ferris wheel stops and Henry and I are in the top car" (173). Here again are the strains that run throughout the chapter: present fulfillment accompanied by a sense of loss, the harmony of contentment and longing that is life itself.

This harmony is played out in the last glimpse we get of Templeton as well. Wilbur is true to his word, and Templeton daily gorges himself full before Wilbur takes his turn at the trough. Consequently, the rat has grown to an enormous size. "Who wants to live forever" (175), he sneers when the old sheep cautions him about too narrow a focus on the pleasures of the present. But Templeton puts off any cautions about the future or remembrances of the past, confining himself to present satisfactions. The illustration of Templeton, grown grotesquely fat, provides a fitting final glimpse of a character unpleasant but critical to the success of Charlotte's plans and Wilbur's ultimate security. Here Templeton is immediately contrasted to Wilbur who honors his vow in the past and looks forward to the future hatching of Charlotte's eggs, about which he is as solicitous as he would be were he "guarding his own children" (175).

At last spring arrives, and Charlotte's eggs hatch. But the profound joy Wilbur feels—his heart pounds; he squeals; he races in circles; he does a back flip—soon turns to grief as profound as his joy was intense. For the hatchlings, Charlotte's long-awaited children, begin to stand on their heads, throw balloons of silk behind them, and waft away in the warm breeze. These balloons connect with the repeated images of flight and launching forth—Charlotte's web, Wilbur's failed one, the children's swing in the barn, Fern's Ferris wheel—which suggest a full engagement with life, a setting forth to define a self and to create a space where that self can come into the fullness of being. "Goodbye," the spiderling aeronauts call to a panicking Wilbur; "This is our moment for setting forth" (179). Joy and sorrow, fulfillment and loss—the dialectics of life are everywhere announced in the chapter. Three of Charlotte's daughters remain for Wilbur, bringing happiness back into his barn.

The chapter's illustrations focus on Wilbur forlorn and Wilbur felicitous. The first of the book's last two illustrations depicts a disappointed Wilbur presiding tearfully over the departure of the spiderlings whose eggs he has so carefully tended through the long winter. This is a depiction of the sadness of life, of leave-taking, of loneliness, and of loss. But true to the rhythms of the chapter, the countervailing tenor of fulfillment, of happiness and joy is also presented in the book's concluding illustration of a contented Wilbur looking up at three webs in the making above the doorway, the springtime world budding and leafing behind him.

As the years pass, the cycles of fulfillment and loss continue. Fern, grown older, seldom visits the barn anymore, being "careful to avoid childish things, like sitting on a milk stool near a pigpen" (183), but Charlotte's children and grandchildren and great grandchildren pass in and out of Wilbur's life in recurrent cycles of welcoming and leave-taking. Though Wilbur loved Charlotte's progeny dearly, none of them displaced the memory of Charlotte from his heart. Happiness and sorrow, contentment and longing, fulfillment and loss—these are the rhythms of life, the chapter reminds us, and its last moving testament to Charlotte as "a true friend and a good writer" (184) is preceded by the great hymn to the barn that the entire book was intended to be. This hymn embraces all the bittersweet complexity of life in a swelling affirmation: "Life in the barn was very good," we are told, and White's catalog of opposites, of the variety and abundance of life is captured in that one word "good"—a word also used by the Creator in Genesis to describe every facet of the creation.

United in that creation are "night and day, winter and summer, spring and fall, dull days and bright days." For Wilbur, the barn, the metaphor for all of life itself, is "the best place to be," and he accepts it all, embraces it as "good," including "the garrulous geese, the changing seasons, the heat of the sun, the passage of swallows, the nearness of rats, the sameness of sheep, the love of spiders, the smell of manure, and the glory of everything" (183). This is White's secular doxology, a great upsurge of love, gratitude, affirmation, and acceptance of the world's abundance and diversity. This coda is a fitting "hymn to the barn," a moving "paean to life," as is the entire novel which it concludes.

Critical Reception

Charlotte's Web is White's greatest work. Since its publication in 1952 it has rightly been accorded the status of a "classic," despite White's uneasiness at its being called this soon after its appearance. That it is a great book was soon recognized, the early reviews being nearly unanimous in their praise. Bennett Cerf, for example, wrote in the *Saturday Review* that though many books published in 1952 will be classified as "more important" than *Charlotte's Web*, "I know that none will delight me—or my young sons . . . — as much." "A more thoroughly entrancing result could not possibly have been achieved," he continued, than this collaboration between White and his illustrator, Garth Williams.[6]

The reviewer for *Booklist* also noted the book's appeal to both children and adults but observed that "younger readers . . . are likely to lose interest as the story moves on, leaving it to adults who enjoy the author's symbolic and philosophic implications."[7] Any such "implications," however, White repeatedly denied, claiming in 1971 that "there is no symbolism in *Charlotte's Web*. And there is no political meaning in the story. It is a straight report from the barn cellar, which I dearly love" (*Letters*, 614). Soon after the novel was published, White was at pains to advise a young reader about how to approach the book: "When you read it," he admonished, "just relax. Any attempt to find allegorical meanings is bound to end disastrously, for no meanings are in there. I ought to know" (*Letters*, 373).

P. L. Travers, author of the Mary Poppins books, accorded the work her highest praise, not for any symbolism or allegory but because it manifests that "tangible magic" characteristic of only the best stories for children. "Such tangible magic is the proper element of childhood," she argued, and *Charlotte's Web* manifests it throughout in its "sense of delight in daily things" and in its insistence on the "goodness and meaning in simply being alive."[8] The *Times Literary Supplement* also praised the book, observing that "an adult reader will admire and enjoy the pungent economy of phrase, [and] a child will feel that this is really how creatures do think and behave."[9] Edward Weeks pithily called the book a "perfect" work for children in the *Atlantic Monthly*.[10] In the same issue of this journal Margaret Ford Kieran expanded Weeks's succinct assessment: *Charlotte's Web*, she wrote, "is a must on your fall list. If there is such a thing as a realistic fantasy, here it is, and though I am not usually attracted by stories that personify animals, this one is absolutely delicious."[11]

One of the most important reviews, and one of the most positive, was penned by Eudora Welty in the *New York Times*. She wrote that the book "has liveliness and felicity, tenderness and unexpectedness, grace and humor and praise of life, and the good backbone of succinctness that only the most highly imaginative stories possess." "As a piece of work," she continued, *Charlotte's Web* "is just about perfect, and perfectly effortless and magical . . . in the doing" (Welty, 205).

The reviewers of *Charlotte's Web* were nearly, but not quite entirely, unanimous in their high estimation of White's second children's book. For example, Anne Carroll Moore, though in retirement, nevertheless penned a generally negative notice of *Charlotte's Web*, as she had of *Stuart Little*. "I may as well confess," she wrote, "that I find . . . *Charlotte's Web* . . . hard to take from so masterly a hand." Moore complained that "Fern, the real center of the book, is never developed" and that the animals, instead of talking, merely "speculate" abstractly. She also thought the book "never came clear from the preoccupation of an adult who had not spent a childhood on a farm."[12] White later quipped that the only unfavorable criticism of his work for children had come "from a couple of librarians, notably Moore," who "regard themselves as child psychologists" (*Letters*, 368). Moore's animus against White's first two books for children is difficult to explain, especially as she had earlier encouraged White to write for children and had repeatedly avowed that there was "no one whose writing I more deeply regard in the adult field" (Moore, 394). Such strange lapses in judgment are difficult to understand in someone whose critical taste was generally sound and whose entire career was devoted to the reading and evaluating of works for young people.

It was not until the 1970s that any serious critical attention was accorded *Charlotte's Web*. Gerald Weales's *New York Times* article on White's children's books remains one of the most insightful early commentaries on *Charlotte's Web*. Weales was one of the first to note the intricacies of White's plotting, the interplay of the rescue of Wilbur with the maturation of Fern, all occurring within the great, natural rhythms of growth and change characterizing the natural world (Weales, 409). Marion Glastonbury also noted in 1973 that White's central achievement in *Charlotte's Web* was grounded on his "solid evocation of shifting seasons, the perpetually changing landscape, the ceaseless mobility of 'here and now'" (7). Edward C. Sampson, one of the first scholars to have access to White's papers at Cornell, argued, accurately I think, that "the key to the structure" is Fern, a late arrival in the evolution of the manuscript, whose growing up counterpoints the main plot's emphasis on Wilbur's avoiding the butcher and his subsequent maturation. With Fern, according to Sampson, there is "growth and transition," while for Wilbur, "the world of childhood continues" (103). Though Sampson was correct in demonstrating Fern's central role in the novel as bridge between the human and animal realms, he seemed to miss the significance of Wilbur's maturation and his negotiation at the end of the book of life's mixed pleasures and sorrows. At novel's end, Wilbur clearly manifests an adult perspective, having experienced the "growth and transition" Sampson attributed only to Fern in the work.

Margaret Blount in *Animal Land* (1975) marked White's success in avoiding the "pitfalls of giving animals moralizing voices, sad or happy thoughts" and noted his achievement in remaining remarkably close to nature, even in a book relying to such a large extent on fantasy (259). Calling *Charlotte's Web* "a gem" and "*the* classic American children's book of the last thirty years," Roger Sale in *Fairy Tales and After* (1978) also observed White's adroit adjustment of realism and fantasy in the novel. She termed *Charlotte's Web* a "full, sustained, serene" book (258) and noted the double hymn sung throughout the work—the first in praise of the beauties of the transient world and the second in celebration of the enduring values of love and friendship that do not admit of change. Sale concluded that *Charlotte's Web* is "a sweet interlude of a book" (267).

Peter Neumeyer argued in "What Makes a Good Children's Book?: The Texture of *Charlotte's Web*" that the novel's generally agreed-upon excellence resulted from its dense, rich texture, evident throughout, "from the discreet word all the way to the mythopoeic dimension" (66). John Griffith, on the other hand, argued that the novel's excellence is attributable to its "consoling fantasy in which a small Everyman survives and triumphs over the pathos of being alone" and examined Wilbur's "desperate existential situation"—his fear of dying, his ennui, and his hunger for friendship and love.[13] Griffith concluded that *Charlotte's Web* posed language as an antidote to Wilbur's yearning, in that the "highest and best love, in this story, is that which expresses itself through words" (117). Janice M. Alberghene also pointed out that the novel features Charlotte's prompting the reader "to consider and experience language in increasingly sophisticated ways, from the literal meanings of words to casting words into stories and speeches."[14]

In "The Creation of *Charlotte's Web*: From Drafts to Book" Peter Neumeyer demonstrated that White achieved his customary brevity and clarity of style only after successive drafts of the novel were completed.

Neumeyer's review of the manuscripts demonstrated White's evolving conceptualization of the novel and the interaction of his characters. Neumeyer's most extensive comments on the work can be found in his entries on White for *Twentieth-Century Children's Writers* (1983) and for the *Dictionary of Literary Biography* volume on *American Writers for Children, 1900–60* (1983). Calling the book "lyrical, suspenseful on its primary level, and philosophical under all," Neumeyer concluded his discussion in *Twentieth-Century Children's Writers* with the assertion that the book "is just about perfect, and just about magical in the way it is done" (1983a, 817), a sentiment he echoed in his *Dictionary of Literary Biography* entry, where he called the work "unquestionably a rich and a contemplative book" devoted to "White's thematic preoccupation with friendship, with the warm glow of the pastoral, and with the cycle of the rural year" (343). Neumeyer concluded by asserting that in *Charlotte's Web* "we may well be seeing E. B. White at his best" (346).

In the 1980s, then, *Charlotte's Web* received the critical attention usually accorded a work accepted as part of the traditional literary canon. Indeed, *Charlotte's Web* was selected as a "touchstone" work by the Children's Literature Association, which compiled a list of those works for children that anyone interested in children's literature must know. In her article for this volume, Sonia Landes concluded that when *Charlotte's Web* is brought to the touchstone that tests for literary quality, the work "comes up gold," proving that it "will be read in other places and years to come" (280).

Other critics commented on the novel during the 1980s as well. For example, Norton D. Kinghorn claimed that the book is essentially about Charlotte, not Wilbur. "If the book has a protagonist," he argued, "she is it" because she effects the outcome of all the plot events, acts heroically, draws together all the themes, and commands reader attention. And, he continued, her web serves as the work's unifying image.[15] Ashraf H. A. Rushdy in "'The Miracle of the Web': Community, Desire, and Narrativity in *Charlotte's Web*" also asserted that Wilbur's salvation is Charlotte's work, that she has wrought the difference between the opening scene where Farmer Arable seeks to dispatch Wilbur to hog heaven with the axe and the closing scene where we are told that Farmer Zuckerman "took fine care of Wilbur all the rest of his days" (183). Charlotte effects this difference by successfully integrating Wilbur into the human community: she bridges the distinctive gap between the animal and human realms through the mechanism of the web and through the agency of language. Charlotte realizes that even though "a community has an established pattern of determining what role anything should take" in that community, "there exists the chance that there can be a different story," and this different story Charlotte tells in the web, thus changing the communal valuation of Wilbur and ensuring his salvation.[16]

From the first appearance of *Charlotte's Web* in 1952 to the present, critics have hailed the book as a children's classic. Critical commentary is nearly unanimously laudatory and demonstrates the plenitude of significances to be found in a novel that richly repays repeated readings. Nearly every American child is familiar with Charlotte and Wilbur, and *Charlotte's Web* has a large international currency, having been translated into more than 25 languages. It has occasioned an animated film, and an opera by Charles Strouse premiered in 1989, with a score that ranges from music hall to rock with ballads thrown in, all played by a piano-synthesizer-percussion ensemble. The novel is clearly one of the great American books for children. It was a runner-up for the Newbery Medal in 1953 and won the Lewis Carroll Shelf Award in 1958, indicating its worthiness to occupy the same shelf with *Alice in Wonderland*, a book it consistently outsells every year. In 1970 the Claremont Reading Conference awarded *Charlotte's Web* the George Stone Center for Children's Books Recognition of Merit Award for its capacity "to arouse in children an awareness of the beauty and complexity of their expanding universe." *Charlotte's Web* has been doing that now for several generations of juvenile readers.

Chapter Four

"To Solve His Problems with Music": *The Trumpet of the Swan*

The Genesis of the Novel

In his review for the *New York Times Book Review,* John Updike judged *The Trumpet of the Swan* "the most spacious and serene" of White's three novels for children, "the one most imbued with the author's sense of the precious instinctual heritage represented by wild nature" (Updike, 4). *The Trumpet of the Swan* celebrates a nature uncircumscribed by human concerns or conveniences, an untamed wilderness to which the central characters repair after necessary sojourns in civilization. Their hearts are clearly in the Canadian wilds, to which they escape only after satisfying the demands of the human world.

This novel thus differs markedly from *Stuart Little*'s focus on the search for Margalo—by car—down roads frequented by humankind, and from *Charlotte's Web*'s celebration of domesticated nature on Zuckerman's idyllic farm. *The Trumpet of the Swan* holds up as an ideal those precious "days in the deep woods, far, far from everywhere—no automobiles, no roads, no people, no noise, no school, no homework, no problems"—except for the problem of getting lost in the vast Canadian wilds, which serve as initial setting for the novel and eventual point of return for the novel's two main characters—the boy Sam Beaver and his friend Louis the trumpeter swan.[1] A second problem both characters face is deciding what they want to do in life that will ensure their frequent return to this rich untamed world.

Despite the book's "spacious and serene" celebration of nature and despite Updike's generous review, the novel represents a falling off from White's first two works for children. Even Updike noted that *The Trumpet of the Swan* was "not quite so sprightly as *Stuart Little,* and less rich in personalities and incident than *Charlotte's Web*" (4). Indeed, the

general consensus among reviewers and critics has been that this third
novel is the weakest of White's works for juveniles—a judgment with
which White himself was in agreement. As Peter Neumeyer aptly indicated in his entry on White in *Twentieth-Century Children's Writers*, *The
Trumpet of the Swan* "would be a splendid accomplishment for a lesser
writer," but it "is not usually thought to stand comparison with White's
earlier two children's books" (1983a, 818).

Some of the book's weaknesses can be explained by its manner of
composition and by White's reasons for undertaking the project in the
first place. According to Scott Elledge, White's biographer, White
undertook the project with the same urgency and for the same reasons
that he began *Stuart Little* 23 years earlier—"the fear of dying and leaving Katharine inadequately provided for" (345). Suffering from osteo-
porosis and confined to a hospital bed, Katharine was attended at home
by nurses round the clock. Her expenses, which the proceeds from this
book were expected to allay, were considerable. White began work on
the manuscript in 1968 and completed it in what was for him record
time—November 1969.

Because he and his wife were then in such poor health, he sent it to
his publisher without submitting it to the extensive rewriting and
rethinking processes (White called these processes "regurgitating it and
swallowing it again" [*Letters*, 583]) that had contributed so greatly to the
artistic success of his first two books. According to Elledge, White "was
dissatisfied with the book, and after he turned it in he wished he had
held it a year and then rewritten it, as he had done with his other children's books" (345). Consequently, the book lacks the compression and
succinctness of the earlier works. The plot sprawls geographically and
episodically, lacking the keenness and tautness that White showed himself capable of in writing his first two books for children. To Garth
Williams on 31 December 1969, White asserted that "I'm not entirely
happy about the text of the book—I am old and wordy, and this book
seems to show it" (*Letters*, 592).

White initiated the book with little background knowledge about
some of his settings and about the nature and habits of trumpeter swans.
"It is very unusual for me to attempt to write about something I don't
know about at first hand," he confided to his old friend and fellow
Cornellian Howard Cushman, "but this goddam little fictional character
has got me into this, and I could break his arm. Or wing" (*Letters*, 568).

White asked Cushman, who then lived in Philadelphia, to send him
photographs of the trumpeter swans in the Philadelphia Zoo; he also

asked Cushman to provide him with background information about nightclub locations in Philadelphia, the layout of the zoo, and the dimensions and appearance of the zoo's Bird Lake. Writing of the book to James Wright on 29 August 1970, White confessed that it "took a lot of gall to write it, as I have never in my life laid eyes on a Trumpeter Swan, either in or out of captivity. But I'll tackle anything in a pinch, and I began to feel the pinch more than a year ago when I looked around and discovered that my house was full of day nurses and night nurses at $28 per day. Or night" (*Letters,* 605). White wrote to Robert Coates on 14 September 1969 that the book "will have to net me about half a million dollars, otherwise I won't be able to pay off all the registered and unregistered nurses that tend K. every day and every night" (*Letters,* 584). By way of explaining the defects in the book, White continuously referred to it as a mercantile venture. To Helen Thurber, White complained that "so far, the book has given me little joy and lots of headaches" (*Letters,* 593).

The qualified success of *The Trumpet of the Swan* and White's dissatisfaction with it thus resulted from the fiscal urgency under which it was written and the lack of an immediate knowledge of his characters and settings. Clearly, part of the success of *Stuart Little* derives from White's exact depiction of life lived in an apartment in New York City where he had sojourned for so many years, and the success of *Charlotte's Web* is due in large part to the immediacy of its hymn to the rural life to which he himself had retired so many years before.

Dorothy Lobrano Guth and Scott Elledge, however, maintain that there are repeated autobiographical elements throughout *The Trumpet of the Swan* that give it whatever sense of authenticity it has. Guth, the editor of White's letters, notes that when White worked as a counselor at Camp Otter in Ontario in the summers of 1920 and 1921, his eyes were opened to true wilderness, as opposed to the rural charm of the Belgrade Lakes of his childhood summers in Maine. "Almost fifty years later," she notes, White "drew on his memories of Camp Otter in his account of 'Camp Kookooskoos' in *The Trumpet of the Swan*" (*Letters,* 21). When White eventually became an investing partner in the camp he employed "a live Chippewa Indian" named Sam Beaver, who in *The Trumpet of the Swan* appears under a different guise and age but with the same name (*Letters,* 88, 94). The name for Camp Kookooskoos comes from a Milicete Indian word meaning "great horned owl."

Elledge argues for a considerably greater autobiographical influence in the novel than White's memories of the Canadian wilds transmuted into the novel's setting. According to Elledge, "the truth of the tale" derives from White's memories of being unable to speak in public and his inability to talk to girls, played out in the novel in Louis's muteness and his consequent inability to court Serena, "the swan of his desiring." In addition, Elledge notes a connection between Louis's father's breaking into the music store to steal a trumpet for Louis and White's own father's apparent extralegal relationship with his Horace Waters Piano Company partners, who eventually sued him for fraud. Elledge thus gives the novel a thorough biographical reading and concludes that one of the weaknesses of the story results from White's "dividing his (and his readers') interest between Louis and Sam, who both portray aspects of White's character and enact events based on White's memories" (347).

A further cause of disappointment in the book for White (and for most readers) was Garth Williams's unavailability to work on illustrations for the volume. In a 31 December 1969 letter to Williams, White lamented that "I had always hoped that Williams and White would be as indestructible as ham and eggs, Scotch and soda, Gilbert and Sullivan" and declared his great unhappiness "about being separated from you after all these many fine and rewarding years" (*Letters,* 591–92). Updike, too, registered disappointment in the change in illustrators: "At first glance, one's heart a little falls to see that wash drawings by Edward Frascino have replaced Garth Williams's finely furry pen-and-ink illustrations," though Updike later concedes that Frascino's looser line is congruent with White's plotting and narrative pace (4). Frascino's black and white and gray wash drawings are certainly expressive and more than merely serviceable, though one cannot help but wonder how much the book's effectiveness is compromised by its not being illustrated by Williams, clearly one of the great illustrators for children and an artist who had already proven a strongly empathetic interpreter of White's works.

Despite the novel's weaknesses and White's dissatisfactions with it, *The Trumpet of the Swan* amounts to much more than a mere potboiler and thus deserves a close reading. In the first place, its action-crammed plot rarely fails in holding reader interest. The novel focuses on Louis, a trumpeter swan born mute. His inability to produce the characteristic "Ko-Hoh" sound alienates him from others of his species and, more important, disqualifies him as a suitable mate since he cannot trumpet the necessary mating cry. Louis, thus disabled, enrolls in school with the help of his friend Sam Beaver, an 11-year-old boy whom he had met soon after hatching. In school Louis learns to read and write and acquires a chalk pencil and a slate which he ties around his neck and which allows him to communicate with people, though not with his fellow swans. To foster this communication with his own species, Louis's father helps Louis to overcome his handicap by crashing through the plate-glass window of a music store in Billings, Montana, and stealing a trumpet, on which Louis learns not only to make the distinctive trumpeter swan "Ko-Hoh" but also to play everything from taps to jazz.

Grateful to his father for his generous and ingenious act but at the same time conscious of his father's essential wrongdoing, Louis sets out to save his family honor by earning enough money to pay for the trumpet and for the store damages. His departure from home is made particularly difficult by his having to leave behind the young swan, Serena, with whom he has fallen in love. Louis holds down a succession of jobs: Sam Beaver recommends him for a summer job at Camp Kookooskoos playing reveille and taps, after which Louis flies to Boston to play trumpet for the entertainment of the passengers on the swan boats in the lagoon of the Public Garden. Next, Louis flies to Philadelphia, where he plays trumpet in a nightclub and offers free programs to zoo visitors on Sunday afternoons. Fortuitously, a sudden storm blows Serena all the way from Montana to the zoo's bird pond. Here Louis's wooing meets with a happy conclusion, and the pair fly happily back to their spring mating in Canada and winter sojourning in Montana, Louis giving his father more than enough money to reimburse the Billings music store owner.

White claimed that *The Trumpet of the Swan* was a love story, though Elledge is more accurate in his assessment of the work as "primarily an adventure story in which the hero's adolescent love is more a preoccupation than it is a motive for his actions" (347). More important than either the love story or adventure aspects of the novel, however, is its focus on the difficult experience of growing up. Updike calls the novel "a parable of growing" (4), and it is perhaps this aspect more than any other that makes the greatest claim for attention from the young reader. The book equates maturation with finding a voice with which to communicate one's needs, desires, and aspirations. Only when Louis can communicate, when he develops an expressive voice can he enter the world, claim a place in it, and live a satisfying and successful life.

This focus on maturation, on finding an empowering voice that grants love, security, and competence may help to explain the continuing popularity of the book among children and the adults who foster their reading. There are other rewards in reading the novel: it deals seriously with overcoming a handicap; it celebrates the survival in the wild of a beautiful but threatened species; it extolls the pleasures and benefits of music and art; it acknowledges the imperative to love and be loved and to find a mate; it explores the relationships between fathers and sons and the age-old tensions and affections between generations; and it acknowledges the fragile beauty of the planet and its wild, natural places. The novel's overall tone is engaging without ever being condescending: it is a respectful book—respectful of its subject, of its readers, and of the issues it addresses. Elledge is right in calling the book remarkable in being "a young book by an old author" (348).

Because of these elements and despite White's dissatisfaction, *The Trumpet of the Swan* was a great commercial success. In November 1970, soon after its publication, the work assumed first position on the *New York Times* best-seller list of children's books, displacing *Charlotte's Web*. The novel retained this position well into 1971, earning White a considerable income in royalties. The book was passed over for the Newbery Award, which was given instead to Betsy Byars's *The Summer of the Swans*. "How's that for a near miss?" quipped White; "I just got one word wrong!" (*Letters,* 615). In late 1971 White condensed the novel into approximately four typewritten pages for a presentation, with music especially written for it, by the Philadelphia Orchestra to benefit the orchestra and the Philadelphia Zoo. Thus, despite White's fears on sending the manuscript forth, *The Trumpet of the Swan* was in almost every way a public and commercial success.

Human Realm/Natural Realm

Despite the relative speed with which White wrote the book, he focused his usual attention on the appropriateness of its illustrations. The design for the dust jacket is White's own: he specified the exact scene, indicating that it "should suggest awe, wonderment, enchantment—not action, except the tiny act of tugging at the [shoe]lace. The boy should probably be rather hunched over, unsmiling" (*Letters,* 591). This initial picture prepares the reader for the important dynamics of the novel. First, Sam Beaver, the boy in the picture's foreground, is obviously a representative of the human realm, while the male swan swimming in the background and keeping a watchful eye on his cygnet is a representative of the natural realm. The emissary between these two alien realms is Louis, pictured at left foreground untying Sam's shoelace.

White seems fascinated by such emissaries between these two realms. Stuart Little, the tiny mouse-boy of White's first novel for children, embodies the two realms, born mouselike to a human family and later falling in love with a bird. Though he converses with representatives of both the human and animal realms, Stuart is not at home in either, and goes on an unfulfilled, though fulfilling, journey to find Margalo and a place for himself in the world. In *Charlotte's Web* White posits Fern as intermediary between the two realms. At first, in her radical innocence, Fern does not discriminate between the human and the animal realms, being unable, for example, to understand her father's distinctions between runt animals and little children. Throughout much of this novel, Fern mediates between barn and farmhouse; she is the link between the animal and human, though in her maturation she comes eventually to acknowledge the essential separation between these realms in her unconscious decision by the end of the novel to live exclusively in the human realm.

In *The Trumpet of the Swan*, however, unlike the earlier novels, White makes no essential pretense as to the separateness of the human and animal realms. He employs no mediators like Stuart and Fern; Louis lives easily in both realms, communicating directly with humans on equal terms just as they communicate with him. If the book is a celebration of wild nature as perceived through Sam Beaver's eyes, it is also a celebration of human culture and inventiveness, which Louis the swan participates in fully. In thus intersecting the animal and the human realms throughout, White imbues the novel with the kind of innocent vision readers share in the opening of *Charlotte's Web,* where Fern's inability to distinguish between the two realms provides the book's initial atmosphere—one of innocence that White retains throughout *The Trumpet of the Swan*.

Thus White took great pains to orchestrate the beginning picture for the book. Human and animal realms meld in the foregrounded interaction between Sam and Louis. In addition, the illustration calls attention to Louis's initial ability to communicate only in actions and not verbally. It also presents Sam being "naturalized" or drawn more fully into nature through the unlacing of his shoe, which symbolizes his human separation from the natural sphere. This illustration thus serves as a carefully prepared entry into the novel.

Chapter 1 immediately introduces a number of issues of importance in the novel as a whole. It opens with Sam Beaver returning from his explorations of a pond a mile and a half from the camp he and his father have set up in the Canadian wilds. Eleven-year-old Sam has seen a nesting pair of trumpeter swans and is hesitant to tell his father about them.

Indeed, he keeps them as a secret from his father, even when his father asks him what he has seen on his explorations. This father-son distancing so repeatedly insisted on in chapter 1 will be played out in the animal realm as well in the relationship between Louis and his father, the old cob. Thus from the beginning the stories of Sam and Louis have clear parallels. The novel indirectly announces its central focus on the growing process as indicated by the changing relationships among the generations, especially between father and son. In chapter 1 Sam is claiming his space in the world: he charts his own path across a treacherous bog his father warns him about and begins to explore the often dangerous world on his own; he claims the swans as his own private secret; he keeps a diary, indicating a separate inner life from his father; and he speculates on what he wants to do when he grows up, a sign of the self-determining decisions he will increasingly be called upon to make as he matures.

Chapter 1 also provides significant nature lore and naturalistic information concerning the nesting habits of the trumpeter swan. Like the first chapter of *Charlotte's Web*, the first chapter of this novel is completely realistic and thus provides a solid grounding for the elaborate and fantastic excursions away from reality that will come to characterize the entire plot.

This initial insistence on reality over fantasy is indicated in the chapter's illustrations as well as its prose. Following a beautifully designed frontispiece and title-page illustration depicting the two naturalistically rendered swans at home in the sedges of their Canadian pond, Frascino begins chapter 1 with an initial illustration depicting Sam consulting his compass as he traverses the swamp. This representation of Sam on his brief journey indicates the larger journey of life he will undertake during the novel and the self-reliance he will gain. He takes his bearings with the direction-indicating compass, not only in the Canadian wilds but also in his life as a whole. This illustration also foreshadows Louis's eventual travels. The last illustration of the chapter, penned by White himself as an example of Sam Beaver's artistic ability, depicts a swan teetering precariously on a large nest containing four eggs. As White indicated, "I decided to do the sketch myself, as my ability with a pencil is just about right for an 11-year-old boy" (*Letters,* 597).

This tailpiece illustration for chapter 1 provides an adroit transition from the human focus on Sam and his maturation and changing relationship with his father to an almost exclusive focus in chapter 2 on the swans themselves, who are nesting on a spring pond "seldom visited by any human being" (7). Chapter 2 is essentially a nature excursion with a kindly naturalist: it begins with a loving description of the slow onset of spring and the subsequent arrival of the migratory birds, most majestic of them all being the trumpeter swans. White is intent on providing his readers careful ornithological descriptions of the swans, including their distinctive calls, their feeding habits, the width of their wingspans, their awesome strength, and, most important, their nesting habits. The narratorial voice in the chapter is part pedagogue and part storyteller. This is in keeping with White's avowed intent that "however fantastical the tale, the behavior of the bird is authentic and violates nothing in the natural world of swans" (Elledge, 346). In the midst of this naturalistic depiction of swan behavior, White inserts the fantasy of the two swans conversing, debating, and weighing the nesting decisions they mutually arrive at. The chapter closes with the swans' joyous trumpeting, heard for a mile and a half around by all wild creatures—and by one pair of ears "that did not belong to a wild creature" (14), a neat tie-in to chapter 1 through this closing reference to Sam Beaver. The only illustration in chapter 2 is a full-page depiction of the swans' arrival at the pond—one flying over and the other splashing down in the foreground (9).

The nature lesson continues in chapter 3 with a close explication of how eggs incubate and of the sacrifices a nesting swan must make in order to ensure the successful hatching of her brood. The nature lesson is in the form of a conversation between the cob and the hen, who is asked questions about her nesting experiences. The tone of these passages extolling the wonders of nature is near-reverent. Indeed, we are told that when Sam was watching the swans "he had the same good feeling some people get when they are sitting in church" (18). An egg, Sam states in his journal, "is the most perfect thing there is. It is beautiful and mysterious" because "it contains life" (23). As he indicated repeatedly in his letters, an egg for White was a "miracle." This same wonder is expressed over the swan's instinctive ability to construct a nest without ever being taught how. These quasi-religious passages have direct antecedents in *Charlotte's Web,* where Dr. Dorian speculates on Charlotte's web-building as a greater miracle than the words she writes in it, and where the minister announces in church that Charlotte's miraculous web instructs all people to be ever receptive to the coming of wonders. In these discussions of nature White comes as close as he ever does to adopting a religious attitude in his works.

Chapter 3 is also significant for bringing together the human and natural realms through the meeting of Sam with the nesting swans. Understandably unnerved to discover a boy sitting silently and observ-

ing them closely, the hen cuts through the cob's furious blustering to
indicate that the boy is, after all, "behaving himself" and is not throwing stones or sticks: "He's simply observing" (16), she assures her mate.
Sam sits on a log, "hardly moving a muscle," "spellbound at the sight of
the swans" (17). Sam is no predator, and he is not tempted into the
depredations usual of boys. Indeed, he behaves at the swans' pond as if
he were in church. This meeting of boy and swans—at first the cause of
such consternation among the swans—eventually proves to be fortunate,
as Sam saves the life of the hen who, in taking a break from the nest, is
stalked by a fox intent on killing her for "a taste of blood" (21). Sam
intervenes at the last moment by throwing a stick, not at the swans, as
the swans had initially feared, but at the fox, their natural predator.
Thus, in a neat inversion of the usual order of things, White presents a
natural predator foiled by a human preserver. Sam has saved the swan's
life, and "the swans felt grateful" (23), saluting him with trumpetings
toned like the notes played on an orchestral French horn. As the swan
returns to her nest, the cob approaches Sam, who "never moved a muscle. His heart thumped from excitement and joy" (23). White at last
juxtaposes, in a bond of friendship, the boy featured in chapter 1 and the
swans focused on in chapter 2. It is an adeptly handled and convincing
union.

The double-page illustration for chapter 3 is masterful, showing the
nesting swan on her break from the nest, preening her feathers, the fox
creeping up on her from behind some bushes. Her utter defenselessness
is intensified by her self-preoccupation and by Frascino's clever place-
ment of the fox on the adjoining page. The frantic cob is in the left background, unobserved by the swan he is ineffectually attempting to warn.
The illustration demonstrates the serious predicament from which Sam
saves the swans as well as Frascino's sympathetic reading of White's text.

The protracted nature lesson continues in chapter 4 with its loving,
meticulous description of egg gestation—an avian process White continually celebrates in his letters. White describes how a cygnet breaks its
way out of a tough-shelled egg, how many days (35) a cygnet remains in
the egg, and what a newly hatched cygnet does first. The tone of the
narrator's science-for-young-people introduction to swan reproductive
biology is echoed in the tone used in the equally commonsense observations of the mother swan, who feels compelled throughout the chapter
to pull the cob back from his flights of poetic fancy to the real world of
the Canadian pond. Here the regenerative miracle of new life is occurring once again in nature.

White, then, cleverly maintains throughout this chapter a tension of voices. The informational and practical voices of prudent, sober narrator and nesting hen are pitched as a basso profundo for the airy wreathings of the cob's verbal arabesques. This engaging interplay of voices in a chapter devoted to the renewal of life is appropriate for a variety of reasons. First, the beginning of new life is both an intensely practical, biological matter involving the survival of a species as well as a poetic event of great beauty in that it suggests renewal, new potential, new hope. The practical, down-to-earth mother swan is clearly attuned to the first significance of the events in the nest; the cob, to the second. In addition, these two voices and the perspectives they represent will become important to the novel's central character, Louis, who must learn how to satisfy his poetic yearnings for art and love at the same time that he responds to the claims made on him by a world he at first seems unequipped to function effectively in. In a larger way, too, White's orchestration in this chapter of the practical and the poetic voices, of the complementary interplay between quotidian demands and the poetic flights above the merely practical and serviceable suggests that fine compromise that Louis learns to make and that White seems to recommend as necessary for successful living.

Though the poetic cob is often made to look foolish, he is nevertheless a largely sympathetic character in the same way that Dickens's Wilkins Micawber (from *David Copperfield*) is sympathetic despite his bombast. White's cob is certainly Micawberish in his use of poetic language and in his inflated sense of self, though improvident he is decidedly not, as later events in the novel prove. The hatching of the cygnets makes the cob feel "poetical and proud": he enjoys speaking "in fancy phrases and graceful language" (26). Despite all the gentle ridicule offered the cob, White gives him one of the most beautiful passages in any of his books.

The cob's welcome speech to his cygnets is a masterpiece of style and tone: it is at once moving and humorous, filled with true poetry and then deflated. The cob makes his speech between the swan's announcement that she will teach the cygnets to swim and her execution of that intention. White again skillfully interweaves the pragmatic and the poetic. The speech is a litany of welcomes to the world's wonders—a welcome "to the pond and the swamp adjacent"; "to the world that contains this lonely pond, this splendid marsh, unspoiled and wild"; "to sunlight and shadow, wind and weather"; "to water!" (30–31). But the cob is pragmatist enough to acknowledge life's darker sides as well, as can be seen in his welcome "to danger, which you must guard against," including the fox, the otter, the skunk, the coyote, and, in a nod to current environmental realities, the lead pellets "that lie on the bottom of all ponds, left there by the guns of hunters" to poison wild birds if ingested (31). Curiously, White's cob *welcomes* the cygnets to life's dangers rather than simply warning them against these dangers, perhaps because life is only fully lived in the negotiation of inevitable dangers as well as in the enjoyment of life's pleasures.

This balanced series of welcomes from the cob is followed by a litany of Polonian advice: "Be vigilant, be strong, be brave, be graceful, and *always* follow me!" (31). This advice is at once true and sententious, and it excellently illustrates White's bravura tonal performance here. The cygnets are then encouraged to enter life in a very beautiful way: "Enter the water quietly and confidently," assured by the swans' loving support as they find their way in the world (31). This high-style speech is soon countered by the hen's severe pragmatism: "glad the speech was over," she ushers the cygnets into the water, launching them into the world. It is the duet of poet-father and pragmatist-mother that ensures the cygnets' happy initiation into life.

The chapter is interesting also for its presentation of Sam as essentially an observer, much like Fern in *Charlotte's Web*. Like Fern, at least initially, Sam is completely enveloped in the natural world. The day recounted in the chapter is one of the most memorable days in Sam's life. In refusing to share what he has seen with his father, he thereby asserts his independence by claiming his experiences as his own. Observing the swans and cygnets, Sam "was perfectly happy" (29), especially when the cob brings the cygnets right up to him for an introduction. This introduction, however, has disturbing overtones: the fifth cygnet, unable to "beep" like the first four, pulls Sam's shoelace by way of alternate greeting. Sam's gradual maturation is hinted at by that evening's diary entry, wherein he poses for himself the perennial question of childhood concerning what he will be when he grows up—a question with which White often ended his own youthful diary entries.

Louis's Problem

The matter of chapter 5 is anticipated by the illustration in chapter 4, where the attention of all—Sam, the cob, and three of the four cygnets—is focused on Louis, who pulls Sam's shoelace in lieu of beeping his greetings as his siblings have done. The first to notice anything amiss with Louis is, of course, the ever-practical hen, who calls the cob's attention to Louis's persistent silence. This third hero of White's children's books shares the condition of his first two: like the mouse-boy Stuart and the runt Wilbur, the mute Louis is ill-equipped to survive in a world where his success in living fully and being loved is dependent upon his use of the signature "Ko-Hoh" of the trumpeter swan.

At first the cob shows a certain selfishness in wishing away "the added strain of having a defective child," one who will interrupt the cob's desire for everything "to go smoothly" in his life so that he can "glide gracefully and serenely . . . without being haunted by worry or disappointment" (36). White depicts the cob as beset by male ego and vanity and thus easily manipulated by the practical swan. She brings the cob into an empathy with Louis by flattering him, reminding him that it was his voice that won her. Thus, gradually, the cob comes to recognize the full implications of Louis's handicap. After proving that Louis is indeed mute, he resolves to rectify nature's omission.

White concludes the chapter with a nice bit of irony: in his attempts to console Louis and encourage him to live life joyously, the cob assures Louis that there is even a slight advantage in being mute, in that "it compels you to be a good listener" (42). In a world full of talkers, the old cob tells Louis, a good listener can pick up more information than one who talks incessantly. Louis is aware of the irony, reflecting, as he has been doing throughout the chapter, on the very great amount of talking his father himself does.

Nonetheless, the cob's breezy eloquence yields some solid—and comforting—assurances and encouragements: Louis must live fully despite fate and "be of good cheer." He must learn to fly, to eat and drink well, and to enjoy the use of his ears and eyes. In short, Louis, in being deprived of one faculty, is not by any means deprived of all, as his father reminds him, closing his speech with the promise that "someday I will make it possible for you to use your voice" (42–43). Thus, though frightened at being different and aware of the cruelty of his fate, Louis immerses himself in life, the chapter closing with him splashing water farther than his siblings, even though unable to join them in crowing about it.

Chapter 6 concerns itself primarily with the aerodynamics of swan flight, much of the chapter being devoted to the cob's flight instructions to the cygnets after his announcement that they must all migrate south to the Red Rock Lakes of Montana in the face of advancing winter. This announcement occasions many questions from the cygnets, "all except Louis." This phrase and its "All but Louis" variant become refrains in the chapter, being repeated no less than five times to emphasize Louis's inability to speak. This handicap temporarily makes Louis distrust his ability to fly as well, though this self-doubt prompts him to try harder at flying than any of the other cygnets, resulting in his becoming "the first of the young cygnets to become airborne, ahead of all his brothers and sisters" (49).

The interplay between self-doubt and achievement, between the incessant reminder of handicap and the overcoming of it is the essence of the chapter, which concludes with the swans flying over Sam Beaver's camp, occasioning the boy's diary ruminations about the miracle of migration and how a bird knows "how to get from where he is to where he wants to go" (52). The chapter is illustrated adroitly with a depiction of the seven swans flying diagonally across two pages of print, the cob in the lead, the hen scudding off the water behind the last of her airborne cygnets. It is one of the most successful illustrations in the book in terms of its inherent design and its spatial relation to the text on the two pages.

Chapter 7 is in many ways one of the book's most interesting and significant. Louis's successful first flight in chapter 6 prepares for a flight in this chapter that is both metaphorically and situationally important, for Louis flies away from the more or less real presentation of swan-life-in-nature to the human realm, which he will participate in fully for most of the remainder of the book. At this point, too, the novel departs dramatically from the earlier nature realism into pure fantasy. The transition is abrupt and daring, and nowhere else in White's children's books does it occur so boldly. In *Stuart Little* White plays with a character who *incorporates* the boundary and who can negotiate both sides—animal and human—though for the most part Margalo and Snowbell are on one side of the boundary and the Littles are on the other. In *Charlotte's Web,* too, animals and humans remain separated by a boundary imposed by nature itself (though the young Fern can cross this boundary for a time and Charlotte herself penetrates it on the occasions in which she writes in her web). But only in *The Trumpet of the Swan* is that boundary shattered so completely as to allow free intercourse between animal and human realms. This novel is, however, similar to the first two in that the two realms are negotiated by one character, in this case Louis.

Until chapter 7 swan lore is restricted to that which occurs, more or less, in nature. Here is a definitive departure from any accurate representation of nature and a blurring of the human and animal lines so clearly respected in *Charlotte's Web.* Louis seeks to overcome his "defectiveness" by learning to read and write, by hanging a small slate and chalk pencil around his neck, thereby acquiring a voice of sorts. Here White propels his novel with full velocity into fantasy: Louis decides to find Sam Beaver and to attend school with him. The finding of Sam somewhere in the state of Montana is sheer plot contrivance: on his second try "lucky" Louis finds Sam splitting wood on his father's ranch and identifies himself by again untying Sam's shoelace. The wondrous proceeds matter of factly: Sam's mother will not allow Louis to share Sam's bedroom but allows Sam to bring Louis with him to school the next day.

This is the second school scene in White's children's books, the first being the episode involving Stuart as a substitute teacher. Mrs. Hammerbotham, the harried first-grade teacher, at first refuses to allow Louis in her class: "No birds!" she exclaims. "I've got enough trouble" (58). But Sam eventually breaks down the narrow anthropocentrism of her belief that "only *people* need to communicate with one another" by demonstrating conclusively that on the contrary, "all birds and animals talk to one another" (58). Sam's inclusiveness, his refusal to support the customary separation of animal and human realms is reminiscent of Fern's initial position in *Charlotte's Web*.

With Louis established in first grade, Sam is ordered to return to his own fifth-grade classroom and its teacher, Miss Annie Snug. White here provides a gratuitous but amusing deconstruction of the infamous "word problems" given children in math class. Sam and his classmates reduce these mathematical word problems to absurdity with the complicity of their teacher. The children resist the narrow, linear language of the problems and insert real-life motivations and experiences to qualify their rigidity and the general unreality of their school work. Asked, for example, how many miles a man can walk in four hours if he walks three miles in the first hour, Sam answers that the man's total mileage during the four hours would depend entirely on how tired he was after the first hour or how comfortable his shoes were or what he might find along the roadside to divert him. This intrusion of real life with its complexities, qualifications, and perennial adjustments into the artificiality of school mathematics provides an echo of White's earlier commentary on education in *Stuart Little*, with its implicit plea for less rigidity and greater human sensitivity in the education of children. This amusing but gratuitous concluding episode of chapter 7 has little to do with Louis or with furthering the plot, except for its implicit commentary on the logic of the classroom. The inherent unreality of the math problems does, however, neatly balance the unreality of having a swan-scholar enrolled in school. Both are normalized in the chapter: Louis is enrolled and accepted in his first-grade class and the fifth-grade teacher acknowledges the insertion of real-life considerations into the problems she presents for the children's consideration.

Louis returns to his family in chapter 8 after 18 months away at school. Determined at last to communicate, he hastily scrawls his greetings on the slate hanging from his neck, only to discover what a little forethought would have revealed to him—none of the swans can read. But all was not for naught as Louis had feared: if the swans cannot read, people can, as he discovers when he communicates with the man who comes to give the birds grain. But this ability to communicate with humans does not head off Louis's real difficulty—his inability to communicate with his own kind. This inability reaches a crisis when Serena, "the swan of his choice, the female of his desiring," rejects Louis and his chalked message of love because he cannot win her with a lusty "Ko-Hoh." This sets the stage for Louis's father to act on Louis's behalf: the closing pages of the chapter detail the cob's flight toward Billings, Montana, to acquire a horn for Louis as a substitute voice. The chapter concludes on a note of tension, the swan wondering how her husband can possibly succeed.

Chapter 8, then, is a transition chapter, successful at moving the plot along, but not particularly convincing in its plot motivations. It is difficult to accept that Louis never figures out that his fellow swans cannot read. It is also a stretch to accept that the old cob has to step in to help Louis at this juncture. Louis has been depicted as inventive, ingenious, and utterly self-reliant up to this point. The chapter's one success is its two-page illustration of the hen watching Serena ignore Louis, his scrawled "I love you" pathetically rejected by his illiterate intended, who needs a vocal assurance of his love.

The Old Cob's Solution

Chapter 9 quickens the pace of the novel again. The chapter is a virtuoso performance: stylistically and emotionally engaging, it features a self-sacrificial action done for love. The cob sets out for Billings, Montana, on a "noble quest," motivated by his determination to do "anything to help my son Louis" (76). The old cob dive-bombs through the plate glass of a music store in order to attain a trumpet for Louis. White is at his best in the chapter: the short sentences capture stylistically the noise and confusion of the cob's caper as glass crashes, the saleswoman faints on the piano keys, the owner's shotgun blasts, the musical instruments bang and clash, plaster falls, and the owner yells that he has been robbed. This slapstick scene, full of action, excitement, and humor, is essentially at odds with the deeper, more serious undercurrent of the cob's love and eventual guilt over the incident.

The cob literally risks all, as his wounded shoulder indicates, and is fully aware of the sacrifice of his "excellent character and high ideals" (80), but he validates his actions in his awareness of his ultimate motive: "I did it to help my son. I did it for love of my son Louis" (80). Here the cob's folly and grandiloquence, his self-admiration and pomposity all are punctured by a nobility of feeling and a moving authenticity. If, as Elledge asserts, this episode concerning the cob contains a veiled allusion to White's own father's apparently extralegal maneuvers in certain business aspects of the Horace Waters Piano Company, it also contains a loving acknowledgment of his father's ultimate motives and a moving tribute of understanding and forgiveness.

The chapter concludes with the cob's ornate presentation speech of the trumpet to Louis, but the cob's pomposity is countered by his legitimacy of feeling. And that is the signal achievement of the chapter. White juggles many often conflicting emotions, character motivations, and audience reactions simultaneously: the action in the chapter is at once truly daring and farcically slapstick, morally illegal and emotionally correct; the cob is both pretentious and deeply moving, long winded and simultaneously exact in expression, a fool and a self-sacrificial saint at the same time. The moral issue is never clouded over—the cob has stolen the trumpet at a loss to the store owner of $900—but this issue is movingly grounded in a father's sacrificial love and in a son's gratitude. The chapter is a remarkable achievement in style and in the complexity of its accumulated comedic, moral, and emotional overtones.

The chapter's illustration, too, is a precise shorthand notation for the confusion, humor, and ultimate nobility of the cob's action; the picture is dominated by an enormous swan, trumpet in beak, hovering over shotgun-wielding store owner, fainting saleswoman, cowering customer, and startled salesman. The cob descends into the human realm like an epiphanic god accompanied by chaos and confusion. The illustration is a concise depiction of action, clamor, and surprise brought on by the cob's sudden descent into the human arena.

Chapter 10 begins with a renewed focus on Louis's differences from other swans, but now we start to see his differences as positive attributes. In the first place, he is "the best-liked young male swan" on the lake—

as well as "the best equipped" (84). The slate, chalk pencil, and brass trumpet hung around his neck—heretofore the marks of his "defectiveness"—now become objects of increasing interest to "the young females" because they make Louis look "entirely different from the other cygnets" (84).

Despite Louis's gradually changing fortunes, he is a very troubled swan at chapter's opening. First, he finds learning to play the trumpet an exceedingly difficult task, though White focuses on his undaunted determination to succeed despite all obstacles. Louis thus presents a role model to all youthful readers facing extraordinary challenges as well as the ordinary ones that loom large in every young life. Frascino's full-page illustration provides an amusing quartet of images of Louis in ludicrous positions as he wrestles with learning to play this alien instrument (85). Louis's second source of unease is his conscience-stricken realization that his trumpet has been stolen. Third, Serena, "the swan of his desiring," has flown north with other swans to the Snake River. Thus, at the beginning of chapter 10, Louis "found himself with a broken heart, a stolen trumpet, and no one to give him any lessons" (86).

Faced with these peculiarly human distresses, Louis again turns to the human realm for help: he flies to Sam Beaver's ranch where he receives a very human suggestion. He needs a job, Sam tells him, because his worst woes spring from a lack of money. Sam's suggestion that Louis become camp bugler at Camp Kookooskoos, playing reveille, mess call, and taps on the trumpet, announces the novel's central joke. It is a multilayered one. First, Louis is a trumpeter swan who learns to play the trumpet. Second, his name is Louis, an obvious reference to the jazz trumpeter Louis Armstrong. Thus the book's central joke encompasses the animal and the human realms and engages the reader in Louis's simultaneous swan and human nature as well. In reflecting on the novel's central joke, John Updike noted that if White "once winked during this accumulation of preposterous particulars, it would all turn flimsy and come tumbling down" (5). It does not quite do that, but the joke does seem strained.

Nevertheless, Louis gets his first job in this chapter, as does Sam Beaver, who also goes to the same camp as a counselor and whose diary reflects his concerns over his future, a repeated refrain in his entries being an anxious, "I wish I knew what I was going to be when I am a man" (90). Thus Sam and Louis venture simultaneously into the adult world of work and responsibility. White clearly keeps their development and maturation in close tandem, thereby emphasizing that this is a novel of maturation but at the same time, unfortunately, diffusing reader interest in Louis and his plight. The chapter ends beautifully, however, with Louis's success with the trumpet. To close the chapter, Louis sounds his trumpet, thrilling all who hear it with the sound "of all the wild and wonderful things and places they had ever known: sunsets and moonrises and mountain peaks and valleys and lovely streams and deep woods" (92). With that concluding note, the two boys—or the swan and the boy—launch out from childhood into the world, Louis reflecting that receiving his first job was as exciting as the day he first learned to fly.

Chapter 11 provides a brief interlude—one filled with nostalgia for White's youthful and adult experiences at Camp Otter, in which he later lost a sizable investment. The chapter details an ordinary day at summer camp. Forty boys sit around a campfire, singing with mouths clogged with marshmallows. One boy is a whiner. The camp director is himself an overgrown boy. The boys, including the camp director, all plan to go swimming in the nude in the morning. And that night, Louis sends them to sleep with his rendition of taps. The closing illustration is apt: Louis, in dark silhouette against a sunset-smeared sky, trumpets taps for a camp already sunk in slumber. The picture provides a nostalgic accompaniment to White's homesick memories of adolescence and its healthy venting in a summer camp in the wilds.

"A Rescue," the title for chapter 12, is actually a misnomer, since the chapter features *two* rescues composed along parallel lines. The chapter is, in addition, a nostalgic retrospection on boy life in a summer camp, with its volleyball games after supper, its canoeing and swimming and nature walks, its shifting allegiances among the boys. But the chapter essentially features the dawning maturity of the two central characters and their growing ability to act effectively in the world.

The first rescue is less dramatic but more interesting than the second. Into camp stumbles a skunk one morning from the dump where it has been foraging and where it gets its head stuck in a tin can. Clearly the skunk is in serious difficulty, doomed to starvation unless the can is removed. The boys in the camp come up with all sorts of cockeyed suggestions, from shooting the can with an arrow tied to a string and pulling the can off to smearing the can with glue and then directing the skunk to a block of wood which could then be used somehow to leverage the can off without the boys' being squirted with the skunk's perfume.

Sam Beaver alone among the boys thinks clearly and competently. He rigs up a noose tied to a pole and waits on the roof of the camp for the skunk to blunder by. He then slips the noose around the can, gives it a yank to tighten it, and the can comes off the skunk's head. Sam alone is capable of mature and thoughtful action here, and his effectiveness is clearly contrasted to the other, less mature boys' harebrained schemes.

The first rescue thus involves a human intervening to save an animal. The second parallels the first, though this time an animal effects the rescue of a human. The set-up for this rescue in some ways parallels the set-up for the first one. Whereas nature has been the primary cause of the skunk's trouble, human interaction is the cause of the second problem. Applegate Skinner, an unpopular boy in camp, is subjected to a barrage of taunts about his name, and in his unhappiness, he takes a canoe out alone on the stormy lake without first having passed his swimming or boating tests. After upsetting the canoe in the rough waters of the lake, Applegate is in serious danger of drowning. The boys all set out to save him in canoes, but they cannot make it in time, leaving Louis to dash forth in a flurry of white wings and frothy water to save the unhappy boy. Louis's competence is thus here contrasted to the other campers' ineffectual responses to the crisis, and Louis, like Sam in the previous rescue, stands out as quick-thinking and mature. His competence gains universal recognition in the camp, unlike Sam's quieter display of this mature quality. A man from Washington comes to Camp Kookooskoos to award Louis the Lifesaving Medal, yet another impediment to hang around Louis's already laden neck.

White thus continues to focus on the maturation of his central characters. Sam's maturation is the stuff of realism—how a real boy grows and develops in competence. Louis's maturation is more spectacular—a fantastic progress within the realm of fantasy. Sam's progression is solid, more substantial; Louis's maturation amounts to wish-fulfillment—the kind of grand achievement belonging to the realm of adolescent imagination. It is the stuff of adolescent daydreams: Louis, by chapter's end, has become the camp's "most distinguished counselor" in addition to being "a great trumpet player, a great bird, a powerful swimmer, and a fine friend" (109). Louis's fame is gradually growing: "People all over were beginning to talk about the swan that could play a trumpet" (110).

Adventures in the Great World

After the perfect plot symmetry of chapter 12, the book returns to an exclusive focus on Louis as Sam again drops out of the picture for a time. Chapter 13 extends Louis's growth in competence: Louis wants to be a musician, not just a bugler with a slender repertoire of bugle calls.

Aspiring to play jazz, country-and-western, rock, and the music of the great composers, Louis prevails upon Sam to slit the webs between his three toes with a razor blade so that he can press the valves of the trumpet and thus play the whole range of notes on the scale. This detail still strikes many readers as discordant, even grisly, and prompted some objections among early readers. White responded to these concerns in a letter, indicating that he included the incident partly "to tell a little bit about the horn and its valves" and partly because he found it "an amusing incident." More important, however, White included the detail to show "that Louis was willing to make a personal sacrifice in order to achieve his goal" (*Letters,* 644).

This last reason is the central one. The chapter focuses on Louis's aspirations—his continuing yearning for Serena, his desire to further his art, his goal of clearing his father's debt and restoring his good name. This web-slitting incident, resulting in Louis's tendency to swim in circles, proves the seriousness of Louis's intent. His ultimate success is captured in the amusing illustration (114) depicting his excitement and pleasure in playing the trumpet. Frascino shows Louis large-eyed with excitement at the new sounds blaring from the full frontal bell of his horn. It is an endearing and amusing depiction, one of the best in the book.

As Louis's success increases, so do his encumbrances. To the assorted accoutrements already weighing Louis down—his slate and chalk pencil, his trumpet, and his lifesaving medal—the camp director adds a money-bag filled with Louis's summer earnings. Just as the slit webs on his right foot make his swimming more difficult, so the growing encumbrances around his neck make his flying less free. The chapter thus offers a commentary on the bittersweet nature of growing up. A growth in maturity is always accompanied by a simultaneous gaining and a giving up, and this Louis is made to realize in chapter 13. He plays the trumpet more proficiently now, but his swimming is compromised; he gains those things he needs to achieve his goals, but his flight is less free, less exhilarating than it was in his early youth. Louis recognizes at the end of this chapter that "the best way to travel, really, is to travel light" (116). But a real growth in his maturity comes with his resigned realization that this original freedom is incompatible with growing responsibility, that the fecklessness of youth must give way to the restraints of maturity. Thus, the chapter recognizes the bittersweet nature of all growth and the sweet/sour distillation accompanying increased responsibility.

In chapter 13 Sam Beaver had suggested that Louis head to Boston for a job leading the Swan Boat in the lagoon of the Public Garden after the closing of Camp Kookooskoos. Chapter 14 details Louis's remarkable success in this new job. The wild sound of his trumpet in the Public Garden in the heart of staid Boston "stirred everyone's blood," ricocheting throughout the urban canyons and infiltrating the traditional genteel refinement of the city. This chapter marks Louis's first public success and thus a further increase in the level of his competence and maturity. This chapter also marks an audacious further flight into the fantastic. Once the first premise of the book is accepted—that a swan can go to school to learn to write—the rest of the fantasy follows in due course, escalating with a crazy kind of logic predicated on earlier events.

The sheer whimsy and sprightliness of chapter 15 make for delightful reading. The swan-boatman fears for Louis's safety on the lagoon in the Public Garden and thus insists that Louis stay in the Ritz-Carlton adjacent to the park. This arrangement provokes some of the least subtle but nonetheless amusing humor in the book, from the night clerk's consternation at his new guest to Louis's ingenious accommodations to his alien environment. The night clerk initially objects to housing a bird at all, but his refusal is reversed upon his discovery that Louis is a celebrity, has luggage (the numerous encumbrances around his neck), does not have lice, and is scrupulous in his personal habits. What finally wins the clerk over is Louis's trumpet rendition of "There's a Small Hotel," the sweet strains of Louis's music filtering throughout the Ritz and charming all listeners. "It was a moment of sheer magic," the narrator asserts (128). Once again, Louis's trumpeting, with its wild, natural accent counterpointing and enhancing the jazz and classical human music he plays, recalls all listeners to something in them that has been lost and evokes again a dim recollection of the original connections between humans and nature. That connection, made diffuse in the expensive sophistication of the Ritz, is again magically evoked by Louis's trumpet rendition. And this is the key that unlocks for Louis a hotel room for the night.

Louis is clearly out of his element at the Ritz-Carlton. In *Stuart Little* White used this device of presenting a character at odds with the world in which he finds himself. Like Stuart, Louis makes heroic and ingenious adjustments to his uncongenial environment. For example, when the bellboy approaches him for his luggage, Louis hands him the impedimenta around his neck to carry and then tips him in his room. Hungry, Louis orders 12 watercress sandwiches and, after the waiter has retired, he scoops out the watercress and abandons the bread. Finally, after reading an account of his success in the Public Garden in the evening paper and after writing a letter to Sam reaffirming his goals of paying off his

father's obligation and of winning Serena, he retires for the night. He runs a bath of cold water in the tub and sleeps there, his bill tucked under his wing, dreaming of small Canadian lakes in springtime and of his love, Serena. Thus, the chapter demonstrates Louis's ever-increasing competence in his art and his growing ability to meet the challenges before him. The chapter also shows, in a humorous way, Louis's ability to adapt to his changing world and to mold circumstances in such an ingenious way as to satisfy his needs even in the most unpromising of situations. What White does more consistently and better in *Stuart Little*, his novel of dauntless adaptability to whatever life offers, he echoes in this novel as well, though more faintly.

After the Swan Boat owner sees Louis's bill at the Ritz, he agrees to let Louis sleep on the lagoon with the other water fowl the following night—an arrangement much more to Louis's liking. Chapter 16 recounts Louis's great success in closing the summer season for the Swan Boat. His fame and renown grow increasingly, and just as he completes his engagement in Boston, he receives a telegram offering him a ten-week engagement in a Philadelphia nightclub at $500 a week. Louis's last day in Boston marks the end of "another chapter in his adventurous life, out in the big world" (142) and moves him closer to achieving the goal ever on his mind. Thus the book features an escalation of challenges for Louis and his concomitant successes.

After Louis flies, clanking and encumbered, to Philadelphia, he makes a dramatic splashdown in Bird Lake in the Philadelphia Zoo, where he immediately feels right at home. White relied upon his friend and fellow Cornellian Howard Cushman for details concerning this zoo, which he had never visited. White felt called upon to defend the positive attitude toward zoos displayed by both Louis and Sam in the novel, arguing that Louis was not at all "insensitive or disloyal" in his agreeing to live in the Philadelphia Zoo's Bird Lake: "Life in a zoo is just the ticket for some animals and birds," White wrote to Alice J. Scott on 23 September 1970. White especially defended the Philadelphia Zoo, which "hatched some Trumpeter cygnets a few years back when the species was threatened with extinction, and helped save them for the world" (*Letters*, 606).

With Louis's increasing success come increasing complications, including dealing with his agent, Abe "Lucky" Lucas, a character out of a Damon Runyon novel, dressed in a purple suit and a Tyrolean hat who demands 10 percent of Louis's earnings and offers to hold Louis's bulging moneybag in his safekeeping. But Louis proves himself shrewd in dealing with a dangerous world: he demands that "Lucky" Lucas pay for his cab fare to and from the nightclub where he will perform and he automatically refuses to entrust his money to "Lucky's" proffered safe-keeping. Louis also accepts a quid pro quo arrangement with the zoo: it will allow him to stay on Bird Lake without pinioning him (amputating the top of one of his wings, which would prevent him from flying) if he will agree to play a free concert every Sunday afternoon for zoo patrons.

The second half of chapter 16, then, demonstrates Louis's ever-increasing competence in handling the complications of the adult world. The conditions of this job in Philadelphia are much more complex than the simple agreements negotiated with Mr. Brickle at Camp Kookooskoos or with the Swan Boat operator. These were like the summer jobs of adolescence; now Louis enters a workaday world characterized by a complex interweaving of interests and an extensive interdependence among people, and it is Louis's adult responsibility to negotiate these demands, which he succeeds in doing in this chapter.

Chapter 17 is clearly the climax of the book, bringing together all the novel's themes and resolving its primary tension. The chapter begins with a recognition of Louis's willingness to sacrifice in order to attain his goals. He plays for 10 weeks, every night but Sunday, in a big, noisy nightclub crowded with loud and self-indulgent people. He "did not like the job at all," we are told, but he continued with it, even though his heart was with his Sunday evening concerts at the zoo and with his occasional guest appearances with the Philadelphia Symphony Orchestra.

After establishing again the extent of Louis's dedication to his goals, White next indulges in a bold sleight of hand as far as plotting is concerned. A violent gale assaults Philadelphia, serendipitously blowing Louis's love Serena across many states to the very zoo where Louis is staying. This obvious manipulation of plot is less than satisfactory, representing a disappointing departure from the near-perfect plotting of *Charlotte's Web* and the much more satisfying episodic architecture of *Stuart Little*. Nonetheless, all of Louis's dreams are met in Serena's arrival and in his subsequent ability, for the first time, to give voice to his previously inchoate longings and to his mute affections. In the dawn soon after her arrival, Louis awakens Serena with his rendition of "Beautiful Dreamer," each note being "like a jewel held to the light" (157). This, as White makes clear, "was the moment of triumph for a young swan who had a speech defect and had conquered it" (158). This point is repeated throughout the remainder of the chapter, unlike the more suggestive and evocative handling of moments of climax in the two earlier—and better—of White's works for children. Again and again, White reiter-

ates the chapter's climactic point: Louis "was the happiest bird alive. He
was a real Trumpeter Swan at last. His defect of being without a voice
had at last been overcome" (163).

Thus by the end of this chapter Louis has achieved competence in his
art and in his ability to negotiate his way in the world. He has also won
love, fame, and fortune. With the acquisition of Serena's love and his
ever-expanding moneybag and the extraordinarily positive responses of
all of Philadelphia to his art, Louis has achieved the mature success he
has worked so hard for. The novel is a maturation tale, and that maturation is complete by the end of chapter 17.

The Fullness of Being

The novel's subsequent four chapters provide a lengthy dénouement, a
reconciling of the issues addressed, and a final coming into the fullness of
maturity for both Louis and Sam. In chapter 18, for example, White
accomplishes the disengagement of Louis and Serena from the zoo,
which, of course, is eager to keep them. The chapter opens with an order
from "the Head Man in Charge of Birds" to have Serena pinioned. Louis
knows immediately that if the keepers succeed, Serena would have to
remain in Philadelphia for the rest of her life—"a horrible fate" (164)—
far from their dreamed-of idyll in lonely northern lakes. His response is
immediate: he determines that no one will clip the wings of love, in
either a metaphorical or an actual sense, and, after freeing himself from
the encumbrances around his neck, he dispatches the two keepers with
blows of his beak and wings. Louis's effective action in the face of this
challenge to his life plans is continued when he enters the Head Man's
office to declare his love for Serena and to resist the offer of a lifetime of
security and comfort in the zoo. The old cob had earlier welcomed his
progeny to the dangers of the world as a necessary part of life, and Louis,
embracing life fully, cannot countenance the elimination of these dangers
for a life circumscribed by the secure but life-limiting walls of the zoo.

Declaring, "I have other plans," Louis plays an old Irving Berlin song,
filling the office "with the sound of love" (168) and solving yet another
problem with music. This is the first of three times in the chapter that
Louis uses his musical talents to bolster his arguments. He solves his
problems with music and logic, appealing to the Head Man on two levels, but reverting to music when the Head Man grows logically intransigent. Louis is the true son of his pragmatic mother and poetic father: he
is equally at home with logic and poetry and uses them interchangeably

to make his way in life successfully. Though the Head Man claims Serena for the people of Philadelphia because she was blown to the zoo by "an act of God," Louis claims her for himself "by reason of the power of love—the greatest force on earth" (168).

The Head Man's second argument revolves around a promised safety for Louis, Serena, and their eventual hatchlings from all the perils to which Louis's father had welcomed his children in that earlier grandiloquent speech made on the hatching of Louis and his siblings. The Head Man promises security from fox, otter, and coyote as well as from hunger, hunter, and lead-pellet poisoning. But Louis asks for more than security: he demands his freedom as a higher value than mere safety and comfort and plays his trumpet a second time. This force of logic and aesthetics leads the Head Man to understand Louis's position and empathize, even if he still refuses to forsake what he sees as his duty to the people of Philadelphia.

Louis negotiates two concessions: he asks for a delay in pinioning Serena until after Christmas, and he persuades the Head Man to allow him to send a wire to Sam Beaver asking him for help. When Sam, now 14, arrives, Louis explains his natural preference for leaving civilization once his debts are paid and returning to a life in the wild. Sam's solution proved controversial for some of White's readers, who objected that Louis sold out when he agreed that in the future he and Serena would supply the zoo with those cygnets they judged weaker in the world and thus in need of "special care and protection" and "extra security" (173). Nevertheless, this compromise, negotiated by Sam after seeing how happy and well the water fowl seemed in the zoo's Bird Lake, is accepted by all parties, and the strict logic of these negotiations is softened for the third time by Louis's music, which reverberates throughout the zoo, making the whole world seem "better and brighter and wilder and freer and happier and dreamier" (173).

Chapter 18, then, is a beautifully developed chapter, uniting Louis and Sam again in solving together Louis's final problem. Their effective negotiations demonstrate the completeness of their maturity. They are able to see problems clearly, probe them for their underlying validity and spoken and unspoken claims, and offer effective solutions that represent a satisfactory resolution of all the issues. This logical ability ensures that they can now broker their own futures in the world. Their logical abilities in ensuring their effectiveness in life are strengthened and complemented by their highly developed aesthetic sensibilities, especially

Louis's. Louis effectively tempers argument with music, logic with emotion, and when reason proves intransigent, he softens it with art. This combination of head and heart, of the practical and the aesthetic, of the reasonable and the beautiful, of the logical and the imaginative produces a fully mature and effective personality and demonstrates the well-rounded character that emerges after what White presents as a successful maturation process. Louis is thus the product of pragmatic mother and poetic father, resolving into a life-enhancing unity the separate but complementary gifts of his two parents.

Chapter 19 is largely Sam's chapter. Earlier in the novel the chapters in which Sam played a major role almost always ended with Sam's perennial reflections on what he wanted to do when he grew up. This repeated refrain is resolved in the first paragraph of chapter 19: the day Sam visits the Philadelphia Zoo is a turning point in his life because while visiting there, "all his doubts vanished. He knew he wanted to work in a zoo" (174).

This decision immediately counterpoints Louis's desire to escape the zoo in search of his freedom. Indeed, when Sam decides to spend his working life at the zoo, he is on a mission to help Louis and Serena escape from that same zoo. Sam even tells the Head Man that he has come to the zoo "to defend freedom" (175), a goal seemingly in opposition to the decision he himself makes then and there concerning what he will do with his life. His defense of Louis's freedom is eloquent, if a bit contradictory, given his choice of professions. He argues that "Louis would pine away in captivity" and proceeds to draw for the Head Man an evocative picture of the wild places Louis must live in, the "little ponds, swamps, cattails, Red-winged Blackbirds in the spring, the chorus of the frogs, the cry of the loon at night" (176). This reanimates the Head Man's own youthful dreams and turns his fixed resistance into a final agreement.

To complicate this counterpointing of zoo with natural freedom, Sam has earlier talked Louis and Serena into supplying the zoo with cygnets on occasion, an action seeming to contradict Louis's determination not to remain in a zoo. Indeed, Louis seems to agree to condemn his own children to a life he rejects for himself, prompting White to note that Louis was not being "insensitive or disloyal." He simply takes Sam's advice, and "Sam is very pro-zoo" because the zoo serves to educate the public on the necessity for the preservation of the natural world. In short, the zoo performs, in Sam's (and White's) view, a higher good. *The*

Trumpet of the Swan thus concludes with an interweaving of intentions and a counterpointing of desires between the novel's two featured characters.

Sam assures the Head Man of Louis's trustworthiness in honoring his bargain with the zoo by providing a detailed financial report on Louis's assets accumulated in order to pay off his father's debt. The long paragraph amounts to a lesson in accounting, with detailed debits and credits for expenses and earnings—down to the last penny. Louis has earned $4,420.78, which he will give to his father, having "no use for money anymore" (178). When the Head Man hears of Louis's imminent divestiture, his turning his back on money entirely, he waxes romantic, imagining a life like Louis's freed from financial encumbrances, from the quotidian duration of earning and spending, buying and selling, the daily round of money made and money expended. This urge to escape the cycle leads the Head Man to leave his office for the day to show Sam the zoo and to commune again with the atavistic freedom from financial concerns that animals manifest.

The chapter concludes with the dual flight of Sam by plane and Louis and Serena by wing. Plane and swans take off in tandem from the airport runway, Sam and Louis waving good-bye to each other. The chapter provides yet another coda to the dual maturation tale the book has unfolded. Sam knows clearly what he will do with his life and the goals he will pursue: the tag question of his journal entries has been answered. Louis, on his honeymoon with his beloved Serena, contemplates his triumphant return to Montana. Penniless when he left there originally, he now returns rich. Unknown on his departure for the world, he returns famous. Alone on leaving, he flies home accompanied by his bride. His goals merely nascent on his departure, he comes back to Montana with medal, trumpet, and hard-earned cash, having accomplished all he had set out to do. The chapter thus ends with a reiteration of the two characters' great successes in achieving the maturation set for them both to accomplish in the early chapters. White provides yet another rhapsodic affirmation of their success, concluding the chapter with Louis's exhilaration: "Freedom felt so wonderful! Love felt so good!" (184).

Chapter 20 serves to tidy up the old cob's adventures in Billings and to restore his honor lost in his robbery of the Billings music store. The chapter is a noisy, action-packed one in which White again expertly balances the pomposity of the old cob with his genuine nobility and poetic sensitivity. The old cob is, in some ways, the best-wrought character in the novel, evoking humor, admiration, and exasperation in just about equal parts.

The chapter begins with the clamorous welcome afforded Louis and Serena on their heroic return to their families on the Red Rock Lakes and Louis's commissioning of the old cob to redeem his honor by carrying the moneybag and an explanatory message inscribed on Louis's slate back to the owner of the music store. The mission is eagerly accepted by the cob, though his sensible mate attempts to puncture his heroic posturing by reminding him of the very real dangers awaiting him. Amid multiple rhetorical flourishes ("My hour has come. . . . My moment of truth is at hand"), the old cob accomplishes his mission, although he creates the same havoc occasioned by his first foray into the human world.

The cob faints away at the sight of the blood trickling from his superficial wing wound, surrounded by a gathered mob all talking at once. The major players in the scene are the music store owner, a game warden who just happens to be in the vicinity, and a policeman, all contending for the money left by the fainting swan. The policeman claims he needs to keep the money safe until the facts of the case can be sorted out. The storekeeper insists the money is his as directed in the swan's slate message. The game warden claims the money by right of confiscation because the storekeeper has illegally wounded an endangered bird. Assorted voices in the surrounding crowd repeatedly make their way into the central discussion.

The simplicity and essential concord of the animal world displayed at the beginning of the chapter is here countered by the dissonant contentiousness of the human world—a discord evoked by this epiphanic intrusion into the human realm of an emissary from the natural one. A judge is called in to arbitrate the disputes and to restore order, which he does by awarding the full sum to the storekeeper: "Everyone is innocent, the swan is honest, the debt is paid, the storekeeper is rich, and the case is dismissed" (196). Frascino's two-page illustration of the scene shows on the first page a tight knot of men all talking at once and in the second the cob on a stretcher being carried into an ambulance. It is an effective rendition of the opposition between the human and the animal realms and their differing attitudes toward money.

White concludes the crowd scene with a plug for the Audubon Society, which he targets as recipient of the storekeeper's largesse. The storekeeper donates the remainder of Louis's accumulation, after his own losses are recovered, to the Audubon Society to help in its efforts to preserve birds threatened with extinction—a condition the store owner explains to a child in the crowd and thus indirectly to White's own child readers. This passage is abundantly transparent: White here inserts a direct ecological message after he has built a strong allegiance between reader and trumpeter swans, a species threatened with the very extinction he takes such pains to define.

The chapter's overt message concluded, the focus shifts again back to the swan luxuriating in a hospital bed attended by nurses. On his return to the lakes he regales his family with an embellishment of his "extraordinary adventure," silencing the logical intrusions of his wife and indulging in the kind of aesthetic embroidery which endears him to White's readers. He notes, for example, how beautifully his black bill contrasted with the snowy white sheets of his hospital bed. The chapter concludes with a concord between cob and hen, who affectionately welcomes her mate home. After a swim and breakfast, the cob pulls the Band-Aid off of his wound and throws it away, having returned fully and for good to the natural realm.

Chapter 21, "The Greening Spring," provides an idyllic coda—a richly satisfying parting glance at the events, characters, and places featured in this tale of the joint maturation of its two central characters. It is a near-perfect ending for what can only be seen as a less-than-perfect book. The chapter, like the lives of Louis and Serena together, begins in love, the two swans flying north in the spring to the same Canadian pond that serves as the novel's opening setting. They fly together in the exhilaration of the budding spring and of their early love, unencumbered by jobs and the necessity for money, without which "Louis felt a great sense of relief" (201).

As Louis and Serena felt "the changing world" from winter to soft spring, "they stirred with new life and rapture and hope" (202). Indeed, the last illustration (206–207) depicts Louis and Serena arriving at the pond where Louis had been hatched. The illustration takes up two complete pages on which there is no text, all other illustrations in the text having been designed in juxtaposition to the written word. This freedom from the text provides the reader with that completely natural realm that Louis here returns to. There is nothing of human culture in the picture; it is solely a depiction of nature. As such, it is a very effective instrument allowing the reader to share in Louis's joy and immersion in a realm natural to him. The perspective of the illustration, however, is not Louis's, for he and Serena are depicted entering the picture plane at upper left. The point of view may be that of Sam, whose later visits to the pond are recorded in this last chapter. This would be in keeping with the dual characterization of Louis and Sam throughout the novel. Or the point of view may be strictly that of the reader, who now, with Louis established in his maturity, is asked to withdraw from intimacy with him as he lives his life with Serena in a realm essentially distinct from the human one. At any rate, the illustration provides the novel with a highly effective pictorial closure.

Sam Beaver shows up at the pond on occasion after Louis's cygnets hatch, and, in subsequent years and after subsequent nestings, Louis and Serena fly back over Louis's earlier route, revisiting the scenes of Louis's adolescence—Camp Kookooskoos, the Public Garden at Boston (where Louis again leads the Swan Boat and he and Serena spend a night at the Ritz), and Bird Lake at the Philadelphia Zoo (where Louis keeps his promise of providing a cygnet and where he visits Sam Beaver then working there). Thus Louis and Serena live a fairy-tale ending: the hero, in the beginning of his maturation tale the least likely to succeed because of his handicap, emerges victorious after his trials, having faced them courageously and energetically and thereby having constructed a pleasant and meaningful life for himself through the strong exercise of his will and through the generosity of those well disposed to him. Louis and Serena thus deserve the happy, long life they are allowed to enjoy together by novel's end. Part of that happy life results from Louis's continued devotion to his art—an important issue in the novel. Ever a musician, Louis values his trumpet and his art for the remainder of his life, sharing his music with his family and, on his yearly flights to old haunts, with a wider audience.

The novel concludes as it began, with Sam sharing a camping trip in the Canadian wilds with his father. Sam, too, like Louis, has successfully forged a happy and meaningful life. He has figured out a way to earn his living doing what he most wants to do and is allowed the final grace note of balancing his city life in Philadelphia with his life of service and continued connection with the earth's diversity of natural creatures sheltered and fostered at the zoo. This last glimpse of Sam in the Canadian wilds shows him matured but continuing the best habits of his boyhood. Sam remains curious and engaged with the life about him, as is reflected in his continuing to keep his journal and in his concluding each day's entry with a question indicating his continued openness to the new and to the world's unfailing wonders.

But the last sentence of the novel is Louis's. White knows how to conclude a novel, and this one ends as successfully as the other two works: Louis reflects on the relationship between reality and art, on their necessary coexistence and how, through their cooperative interchange, life is given meaning and structure. Preparing for sleep, Louis reflects on "how lucky he had been to solve his problems with music," a resolution bringing together reality and art in a cooperative interchange. This interchange allows Louis "to look forward to another night of sleep and another day tomorrow, and the fresh morning, and the light that returns with the day" (210). White's last book for children thus ends with the hope and the promise that every good children's book provides its youthful readers, situated as they are just at the beginning of life and just about to venture.

Critical Reception

The Trumpet of the Swan was reviewed in almost every major periodical on its appearance in 1970, largely because of E. B. White's reputation in American letters and because of the enormous success, both critically and commercially, of his two previous works for children. But this third work by White has subsequently been ignored by most critics of children's literature, who generally judge it much as White did—as a definite falling off from the artistic achievement of its two predecessors. Usually deprecatory in referring to his work, White was exceptionally so about *The Trumpet of the Swan*, noting in his letters how unusual it was for him to be writing about something he did not know firsthand and about a setting with which he was completely unfamiliar (*Letters*, 568, 583). He also repeatedly judged the book too long and seemed to apologize for writing it by explaining that it was undertaken to earn the money needed to pay off Katharine's medical expenses (*Letters*, 602, 584, 605). He was also saddened by Garth Williams's inability to provide the book's illustrations. He further argued that the book was often misjudged because frequently given to children too young for it: "I am always distressed when I hear of a second grade teacher reading 'The Trumpet' to her class—it really belongs more in the fourth and fifth grade level" (*Letters*, 645).

White's reservations about the book were not reflected in the initial critical responses to it penned by reviewers or by its considerable success in the marketplace. White noted with irony in November 1970 that *The Trumpet of the Swan*, then number one on the children's best-seller list, had bumped *Charlotte's Web* down to fourth place: "So there I was," he wrote to Hamish Hamilton, "betraying my own best friend, in cold type" (*Letters,* 608). The book's early reviews must have been as gratifying to White as was the book's early success with the public.

In an early review Polly Goodwin noted that White had poured into the book "a blend of tenderness, humor, wisdom and imagination that should guarantee it a long life in children's hearts" and that the book, consequently, "will enchant any age."[2] Zena Sutherland pronounced the plot of the book "diverting" and noted that "the half-tone illustrations reflect its humor," but, for her, "it is the style that makes the book a masterpiece."[3]

Perhaps the most important of the early reviews of *The Trumpet of the Swan* was that penned by John Updike in the 28 June 1970 *New York Times Book Review.* Updike, a former *New Yorker* colleague of White, asserted that this new book for children joins White's "two others on the shelf of classics" and, with them, shares an "inimitable tone," including "the simplicity that never condescends, the straight and earnest telling that happens upon, rather than veers into, comedy" (4). Updike noted an "accumulation of preposterous particulars" in the story of a mute trumpeter swan, and remarked on White's ability to keep the story buoyant, never once winking over the heads of his child audience and thereby turning the plot flimsy and causing it to tumble down. Updike further noted how White's eye and ear for the concrete particular "engenders textures of small surprise and delightful rightness" (5). Updike concluded by noting that the novel "glows with the primal ecstasies of space and flight, of night and day, of nurturing and maturing, of courtship and art" (24). White, according to his letter of response, was grateful for Updike's generous review.

Edmund Fuller, writing in the *Wall Street Journal,* noted that *The Trumpet of the Swan* joins White's two previous books in passing "the unfailing test of a fine book for children," specifically that children "shall really love it and that adults whose spirits have not withered on the vine shall enjoy it also." Fuller notes White's use of "a great deal of solid fact about Trumpeter Swans" and his "sound nature writing as a grounding for the fantasy."[4]

Calling the book "a prizewinner" and "a quiet joy," the reviewer for the *Christian Science Monitor* noted that *The Trumpet of the Swan* "is a work of poetry and humor, delicacy, and just sufficient echo of earth to be (however incredible) credible."[5] In the *Horn Book* Paul Heins noted White's "characteristically understated style, which extracts the essential humor from the most unprepossessing of situations"; Heins was, however, the first of the early reviewers to note that this book was "not . . . the equal of *Charlotte's Web*."[6]

Michele Murray in the *National Observer* summarized the novel as being about "the power of desire when it is linked to endurance and about the triumph over adversity of the bold and loving heart." She further noted, however, that "the novel is possibly too long to sustain the single tone of pastoral elegy in which it is written" and that it suffers in comparison to White's two previous books for children.[7] The *Instructor*, however, noted that the novel "is a worthy companion for *Charlotte's Web* and *Stuart Little*," for which "there is no higher praise."[8]

A second major review, penned by Edward Weeks in the *Atlantic Monthly*, noted that *The Trumpet of the Swan* bears repeated reading because the situations recounted in it, like those in *The Voyages of Doctor Dolittle*, "are so preposterous yet so plausible that the imagination is not content with the first impression; it must go back to relive and cherish the details." Weeks noted White's "special kind of genius" that allowed him "to create the perfect blend of fantasy and belief" in the novel. In an idiosyncratic judgment, Weeks proclaimed Louis's mother, the tart-mouthed swan addicted to reality and to puncturing the pompous verbosity of her husband, "the real heroine of the book."[9]

Amy Kellman in *Grade Teacher* observed that the novel's "nature-fantasy plot is sometimes strained, leaning too hard on the long hand of coincidence," and further noted the minimal characterization afforded the human characters in preference for the depiction of the swans, which she termed "fully realized creatures."[10] The reviewer for *America* read the novel from a different perspective, calling White's plot "a witty, credible, sophisticated story with remarkable swan dialogue."[11]

The most unabashedly positive review came from Jean Stafford, a friend of the Whites and a fellow contributor to the *New Yorker*, which published her review on 5 December 1970. Stafford called the publication of White's book "the big news of 1970" and termed the work "very nearly perfect." She predicted that Louis "is bound to be as dearly loved as Charlotte and Stuart Little."[12] The reviewer for the *New York Times Book Review* urged caution as to a premature judgment of the book, arguing that only children could decide whether or not this novel would join its two predecessors in the ranks of modern classics. The reviewer acknowledged the work's "felicitous, graceful telling" and "its charming improbability that Mr. White makes seem possible."[13] The reviewer for the *Times Literary Supplement*, however, dismissed the book with scant notice and faint praise, calling Louis "a sort of feathered Louis Armstrong" and observing coolly that "whether you care for this sort of thing or not depends on your sense of humour."[14]

Margot Hentoff, writing in the *New York Review of Books*, felt that the verdict was already in on the novel and that it was not as successful as either *Charlotte's Web* or *Stuart Little*. She also faulted the book for its lack of humor, noting that perhaps "the mutilation here is too serious, too possible; the swan flying through the air weighed down with trumpet and slate is too orthopedic an image to fuse easily with the freedom and beauty of a wild bird."[15] Thus, the initial reviews of *The Trumpet of the Swan* were by and large strongly positive, though a number of these reviewers distinguished, early on, many of the factors that prevent White's third novel for juveniles from equaling in quality his first two.

The Trumpet of the Swan has occasioned little critical commentary beyond the initial reviews following its publication in 1970, and what commentary it has evoked is usually to be found in general critical assessments of White's career. For example, in his book on White, Edward C. Sampson accorded *The Trumpet of the Swan* a scant paragraph, albeit a perceptive one. Sampson observed that White's third book for children was "a curious combination" of his first two in that Louis's adventures in Boston and Philadelphia remind a reader of some of the adventures encountered by Stuart on his journey, and the relation between Louis the Swan and Sam Beaver, a boy maturing into the world of adults, is reminiscent of the relationship between Wilbur and Fern. Despite these similarities and the inclusion in *The Trumpet of the Swan* of many of White's usual themes, Sampson observed that "the book never reaches the level of the first two," that "there is something missing." Perhaps, he argued further, a swan's stealing a trumpet or playing jazz in a nightclub is harder to accept than Stuart's or Wilbur's fanciful adventures. He judged the book "a success," however, and recognized that "for another writer it might have been a triumph" (103–104).

Roger Sale in *Fairy Tales and After* did not even judge the novel a qualified success. He lumped *The Trumpet of the Swan* with *Stuart Little* in a single dismissive sentence, asserting that neither book "is even good enough to be called a distinguished or considerable failure" (Sale, 258). Most readers of either book would feel that this judgment is too harsh. Peter F. Neumeyer's judgment in *Twentieth-Century Children's Writers* (1983) was more tempered: he admitted that though the novel "would be a splendid accomplishment for a lesser writer," it "is not usually thought to stand comparison with White's earlier two children's books," perhaps because the "genial commerce between animals and human beings seems, in this book, a bit more labored, less inevitable, than in the first two." Whereas White violates the laws of nature "ambiguously only, and with the greatest of restraint" in *Charlotte's Web*, he "seems to throw down the gauntlet almost with bravado with his implausible musical swan" who reads and writes, plays trumpet, and "moves easily in a world of human beings" (Neumeyer 1983a, 818).

In his expanded discussion of *The Trumpet of the Swan* in the *Dictionary of Literary Biography* volume on *American Writers for Children, 1900–1960*, Neumeyer observed that the difference between "the plausible and the implausible is not an issue whatsoever in this story" and that many of the adventures, at least in the book's first half, "seem arbitrary." Despite its faults, according to Neumeyer, the book is "adventurous, imaginative," and at times "touching" (Neumeyer 1983b, 347–48). In a later article, however, Neumeyer quoted from a letter White wrote in 1972 to his friend Reginald Allen in which he painfully admitted "how terribly ashamed and humiliated" he was about the novel, which he claimed to have published without having "tried hard enough" to perfect. Neumeyer, after studying the manuscripts for the novel, concluded instead that White "tried terribly hard" and that if the book is not his most successful, it was not for lack of exertion. Indeed, White's notes, worksheets, and prodigious research indicate that he "tried too hard." "He was buried under his sources and his research," concluded Neumeyer: the problem with the novel "is that White did not personally, intimately, know a Louis, nor trumpeter swans, nor the Philadelphia Zoo, as he knew most profoundly his own pig, his own spider, and his own barn."[16]

By far the most significant discussion of the book is to be found in Scott Elledge's literary biography of White. Elledge challenged White's assertion that despite the novel's fantastic plot, nothing in it violates authentic swan behavior. Elledge objected that "the natural behavior of the trumpeter swan hardly shows in the plot" or in White's "anthropomorphic characterization of Louis" (346). Instead, Elledge argued, whatever truth the story contains is a reflection of White's own life experiences. Thus Elledge provided a biographical reading of the work, including tracing many of the novel's scenes to similar ones garnered during White's youthful trip across the country in his Model T and during his years working at Camp Otter in Ontario. According to Elledge, White's memories of the Horace Waters Piano Company colored his portrayal of the music store in Billings, and his recollections of his Victorian father are transmuted into his portrayal of the old cob.

But Elledge did more than provide autobiographical parallels with the novel. His judgment that this novel "is less moving than White's preceding children's stories because its humor has fewer serious undertones, its sense of life is less profound, and (most important) its characters are less convincing" has about it the ring of accuracy, as does Elledge's assertion that the book primarily concerns "the process of winning the independence of adulthood" (347). This serious theme, however, is treated more in the mode of "musical comedy" than in the manner of a thorough exploration of the maturation process. Elledge concluded that the book can be considered "an extraordinary children's story" primarily because of the treatment "of the relationship between father and son": "Louis's sense of responsibility for his father's honor, and Sam's love for a father from whom he must distance himself, are the truest and most convincing emotions we meet in *The Trumpet of the Swan*" (348).

Elledge concluded his perceptive discussion of the novel by noting that in it White speaks to young people "not just for an endangered species, but for an endangered civilization and an endangered planet" (348). *The Trumpet of the Swan* is White's clearest enunciation of the dangers that lie before human beings as one interdependent species among many and his clearest declaration of hope for the preservation and continuance of the beautiful world he dearly loved and always saw as steeped in wonder. This is the vision of all three of White's books for children, and it is, perhaps, articulated most clearly in this last one.

Chapter Five

"What Do Our Hearts Treasure?": A Retrospective

At the outset of his career as a writer of children's novels, White published two seminal essays. In "A Boy I Knew" (1940) and in "Children's Books" (1938) he provided an inventory of the major themes and issues that inform his children's books and codified his early critical speculations concerning the writing of literature for juveniles. These essays offer the reader of White's works a near complete summary of his major themes and critical approaches; they thus also provide a convenient coda for a consideration of his works for children.

Surprisingly, "A Boy I Knew" is seldom referred to in White criticism, perhaps because he published it in *Reader's Digest* and not the usual journals reserved for his most significant statements in essay form; nor did he gather it into any of the numerous collections of his essays and shorter works published during his lifetime. The date of the essay is significant: it appeared five years before the publication of *Stuart Little* in 1945, just as White was entering middle age and was simultaneously beginning to think about writing for children. Though not well known, this essay is nevertheless a crucial one in understanding the genesis of the major themes and issues informing *Stuart Little*, *Charlotte's Web*, and *The Trumpet of the Swan*.

The essay represents White's attempt to reconnect with the boy he once was, to understand what was important to that boy, what that boy's interests and concerns were, and how he looked at life. In "A Boy I Knew" White circles the ring of time, alternately seeing his father in himself and himself in his son. "A Boy I Knew" is a moving discussion of what has remained important during the 30 years that separate man and boy, a reexamination of those values and ideals that connect the adult writing the essay with the boy he writes about.

What White attempts in this essay is, perhaps, a necessary antecedent for anyone who hopes to succeed in writing for children. It represents that effort to connect again with a childhood long past so as to achieve an authentic voice—one that will allow White to speak to children of issues important to them and in language they will listen to. Without this connection to the boy he once was, as White claims, "I should indeed be lost," certainly as a writer for children.[1] In 1952, the year he published *Charlotte's Web*, White referred to a comment by P. L. Travers, author of the Mary Poppins books, that "anyone who writes for children successfully is probably writing for one child—namely the child that is himself." According to White, "this comes close to the truth, and if any 'barrier' operates it is the internal barrier that separates the child from the man" (*Letters*, 368). In a 1974 interview at what turned out to be the end of his career as a writer for children, White was reiterating what he had come to realize at the beginning of his career, that "it is a great help" for the writer of children's books "if one has managed never really to grow up" (*Pied Piper*, 127). This essay is White's attempt to remove the barrier between child and adult at the beginning of his intent to write for children.

"A Boy I Knew" offers a compendium of issues and concerns—for both phantom boy and reflective writer—that White later considers and develops in his children's novels. Each of White's works for children—indeed, every piece of writing he produced—can be seen as an attempt to answer two crucial questions. The first is asked of the children in his fifth-grade classroom by Stuart Little as substitute teacher: "How many of you know what's important?" (92). The second question served as the title for a 1966 Christmas essay penned in Florida: "What Do Our Hearts Treasure?"[2] In "A Boy I Knew," White offers answers to these questions—answers he knew instinctively as a boy and that he was to formulate more fully as an adult.

"A Boy I Knew" opens with a description of that strange suspension of time that White also described so movingly in "Once More to the Lake," perhaps his best essay. His own father, his son, and he himself exchange positions in a "transmigration, one generation with another" (33), so that White sees himself in his son and, alternately, in his father. This essay opening prefigures the major issues in *The Trumpet of the Swan* and in *Charlotte's Web*, both of which deal with maturation, the passage of time, and generational interactions. *The Trumpet of the Swan*, for example, focuses on father-son relationships between Louis and the old cob and between Sam Beaver and his father and the necessity to clarify those relationships during the course of the maturation process. The issue of maturation is also featured in *Charlotte's Web*, with its depiction of Wilbur's coming into competence against the great cyclical backdrop of the rotation of the seasons and the subsequent generations of Charlotte's progeny. "A Boy I Knew" thus anticipates these novels in its discussion of the swift passage of time, the bittersweet process of growing into maturity, the great wheeling cycle of change and growth everywhere celebrated in *Charlotte's Web* and employed as the central structural device of *The Trumpet of the Swan*.

In one of the most beautiful passages in "A Boy I Knew," White recounts a night journey he once made with his son who slept in the lower berth of a Pullman car they shared. White awoke early in the morning to observe his son, in whom he now again catches a glimpse of his youthful self, "ingesting the moving world" in wonder (33). The boy, conjoining father and son here, looks out just as the sky is growing light and absorbs "the incredible wonder of fields, houses, bakery trucks, the before-breakfast world, tasting the sweetness and scariness of things seen and only half understood" (34). Settings, themes, and even stylistic devices used in White's children's books are clearly foreshadowed in this passage. Dawn, for example, with its pale, cold light, is Stuart Little's and Louis's favorite time of day, a time of reflection and meditation upon the world's mysteries. This "before-breakfast world" described in the passage is also the setting for the opening of *Charlotte's Web*, the first chapter of which is entitled "Before Breakfast." In addition, the listing of "incredible wonders" in the passage is the central stylistic device White would later employ in *Charlotte's Web*, which almost obsessively inventories the variety and abundance of the world's beauties and wonders. "The sweetness and scariness" of the world that White writes of in "A Boy I Knew" provides an early indication of the bittersweetness of the ending of *Charlotte's Web*, with its poignant recognition of life as an alternation of loss and gain. White's great themes for the children's books are thus everywhere nascent in this 1940 essay.

This boy that once was White knew "the satisfactions of life's interminable quest." In passages that essentially summarize the central import of *Stuart Little*, White describes the boy that was himself as "always looking for something that had no name and no whereabouts, and not finding it." Like Stuart on his lifelong quest for beauty and meaning, this phantom boy "either knew instinctively or he soon found out that seeking was more instructive than finding, that journeys were more rewarding than destinations" (34). In addition, this boy, like the protean Stuart, "traveled light, so that he was always ready for a change of pace or of direction and was in a position to explore any opportunity and become a part of any situation, unhampered" (34). In this passage from "A Boy I Knew," White seems already to have formulated the central quest structuring his first work for children, *Stuart Little*. White further describes the boy in his essay as "saddled with an unusual number of worries," an autobiographical situation played out in the children's novels as well (34). White burdened each of the central characters in these novels with trials beyond the common ones usually associated with their positions in life. Stuart, perhaps the most encumbered of all White's juvenile heroes, is a two-inch mouse-boy born into a human family, negotiating whatever he encounters in his strange life with pluck, aplomb, and an underlying faith that he will win through. Wilbur is born a runt and is burdened throughout the novel with a Damoclean death sentence, while Louis, hatched a trumpeter swan, is mute and thus cannot enter fully into the life of his species. Though "saddled with an unusual number of worries," like White as a boy, these three central characters win through to a position where they can live fully and richly. The essay thus foretells the most significant character features of White's three unlikely heroes.

Though this boy featured in "A Boy I Knew" had to negotiate worries beyond the usual compass, he was buoyed by "a faith nourished by the natural world rather than by the supernatural or the spiritual," so that a lakeside granite rock, "upholstered with lichen" becomes the boy's pew, "and the sermon went on forever" (34). This passage explicitly prepares for Stuart's Thoreauvian telephone repairman who rhapsodizes with a religious fervor about the wonders of traveling north and also for the great secular doxology that is *Charlotte's Web*. In *The Trumpet of the Swan* Sam Beaver has a similar experience of "natural religion": while watching the swans, Sam "had the same good feeling some people get when they are sitting in church" (18). Everywhere in his books for children White infuses this "faith nourished by the natural world"—a faith helping to counter the worries of the boy White had been and of the characters central in his children's books.

Like Fern in the early chapters of *Charlotte's Web* and like Stuart throughout his novel, the phantom boy in White's essay "was an idealist of shocking proportions" (34). Indeed, *Stuart Little* features a character who never loses this idealism, who uses it as a road map for life's journey, resisting the seductions of the secure life and the accommodations necessitated by job, marriage, family, and social position. Fern's innate idealism allows her father a momentary glimpse of a springtime, innocent world incorporating ideal justice. Fern, of course, loses this initial radical idealism in order to establish a place firmly in the human community, ruled by expediency and practicality. This necessary conflict between the ideal and the real played out in White's books for juveniles is given its first tentative explorations in this seminal essay written at the beginning of White's career as a children's novelist.

Schools and classrooms are prominently featured in *Stuart Little* and *The Trumpet of the Swan*. White's treatment of the classroom and of education for young children is partially satirical, involving an implicit commentary on its dullness and its lack of relevance in light of the larger issues children will grow up to face. Thus, Stuart subverts the classroom and radically revises the traditional curriculum when he substitutes for a sick teacher. In another classroom in *The Trumpet of the Swan*, Sam Beaver's teacher, Miss Snug, grants the logic of her students' objections to the rigidity of traditional math problems. These concerns are prefigured in "A Boy I Knew," where White says of his 16 years in public schools that he "was uneasy and full of dread the entire time." Largely because he hated being called upon to speak in assembly, "every term was a nightmare of suspense" for him (35). In the children's books White revises the public school he so dreaded as a boy, humanizing it so as to give every student a voice and the confidence to employ that voice in the classroom.

"A Boy I Knew" is, then, a quarry that White mined for scenes, themes, and incidents later incorporated in the children's novels. A particularly rich vein in that essay, one exploited extensively in White's books for juveniles, involves the role animals played in the life of the boy White had been. This boy "felt for animals a kinship he never felt for people"; this phantom boy thus serves as an antecedent for Sam Beaver, who sits, watching quietly the hatching of the cygnets, and especially for Fern Arable. Indeed, Fern as observer of animal life in the barnyard is exactly prefigured by the boy White resurrects in his essay: "The total number of hours he spent just standing watching animals . . . would be impossible to estimate; and it would be hard to say what he got out of it" (35).

This boy also "felt a sympathetic vibration with earth's renascence" in spring (35)—a vibration that was to resonate throughout the springtime world of *Charlotte's Web*, especially in the hatching of the goose's eggs in chapter 6 and the later hatching of Charlotte's eggs in the returning spring of the book's closure. These important plot episodes are prepared for in "A Boy I Knew," where White attributes a "stange compulsion" in the boy he once was "to assist the processes of incubation and germination, as though without him they might fail and the earth grow old and die." This boy symbolically assures this renewal by setting a hen, for to him "a miracle was essentially egg-shaped" (35). White's boyish compulsion to ensure the seasonal processes of renewed life as featured in the essay finds its direct corollary in all of his works for children, from Stuart Little's concluding journey north, initiated at the dawn of a new day and a renewed world, to *The Trumpet of the Swan*'s concluding summary of springtime renewal in the successive seasonal hatchings of Louis and Serena's cygnets. This theme finds its most beautiful and moving articulation in *Charlotte's Web*, however, a novel that can be seen as a ritual of affirmation, a verification of continuous creation, an assurance that regeneration and the earth's renascence are cyclical and constant. This assurance of renewal is, perhaps, the most important of all issues for White as a writer and underlies all of his works for children.

White concludes the essay with a final allusion to the ultimately unattainable quest for beauty and love. According to White, this quest is no less than a human being's primary endeavor to make life meaningful and worth living. As White notes in "A Boy I Knew," the phantom boy's "search for beauty was always vaguely identified with his search for the ideal of love" (36), a description that perfectly summarizes the essential plots of *Stuart Little* and *The Trumpet of the Swan*. It also captures Charlotte's meaning when she tells Wilbur that she helped him because she "was trying to lift up [her] life a trifle," to give her life meaning and validity beyond the daily physical requirements of merely living in the world (164). Charlotte's quest for her life's meaning ends in love and generosity to another in need.

"A Boy I Knew" thus provides both preamble and coda for White's works for children. The essay is equally a preparatory piece and a summation of the major themes, issues, and character types in *Stuart Little*, *Charlotte's Web*, and *The Trumpet of the Swan*. The essay provides an excellent place to begin any reading of White's novels for juveniles and also serves as an appropriate point for a concluding retrospective.

In "Children's Books," written two years before "A Boy I Knew" and published as a "One Man's Meat" essay in *Harper's*, White commented in a casual way about his reading of children's literature. If "A Boy I Knew" is a rehearsal of the themes he would later use, "Children's Books" represents his first attempt at a critical or theoretical understanding of those elements that make for successful children's literature. White's critical position in regard to this literature was more intuitive than clearly formulated or rigorously informed. Rarely does he theorize about children's literature or offer a consistent critical position. Nonetheless, in this 1938 essay he was clearly investigating the field he was soon to enter.

The essay was prompted by the more than 200 review copies of children's books lying around White's Maine farmhouse, sent to Katharine for her annual December article for the *New Yorker* on the best children's books published that year. Though White laments the overrunning of his household—the books are literally everywhere he looks—he nevertheless claims to have come "to know something about children's books from living so close to them" and concludes that such close physical contact "with the field of juvenile literature leads me to the conclusion that it must be a lot of fun to write for children—reasonably easy work, perhaps even important work."[3] With this realization, and with the encouragement of Anne Carroll Moore, former librarian of the New York Public Library's children's collection, White embarked on his career as a writer for children, though he was to find that writing his children's novels was far from being "reasonably easy work" or even much fun.

In this essay White attempts to understand his task as a writer for children. Many of the children's books scattered throughout his rooms produced in him a mild distaste and provided him with examples of what to avoid in his own works. For example, he subtly satirizes the varieties of exotic places, periods, and objects featured in the children's books under his scrutiny. The Valley of the Euphrates, Czechoslovakia, the Scotland of the MacGregors, the depression of 1817 on the Ohio River, Ecuador, Bali, yaks in London—all these provide settings and subjects for the review copies he peruses. One writer, he recounts, apparently "shut his eyes, opened an atlas, and let his finger fall on the Louisiana bayous" (20). White implies that strangeness of geographical scope or focus seems, in so many of these works, to be an end in itself.

White's implicit criticism of this penchant for exotic locales and offbeat topics later evolves into a clear understanding of setting and subject in his own works. His settings eschew the extraordinary: the Littles' New York apartment could be next door to the ones White inhabited for so many years; Stuart's northerly route up the criss-crossing roads of New England was negotiated by the Whites on their frequent trips to their farmhouse in Maine. *Charlotte's Web* features the usual animals one would find on a farm like White's own. And Louis, most at home in the Canadian wilds White loved, nevertheless accommodates himself to life in large cities. White's settings are decidedly ordinary, making the miracles of love and friendship and maturation that occur within them so much more extraordinary and moving.

White also noted, with deflating humor, the "polyglot character of this literature," the "smattering of many tongues and dialects" in the books he has been reviewing. His perusal of the children's books spilling out of cupboards in his farmhouse has, according to White, "left me gibbering" (21). Another feature of these books that White notes is their penchant for scientific accuracy. Books for children, he observes, reflect the period in which they are published. Since science seems to dominate life in twentieth-century America, "books for young people are largely scientific in their approach to their subject matter, whatever it may be." White further observes that even "cute animals of the nonsense school move against impeccable backgrounds of natural history." "Even a female ant," he continues, "who is sufficiently irregular to be able to talk English lays her eggs at the proper time and in the accepted manner" (22). This crucial observation precedes White's own approach to his talking animals: even though his animal characters interact according to human paradigms, they are subject to the natural imperatives of their species. Charlotte lives her season, constructs her egg sac, and dies on schedule despite the lachrymose responses of child readers; Louis's loquacious parents nest in remote Canadian pools, are stalked by predators, and migrate when it is their time. White's early observations of this realism at the heart of the animal fantasies he was then reading determined the dominant approach to the animals he was to take in his own works.

White also found the stuffiness of adult morality to congest a majority of these books for children. He noted that many of the moral truisms and "grown-up conclusions" about life and the way of the world "often rest on perilously soft bottom," and he confessed that often, when "trying to act like a parent," he would tell his son things he himself "didn't thoroughly comprehend," urging his son "toward conventional attitudes of mind and spirit [he] only half believed in and would [himself] gladly chuck overboard" (23).

This early aversion to moral preaching in children's books explains the absence of didacticism in White's own books for juveniles. As Edward C. Sampson rightly observed, the stories of Stuart, Charlotte, and Louis "are refreshingly free of studied attempts to improve young minds" (95). Frequently in his letters, White would insist that youthful readers—and their teachers as well—read his books without searching for messages or moral implications. To Gene Deitch, a director then considering a film adaptation of *Charlotte's Web*, White wrote on 12 January 1971 that he hoped Deitch was not intending "to turn *Charlotte's Web* into a moral tale. It is not that at all." It is, he continued, "an *appreciative* story, and there is quite a difference." He concluded by asserting that the work "is essentially amoral, because animals are essentially amoral, and I respect them, and I think this respect is implicit in the tale." Calling Templeton "the perfect opportunist and a great gourmand," White implored Deitch not "to elevate Templeton to sainthood" or to some kind of negative exemplar of moral lessons (*Letters,* 613).

White concluded his observations concerning children's books with an inventory of the pitfalls suffered by many of the writers whose works he was considering. He saw a large number of these books as being "dull, prosy stuff, by writers who mistake oddity for fantasy and whose wildly beating wings never get them an inch off the ground" (23). Some of these books White cited as "patronizing" and others as "mushy." White was clearly aware, then, of the difficulties facing writers who select children as their primary audiences—difficulties of finding an appropriate tone and voice, of selecting an engaging subject matter, and of avoiding sentimentality, a too-studied whimsy, and false sprightliness. On this point, White was adamant, first to last. In his 1970 acceptance speech for the Laura Ingalls Wilder Award, given every five years by the American Library Association, White admired the "natural simplicity and goodness" of Wilder's prose, in which "there are no traces of condescension—no patronage, no guile, and no cuteness," only "a dramatic force that derives from honesty and accuracy" (349). Again, in his 1974 interview he spoke disapprovingly of those who "write *down* to children": "That way lies disaster," he concluded (127).

In "A Boy I Knew" and in "Children's Books" White rehearses the themes he will develop in his works for juveniles and scans the field to learn more about the nature of writing for children. Although he claimed in the 1974 interview that "I am not well-read in contemporary literature for children and am not in a good position to comment on other authors" (131), his 1938 essay surveying the books his wife was reviewing suggests otherwise, at least early on. These two essays provide a comprehensive review of themes and theories operative in what some contemporary critics have come to consider White's most important literary achievement—one that was to influence writers of children's books to follow. White's works were recognized for their unconventional inclusions from the first, occasioning, for example, the vigorous censure of Anne Carroll Moore, former head of the children's collection at the New

York Public Library and one of the most informed and influential readers of works for children of her time. Her objections to White's first two works for children, especially *Stuart Little*, stemmed from White's intentional violation of an orthodox set of literary conventions governing writing for children that Moore had obviously internalized. As has been recorded, she objected to Stuart's anomalous arrival in a human family, for example, and especially to Stuart's inconclusive quest; these features were anathema to Moore because they broke with expected patterns and conventions in children's books.

The outcry against Charlotte's remarkably unsentimentalized death in White's second novel for juveniles stemmed from the same sense of a broken taboo in children's books—namely, that characters presented as fully alive and with whom children make a vital connection while reading must not die, especially in such a stark, uncushioned way. Too, Louis's slicing of his webbed feet in *The Trumpet of the Swan* and his being made to share so fully in his father's moral dilemma was a bold inclusion in books for young readers. This willingness on White's part to deviate from the expected codes and to experiment with plot construction and event inclusion not usual in children's stories at the same time reflected what was then occurring in the writing of juvenile literature and freed those who followed him to even greater experimentation and bolder innovation.

White is poised historically right before the post-1960s "New Realism" of which his first two books serve as harbingers. This New Realism represents a change in understanding of what is appropriate in children's books. Issues like drugs, divorce, death, gangs, familial and social violence, child abuse, racial prejudice, and sex began to appear with greater frankness during and after the 1960s, whereas before these matters had been considered inappropriate subjects for young readers. Though White's works at the mid-point of the century seem now in every way unobjectionable to contemporary readers, at the time of their publication they were seen as departures from convention.

Thus, in his own mildly iconoclastic way, White helped to prepare for the greater liberties to follow, the authorial freedoms now exercised in a literature for juveniles considerably revitalized by the recognition that children do not exist in golden envelopes of security and protection, that they are, instead, engaged in the complexities of life and inhabit a world alternately beautiful and dangerous, salutary and seriously problematic by turns, and that their literature, to be responsive to children's lives, must recognize and fully address these complexities and dualities.

Though White was himself aware of some of these deviations from usual codes governing works for children, he seems not to have recognized the extent of his subsequent influence, perhaps because he did not consider himself to be primarily a writer of children's stories. He was adamant in reminding his 1974 interviewers that for "every children's book I've written, I have written four adult books" (130). Nonetheless, many contemporary literary critics consider his contributions to children's literature his most significant literary achievements and, along with a number of his personal essays, the basis for an enduring reputation. In his August 1970 acceptance speech for the Laura Ingalls Wilder Award, White noted that "in the world of children's books, I am a wanderer. It is a strange world—one I never seriously considered entering. I arrived there by stumbling into it, as one stumbles into a new place in the forest after losing one's way" (349). E. B. White was a man who always acknowledged his luck. He did so at the beginning and at the end of this acceptance speech, claiming to be "thankful that I was a book writer lucky enough to have had time to write" several books for children and that his life "has been greatly enriched" by having done so (351). For generations of child and adult readers alike, the luck has been on their side.

Notes and References

Preface

1. "Laura Ingalls Wilder Acceptance," *Horn Book* 46 (August 1970): 349; hereafter cited in text.
2. Peter F. Neumeyer, "E. B. White," in *Twentieth-Century Children's Writers*, ed. D. L. Kirkpatrick (New York: St. Martin's Press, 1983), 817; hereafter cited in text as 1983a.
3. Eudora Welty, "E. B. White's *Charlotte's Web*," in *The Eye of the Story* (New York: Random House, 1978), 205; hereafter cited in text.
4. John Rowe Townsend, *Written for Children* (Philadelphia: J. B. Lippincott, 1974), 242; hereafter cited in text.
5. John Updike, "The Trumpet of the Swan," *New York Times Book Review*, 28 June 1970, 4.

Chapter One

1. "Notes and Comment," *New Yorker*, 17 February 1945, 13.
2. *Letters of E. B. White*, ed. Dorothy Lobrano Guth (New York: Harper & Row, 1976), 302; hereafter cited in text as *Letters*.
3. Scott Elledge, *E. B. White: A Biography* (New York: Norton, 1984), 88; hereafter cited in text. Quoted from a letter from White to Alice Burchfield, 26 March 1923.
4. In the essay "The City and the Land" White recounts this early journalistic discovery of a "Mr. Volente," his alter ego. See *The Second Tree from the Corner* (New York: Harper, 1954), 214.
5. *One Man's Meat* (New York: Harper, 1942), Foreword; hereafter cited in text as *Meat*.
6. Henry David Thoreau, *Walden* (New York: Harper & Row, 1961), 2.
7. "Visitors to the Pond," *New Yorker*, 23 May 1953, 28.
8. *Essays of E. B. White* (New York: Harper & Row, 1977), 195; hereafter cited in text as *Essays*.
9. "Notes and Comment," *New Yorker*, 24 January 1953, 19.
10. "A Boy I Knew," *Reader's Digest*, June 1940, 35.
11. "Danbury Fair," *New Yorker*, 18 October 1930, 9.
12. Brendan Gill, *Here at the New Yorker* (New York: Random House, 1975), 290; hereafter cited in text.
13. "Notes and Comment," *New Yorker*, 25 November 1933, 10.

14. Ralph Ingersoll, "The *New Yorker*," *Fortune*, August 1934, 85, 86, 97, 152.

15. "Notes and Comment," *New Yorker*, 17 February 1945, 13.

16. *The Wild Flag* (Boston: Houghton Mifflin, 1946).

17. *The Elements of Style*, 3d ed. (New York: Macmillan, 1979), 69; hereafter cited in text as *Style*.

Chapter Two

1. "The Librarian Said It Was Bad for Children," *New York Times*, 6 March 1966, sec. X, p. 19; hereafter cited in text.

2. Peter F. Neumeyer, "*Stuart Little:* The Manuscripts," *Horn Book* (September–October 1988): 600; hereafter cited in text as "Manuscripts."

3. Gerald Weales, "The Designs of E. B. White," in *Authors and Illustrators of Children's Books*, ed. Miriam Hoffman and Eva Samuels (New York: R. R. Bowker, 1972), 408; hereafter cited in text.

4. *Stuart Little* (New York: Harper & Row, 1973), 1; hereafter cited in text.

5. Peter F. Neumeyer, "E. B. White," in *Dictionary of Literary Biography*, vol. 22, *American Writers for Children, 1900–1960*, ed. John Cech (Detroit: Gale Research, 1983), 342; hereafter cited in text as 1983b.

6. *The Pied Pipers: Interviews with the Influential Creators of Children's Literature*, ed. Justin Wintle and Emma Fisher (New York: Paddington Press, 1974), 127; hereafter cited in text as *Pied Pipers*.

7. *The History of Tom Thumbe*, ed. Curt F. Buhler (Evanston, Ill.: Northwestern University Press, 1965), 5.

8. Malcolm Cowley, "Stuart Little: Or New York through the Eyes of a Mouse," *New York Times Book Review*, 28 October 1945, 7; hereafter cited in text.

9. Marion Glastonbury, "E. B. White's Unexpected Items of Enchantment," *Children's Literature in Education* (May 1973): 6; hereafter cited in text.

10. Ursula Nordstrom, "Stuart, Wilbur, Charlotte: A Tale of Tales," *New York Times Book Review*, 12 May 1974, 8, 10.

11. *Saturday Review*, 10 November 1945, 56.

12. Rosemary Carr Benét, *Saturday Review*, 8 December 1945, 26.

13. *Horn Book* 21 (November 1945): 455.

14. *Time*, 31 December 1945, 92.

15. *Kirkus Review* 13 (15 July 1945): 314.

16. Edward C. Sampson, *E. B. White* (New York: Twayne Publishers, 1974), 95; hereafter cited in text.

17. Margaret Blount, *Animal Land: The Creatures of Children's Fiction* (New York: William Morrow, 1975), 240; hereafter cited in text.

18. Roger Sale, *Fairy Tales and After: From Snow White to E. B. White* (Cambridge, Mass.: Harvard University Press, 1978), 258; hereafter cited in text.

Chapter Three

1. Peter F. Neumeyer, "The Creation of *Charlotte's Web*: From Drafts to Book," *Horn Book* (October 1982): 491.
2. Peter F. Neumeyer, "What Makes a Good Children's Book?: The Texture of *Charlotte's Web*," *South Atlantic Bulletin* (May 1979): 73; hereafter cited in text.
3. *Charlotte's Web* (New York: Harper Collins, 1952, 1980), 43; hereafter cited in text.
4. Perry Nodelman, "Text as Teacher: The Beginning of *Charlotte's Web*," *Children's Literature* (1985): 116.
5. Sonia Landes, "E. B. White's *Charlotte's Web:* Caught in the Web," in *Touchstones: Reflections on the Best in Children's Literature*, vol. 1 (West Lafayette, Ind.: Children's Literature Association, 1985), 270.
6. Bennett Cerf, *Saturday Review*, 15 November 1952, 6.
7. *Booklist* 49 (1 September 1952): 2.
8. P. L. Travers, "Tangible Magic," *New York Herald-Tribune Book Review*, pt. 2, 16 November 1952, 1, 38.
9. *Times Literary Supplement,* 28 November 1952, 7.
10. Edward Weeks, "The Peripatetic Reviewer," *Atlantic Monthly,* 190 (December 1952), 88.
11. Margaret Ford Kieran, *Atlantic Monthly,* December 1952, 101.
12. Anne Carroll Moore, "The Three Owls' Notebook," *Horn Book* 28 (December 1952): 394.
13. John Griffith, "*Charlotte's Web:* A Lonely Fantasy of Love," *Children's Literature* (1980): 111, 113.
14. Janice M. Alberghene, "Writing in *Charlotte's Web*," *Children's Literature in Education* 16 (1985): 33.
15. Norton D. Kinghorn, "The Real Miracle of *Charlotte's Web*," *Children's Literature Association Quarterly* 11 (1986): 5.
16. Ashraf H. A. Rushdy, "'The Miracle of the Web': Community, Desire, and Narrativity in *Charlotte's Web*," *Lion and the Unicorn* 15 (1991): 57.

Chapter Four

1. *The Trumpet of the Swan* (New York: Harper & Row, 1970), 4; hereafter cited in text.
2. Polly Goodwin, "Ages 8 to 12," *Chicago Sunday Tribune Children's Book World,* 17 May 1970, 5.
3. Zena Sutherland, *Saturday Review,* 27 June 1970, 39.
4. Edmund Fuller, "E. B. White's Tale of Swans and Children Delights and Instructs," *Wall Street Journal,* 14 July 1970, 16.
5. "Another Louis Takes Up the Horn," *Christian Science Monitor,* 25 July 1970, 15.

6. Paul Heins, *Horn Book* (August 1970): 391.

7. Michele Murray, "Mr. White's *Trumpet of the Swan* Is an Elegiac If One-Key Pastorale, " *National Observer,* 10 August 1970, 21.

8. *Instructor* 80 (August–September 1970): 173.

9. Edward Weeks, *Atlantic Monthly,* September 1970, 123–24.

10. Amy Kellman, *Grade Teacher* 88 (November 1970): 120.

11. *America* 123 (5 December 1970): 496.

12. Jean Stafford, *New Yorker,* 5 December 1970, 217–18.

13. *New York Times Book Review,* 6 December 1970, 58.

14. "Fish-Scales, Fur and Feathers," *Times Literary Supplement,* 11 December 1970, 1458.

15. Margot Hentoff, "Little Private Lives," *New York Review of Books,* 17 December 1970, 11.

16. Peter F. Neumeyer, "The Creation of E. B. White's *The Trumpet of the Swan:* The Manuscripts," *Horn Book* (January–February 1985): 28.

Chapter Five

1. "A Boy I Knew," *Reader's Digest,* June 1940, 33; hereafter cited in text.

2. "What Do Our Hearts Treasure?" in *Essays of E. B. White.*

3. "Children's Books," in *One Man's Meat,* 19–20; hereafter cited in text.

Selected Bibliography

PRIMARY WORKS

Is Sex Necessary? Or, Why You Feel the Way You Do. With James Thurber. 1929.
  New York: Harper & Brothers, 1950.
The Lady Is Cold. New York: Harper & Brothers, 1929.
Ho Hum: Newsbreaks from the New Yorker. New York: Farrar & Rinehart, 1931.
Another Ho Hum: More Newsbreaks from the New Yorker. New York: Farrar &
  Rinehart, 1932.
Alice through the Cellophane. New York: John Day Co., 1933.
Every Day Is Saturday. New York: Harper & Brothers, 1934.
Farewell to Model T. New York: G. P. Putnam's Sons, 1936.
The Fox of Peapack and Other Poems. New York: Harper & Brothers, 1938.
Quo Vadimus? Or, The Case for the Bicycle. New York: Harper & Brothers, 1939.
A Subtreasury of American Humor. Edited by E. B. White and Katharine White.
  New York: Coward MacCann, 1941.
One Man's Meat. 1942. New York: Harper & Brothers, 1982.
Stuart Little. New York: Harper & Brothers, 1945.
The Wild Flag. Boston: Houghton Mifflin, 1946.
Here Is New York. New York: Harper & Brothers, 1949.
Charlotte's Web. New York: Harper, 1952.
The Second Tree from the Corner. New York: Harper, 1954, 1962.
The Elements of Style. By William Strunk, Jr. With revisions, an introduction, and a
  new chapter on writing by E. B. White. 1959. New York: Macmillan, 1972.
The Points of My Compass. New York: Harper & Row, 1962.
An E. B. White Reader. Edited by William W. Watt and Robert W. Bradford.
  New York: Harper & Row, 1966.
The Trumpet of the Swan. New York: Harper & Row, 1970.
Letters of E. B. White. Edited by Dorothy Lobrano Guth. New York: Harper &
  Row, 1976.
Essays of E. B. White. New York: Harper & Row, 1977.
Poems and Sketches of E. B. White. New York: Harper & Row, 1981.
Writings from the New Yorker, 1925–1976. Edited by Rebecca M. Dale. New
  York: Harper Collins, 1990.

Collections

E. B. White's papers are held in the Cornell University Library Department of
  Rare Books in Ithaca, New York. Katharine White's papers are held in the
  Bryn Mawr College Library's Special Collections, Bryn Mawr, Pennsylvania.

SECONDARY WORKS

Anderson, A. J. *E. B. White: A Bibliography*. Metuchen, N.J.: Scarecrow Press, 1978. A bibliography particularly useful for its inclusion of secondary sources, such as book reviews of White's works.

Elledge, Scott. *E. B. White: A Biography*. New York: W. W. Norton, 1984. The standard biography.

Hall, Katharine Romans. *E. B. White: A Bibliographic Catalogue of Printed Materials in the Department of Rare Books, Cornell University Library*. New York: Garland Publishing, 1979. A bibliography providing complete information concerning White's published books and articles. No secondary sources are included.

Neumeyer, Peter F. "The Creation of *Charlotte's Web*: From Drafts to Book." *Horn Book* (October 1982): 489–97 (part 1); (December 1982): 617–25 (part 2). Explores the composing process and evolution of White's most important work.

———. "The Creation of E. B. White's *The Trumpet of the Swan*: The Manuscripts." *Horn Book* (January–February 1985): 17-28. Explores the composing process of White's last novel.

———. "E. B. White." In *Dictionary of Literary Biography: American Writers for Children, 1900-1960*. Vol. 22. Detroit: Gale Research, 1983. A succinct biographical and critical examination of White's life and career as a writer for children.

———. "E. B. White." In *Twentieth-Century Children's Writers*, edited by D. L. Kirkpatrick. New York: St. Martin's Press, 1983. A brief but complete survey of White's works and career as a writer for juveniles.

———. "*Stuart Little*: The Manuscripts." *Horn Book* (September–October 1988): 593–600. An examination of White's composing process through the manuscripts of his first novel for children.

Nodelman, Perry. "Text as Teacher: The Beginning of *Charlotte's Web*." *Children's Literature* (1985): 109–27. An insightful examination of the structure of the novel.

Russell, Isabel. *Katharine and E. B. White: An Affectionate Memoir*. New York: W. W. Norton, 1988. A portrait of the Whites in their last days by a former employee.

Sampson, Edward C. *E. B. White*. New York: Twayne Publishers, 1974. The only full-length study of White's works.

Wintle, Justin, and Emma Fisher, eds. "E. B. White." In *The Pied Pipers: Interviews with the Influential Creators of Children's Literature*. New York: Paddington Press, 1974. White assesses his career as a writer for children and discusses his works.

Index

The Author

Lucien L. Agosta received his B.A. from Louisiana State University and his M.A. and Ph.D. from the University of Texas at Austin. He taught at Kansas State University, Manhattan, from 1977 to 1987 and is currently professor of English at California State University, Sacramento, where he teaches literature for children as well as nineteenth-century British literature. He has published a book on the American writer and illustrator Howard Pyle and articles on the Brownings, Dante Gabriel Rossetti, Thomas Hughes, Richard Wright, Kurt Vonnegut, and Thornton Waldo Burgess, among other authors.

The Editor

Ruth K. MacDonald is associate dean of Bay Path College. She received her B.A. and M.A. in English from the University of Connecticut, her Ph.D. in English from Rutgers University, and her M.B.A. from the University of Texas at El Paso. She is author of the volumes on Louisa May Alcott, Beatrix Potter, and Dr. Seuss in Twayne's United States and English Authors Series and of the book *Literature for Children in England and America, 1646–1774* (1982).